BLACK LEGACY PRESS™
WWW.BLACKLEGACYPRESS.ORG

SLAVE NARRATIVES

Volume XVI

Texas Narratives

Part 1

By

United States

Work Projects Administry

Copyright © 2024 by BLACKLEGACYPRESS.ORG

All rights reserved. No part of this publication may be reprduced or transmitted in any form or by any means electronic or mechanical, including information storage and retrieval systems without permission in writing from the publisher, except for student research using the appropriate citations.

ISBN: 978-1-63652-194-7

SLAVE NARRATIVES

A Folk History of Slavery in the United States From
Interviews with Former Slaves

UNITED STATES
WORK PROJECTS ADMINISTRY

TYPEWRITTEN RECORDS PREPARED BY
THE FEDERAL WRITERS' PROJECT
1936-1938
ASSEMBLED BY
THE LIBRARY OF CONGRESS PROJECT
WORK PROJECTS ADMINISTRATION
FOR THE DISTRICT OF COLUMBIA
SPONSORED BY THE LIBRARY OF CONGRESS

ILLUSTRATED WITH PHOTOGRAPHS
WASHINGTON 1941

VOLUME XVI

TEXAS NARRATIVES
PART 1

PREPARED BY THE FEDERAL WRITERS' PROJECT OF THE WORKS PROGRESS ADMINISTRATION FOR THE STATE OF TEXAS

CONTENTS

Will Adams 1
William Adams 5
William M. Adams 11
Sarah Allen 15
Andy Anderson 17
Wash Anderson 21
"Uncle Willis Anderson" 25
Mary Armstrong 29
Sterlin Arnwine 35
Sarah Ashley 39
Agatha Babino 43
Mrs. johnbarclay 47
John Barker 49
Joe Barnes 53
Armstead Barrett 55
Harriet Barrett 57
John Bates 59
Harrison Beckett 63
Frank Bell 69
Aunt Virginia Bell 73
Edgar And Minerva Bendy 77
Minerva Bendy 79
Sarah Benjamin 81
Jack Bess 83
Ellen Betts 87
Charlotte Beverley 97
Francis Black 101
Olivier Blanchard 105
Julia Blanks 109
Elvira Boles 121

Betty Bormer(Bonner)	125
Harrison Boyd	129
Issabella Boyd	133
James Boyd	137
Jerry Boykins	141
Monroe Brackins	145
Gus Bradshaw	153
Wes Brady	157
Jacob Branch	161
William Branch	167
Clara Brim	173
Sylvester Brooks	175
Donaville Broussard	179
Fannie Brown	183
Fred Brown	185
James Brown	189
Josie Brown	193
Zek Brown	197
Madison Bruin	201
Martha Spence Bunton	207
Ellen Butler	211
Henry H. Buttler	215
William Byrd	219
Louis Cain	223
Jeff Calhoun	227
Simp Campbell	231
James Cape	235
Richard Carruthers	239
Cato Carter	243
Jack Cauthern	253
Sally Bankschambers	255
Jeptha Choice	259
Amos Clark	263
Anne Clark	267

Thomas Cole	271
Eli Coleman	283
Preely Coleman	287
Harriet Collins	289
Andrew Columbus (Smoky)	293
Steve Conally's house	297
Valmar Cormier	301
Laura Cornish	303
John Crawford	307
Green Cumby	311
Tempie Cummins	315
Adeline Cunningham	319
Will Daily	323
Julie Francis Daniels	327
Katie Darling	333
Carey Davenport	337
Campbell Davis	341
William Davis	345
Eli Davison	351
Elige Davison	355
John Day	359
Nelsen Denson	363
Victor Duhon	365

WILL ADAMS

WILL ADAMS was born in 1857, a slave of Dave Cavin, in Harrison Co., Texas. He remained with the Cavins until 1885, then farmed for himself. Will lives alone in Marshall, Texas, supported by a $13.00 monthly pension.

"My folks allus belongs to the Cavins and wore their name till after 'mancipation. Pa and ma was named Freeman and Amelia Cavin and Massa Dave fotches them to Texas from Alabama, along with ma's mother, what we called Maria.

"The Cavins allus thunk lots of their niggers and Grandma Maria say, 'Why shouldn't they—it was their money.' She say there was plenty Indians here when they settled this country and they bought and traded with them without killin' them, if they could. The Indians was poor folks, jus' pilfer and loaf 'round all the time. The niggers was a heap sight better off than they was, 'cause we had plenty to eat and a place to stay.

"Young Massa Tom was my special massa and he still lives here. Old Man Dave seemed to think more of his niggers than anybody and we thunk lots of our white folks. My pa was leader on the farm, and there wasn't no overseer or driver. When pa whip a nigger he needn't go to Massa Dave, but pa say, 'Go you way, you nigger. Freeman didn't whip you for nothin'.' Massa Dave allus believe pa, 'cause he tells the truth.

"One time a peddler come to our house and after supper he goes to see 'bout his pony. Pa done feed that pony fifteen ears of corn. The peddler tell massa his pony ain't been fed nothin', and massa git mad and say, 'Be on you way iffen you gwine 'cuse my niggers of lyin'.'

"We had good quarters and plenty to eat. I 'members when I's jus' walkin' round good pa come in from the field at night and taken me out of bed and dress me and feed me and then play with me for hours. Him bein' leader, he's gone from 'fore day till after night. The old heads got out early but us young scraps slep' till eight or nine o'clock, and don't you think Massa Dave ain't comin' round to see we is fed. I 'members him like it was yest'day, comin' to the quarters with his stick and askin' us, 'Had your breakfas'?' We'd say, 'Yes, suh.' Then he'd ask if we had 'nough or wanted any more. It look like he taken a pleasure in seein' us eat. At dinner, when the field hands come in, it am the same way. He was sho' that potlicker was fill as long as the niggers want to eat.

"The hands worked from sun to sun. Massa give them li'l crops and let them work them on Saturday. Then he bought the stuff and the niggers go to Jefferson and buy clothes and sech like. Lots saved money and bought freedom 'fore the war was over.

"We went to church and first the white preacher preached

and then he larns our cullud preachers. I seed him ordain a cullud preacher and he told him to allus be honest. When the white preacher laid his hand on him, all the niggers git to hollerin' and shoutin' and prayin' and that nigger git scart mos' to death.

"On Christmas we had all we could eat and drink and after that a big party, and you ought to see them gals swingin' they partners round. Then massa have two niggers wrestle, and our sports and dances was big sport for the white folks. They'd sit on the gallery and watch the niggers put it on brown.

"Massa didn't like his niggers to marry off the place, but sometimes they'd do it, and massa tell his neighbor, 'My nigger am comin' to you place. Make him behave.' All the niggers 'haved then and they wasn't no Huntsville and gallows and burnin's then.

"Old massa went to war with his boy, Billie. They's lots of cryin' and weepin' when they sot us free. Lots of them didn't want to be free, 'cause they knowed nothin' and had nowhere to go. Them what had good massas stayed right on.

"I 'members when that Ku Klux business starts up. Smart niggers causes that. The carpet-baggers ruint the niggers and the white men couldn't do a thing with them, so they got up the Ku Klux and stirs up the world. Them carpet-baggers come round larnin' niggers to sass the white folks what done fed them. They come to pa with that talk and he told them, 'Listen, white folks, you is gwine start a graveyard if you come round here teachin' niggers to sass white folks." Them carpet-baggers starts all the trouble at 'lections in Reconstruction. Niggers didn't know anythin' 'bout politics.

"Mos' the young niggers ain't usin' the education they got now. I's been here eighty years and still has to be showed and told by white folks. These young niggers won't git told by whites or blacks either. They thinks they done knowed it all and that gits them in trouble.

"I stays with the Cavins mos' twenty years after the war. After I leaves, I allus farms and does odd jobs round town here. I's father of ten chillen by one woman. I lives by myself now and they gives me $13.00 a month. I'd be proud to git it if it wasn't more'n a dollar, 'cause they ain't nothin' a old man can do no more.

WILLIAM ADAMS

WILLIAM ADAMS, 93, was born in slavery, with no opportunity for an education, except three months in a public school. He has taught himself to read and to write. His lifelong ambition has been to become master of the supernatural powers which he believes to exist. He is now well-known among Southwestern Negroes for his faith in the occult.

"Yous want to know and talk about de power de people tells you I has. Well, sit down here, right there in dat chair, befo' we'uns starts. I gits some ice water and den we'uns can discuss de subject. I wants to 'splain it clearly, so yous can understand.

"I's born a slave, 93 years ago, so of course I 'members de war period. Like all de other slaves I has no chance for edumacation. Three months am de total time I's spent going to school. I teached myself to read and write. I's anxious to larn to read so I could study and find out about many things. Dat, I has done.

"There am lots of folks, and edumacated ones, too, what says we'uns believes in superstition. Well, its 'cause dey don't understand. 'Member de Lawd, in some of His ways, can be mysterious. De Bible says so. There am some things de Lawd wants all folks to know, some things jus' de chosen few to know, and some things no one should know. Now, jus' 'cause yous don't know 'bout some of de Lawd's laws, 'taint superstition if some other person understands and believes in sich.

"There is some born to sing, some born to preach, and some born to know de signs. There is some born under de power of de devil and have de power to put injury and misery on people, and some born under de power of de Lawd for to do good and overcome de evil power. Now, dat produces two forces, like fire and water. De evil forces starts de fire and I has de water force to put de fire out.

"How I larnt sich? Well, I's done larn it. It come to me. When de Lawd gives sich power to a person, it jus' comes to 'em. It am 40 years ago now when I's fust fully realize' dat I has de power. However, I's allus int'rested in de workin's of de signs. When I's a little piccaninny, my mammy and other folks used to talk about de signs. I hears dem talk about what happens to folks 'cause a spell was put on 'em. De old folks in dem days knows more about de signs dat de Lawd uses to reveal His laws den de folks of today. It am also true of de cullud folks in Africa, dey native land. Some of de folks laughs at their beliefs and says it am superstition, but it am knowin' how de Lawd reveals His laws.

"Now, let me tell yous of something I's seen. What am seen, can't be doubted. It happens when I's a young man and befo' I's realize' dat I's one dat am chosen for to show de power. A mule had cut his leg so bad dat him am bleedin' to death and dey couldn't stop it. An old cullud man live near there dat dey turns to. He comes over and passes his hand over de cut. Befo' long de bleedin' stop and dat's de power of de Lawd workin' through dat nigger, dat's all it am.

"I knows about a woman dat had lost her mind. De doctor say it was caused from a tumor in de head. Dey took an ex-ray picture, but dere's no tumor. Dey gives up and says its a peculiar case. Dat woman was took to one with de power of de good spirit and he say its a peculiar case for dem dat don't understand. Dis am a case of de evil spell. Two days after, de woman have her mind back.

"Dey's lots of dose kind of cases de ord'nary person never hear about. Yous hear of de case de doctors can't understand, nor will dey 'spond to treatment. Dat am 'cause of de evil spell dat am on de persons.

"'Bout special persons bein' chosen for to show de power, read yous Bible. It says in de book of Mark, third chapter, 'and He ordained twelve, dat dey should be with Him, dat He might send them forth to preach and to have de power to heal de sick and to cast out devils.' If it wasn't no evil in people, why does de Lawd say, 'cast out sich?' And in de fifth chapter of James, it further say, 'If any am sick, let him call de elders. Let dem pray over him. De prayers of faith shall save him.' There 'tis again, Faith, dat am what counts.

"When I tells dat I seen many persons given up to die, and den a man with de power comes and saves sich person, den its not for people to say it am superstition to believe in de power.

"Don't forgit—de agents of de devil have de power of evil. Dey can put misery of every kind on people. Dey can make trouble with de work and with de business, with de fam'ly and with de health. So folks mus' be on de watch all de time. Folks has business trouble 'cause de evil power have control of 'em. Dey has de evil power cast out and save de business. There am a man in Waco dat come to see me 'bout dat. He say to me everything he try to do in de las' six months turned out wrong. It starts with him losin' his pocketbook with $50.00 in it. He buys a carload of hay and it catch fire and he los' all of it. He spends $200.00 advertisin' de three-day sale and it begin to rain, so he los' money. It sho' am de evil power.

"'Well,' he say, 'Dat am de way it go, so I comes to you.'

"I says to him, 'Its de evil power dat have you control and we'uns shall cause it to be cast out.' Its done and he has no more trouble.

"You wants to know if persons with de power for good can be successful in castin' out devils in all cases? Well, I answers dat, yes and no. Dey can in every case if de affected person have de faith. If de party not have enough faith, den it am a failure.

"Wearin' de coin for protection 'gainst de evil power? Dat am simple. Lots of folks wears sich and dey uses mixtures dat am sprinkled in de house, and sich. Dat am a question of faith. If dey has de true faith in sich, it works. Otherwise, it won't.

"Some folks won't think for a minute of goin' without lodestone or de salt and pepper mixture in de little sack, tied round dey neck. Some wears de silver coin tied round dey neck. All sich am for to keep away de effect of de evil power. When one have de faith in sich and dey acc'dently lose de charm, dey sho' am miserable.

"An old darky dat has faith in lodestone for de charm told me de 'sperience he has in Atlanta once. He carryin' de hod and de fust thing he does am drop some brick on he foot.

De next thing, he foot slip as him starts up de ladder and him and de bricks drap to de ground. It am lucky for him it wasn't far. Jus' a sprain ankle and de boss sends him home for de day. He am 'cited and gits on de street car and when de conductor call for de fare, Rufus reaches for he money but he los' it or fergits it at home. De conductor say he let him pay nex' time and asks where he live. Rufus tells him and he say, 'Why, nigger, you is on de wrong car.' Dat cause Rufus to walk further with de lame foot dan if he started walkin' in de fust place. He thinks there mus' be something wrong with he charm, and he look for it and it gone! Sho' 'nough, it am los'. He think, 'Here I sits all day, and I won't make another move till I gits de lodestone. When de chillen comes from school I sends dem to de drugstore for some of de stone and gits fixed.'

"Now, now, I's been waitin' for dat one 'bout de black cat crossin' de road, and, sho' 'nough, it come. Let me ask you one. How many people can yous find dat likes to have de black cat cross in front of 'em? Dat's right, no one likes dat. Let dis old cullud person inform yous dat it am sho' de bad luck sign. It is sign of bad luck ahead, so turn back. Stop what yous doin'.

"I's tellin' yous of two of many cases of failure to took warnin' from de black cat. I knows a man call' Miller. His wife and him am takin' an auto ride and de black cat cross de road and he cussed a little and goes on. Den it's not long till he turns de corner and his wife falls out of de car durin' de turn. When he goes back and picks her up, she am dead.

"Another fellow, call' Brown, was a-ridin' hossback and a black cat cross de path, but he drives on. Well, its not long till him hoss stumble and throw him off. De fall breaks his leg, so take a warnin'—don't overlook de black cat. Dat am a warnin'.

United States.Work Project Administration

WILLIAM M. ADAMS

WILLIAM M. ADAMS, spiritualist preacher and healer, who lives at 1404 Illinois Ave., Ft. Worth, Texas, was born a slave on the James Davis plantation, in San Jacinto Co., Texas. After the war he worked in a grocery, punched cattle, farmed and preached. He moved to Ft. Worth in 1902.

"I was bo'n 93 years ago, dat is whut my mother says. We didn' keep no record like folks does today. All I know is I been yere a long time. My mother, she was Julia Adams and my father he was James Adams. She's bo'n in Hollis Springs, Mississippi and my father, now den, he was bo'n in Florida. He was a Black Creek Indian. Dere was 12 of us chillen. When I was 'bout seven de missus, she come and gits me for her servant. I lived in de big house till she die. Her and Marster Davis was powerful good to me.

"Marster Davis he was a big lawyer and de owner of a plantation. But all I do was wait on ole missus. I'd light her pipe for her and I helped her wid her knittin'. She give me money all de time. She had a little trunk she keeped money in and lots of times I'd have to pack it down wid my feets.

"I dis'member jus' how many slaves dere was, but dere was more'n 100. I saw as much as 100 sold at a time. When dey tuk a bunch of slaves to trade, dey put chains on 'em.

"De other slaves lived in log cabins back of de big house. Dey had dirt floors and beds dat was made out of co'n shucks or straw. At nite dey burned de lamps for 'bout an hour, den de overseers, dey come knock on de door and tell 'em put de light out. Lots of overseers was mean. Sometimes dey'd whip a nigger wid a leather strap 'bout a foot wide and long as your arm and wid a wooden handle at de end.

"On Sat'day and Sunday nites dey'd dance and sing all nite long. Dey didn' dance like today, dey danced de roun' dance and jig and do de pigeon wing, and some of dem would jump up and see how many time he could kick his feets 'fore dey hit de groun'. Dey had an ole fiddle and some of 'em would take two bones in each hand and rattle 'em. Dey sang songs like, 'Diana had a Wooden Leg,' and 'A Hand full of Sugar,' and 'Cotton-eyed Joe.' I dis'member how dey went.

"De slaves didn' have no church den, but dey'd take a big sugar kettle and turn it top down on de groun' and put logs roun' it to kill de soun'. Dey'd pray to be free and sing and dance.

"When war come dey come and got de slaves from all de plantations and tuk 'em to build de breastworks. I saw lots of soldiers. Dey'd sing a song dat go something like dis:

"'Jeff Davis rode a big white hoss,

Lincoln rode a mule;

Jess Davis is our President,

Lincoln is a fool.'

"I 'member when de slaves would run away. Ole John Billinger, he had a bunch of dogs and he'd take after runaway niggers. Sometimes de dogs didn' ketch de nigger. Den ole Billinger, he'd cuss and kick de dogs.

"We didn' have to have a pass but on other plantations dey did, or de paddlerollers would git you and whip you. Dey was de poor white folks dat didn' have no slaves. We didn' call 'em white folks dem days. No, suh, we called dem' Buskrys.'

"Jus' fore de war, a white preacher he come to us slaves and says: 'Do you wan' to keep you homes whar you git all to eat, and raise your chillen, or do you wan' to be free to roam roun' without a home, like de wil' animals? If you wan' to keep you homes you better pray for de South to win. All day wan's to pray for de South to win, raise the hand.' We all raised our hands 'cause we was skeered not to, but we sho' didn' wan' de South to win.

"Dat night all de slaves had a meetin' down in de hollow. Ole Uncle Mack, he gits up and says: 'One time over in Virginny dere was two ole niggers, Uncle Bob and Uncle Tom. Dey was mad at one 'nuther and one day dey decided to have a dinner and bury de hatchet. So day sat down, and when Uncle Bob wasn't lookin' Uncle Tom put some poison in Uncle Bob's food, but he saw it and when Uncle Tom wasn't lookin', Uncle Bob he turned de tray roun' on Uncle Tom, and he gits de poison food.' Uncle Mack, he says: 'Dat's what we slaves is gwine do, jus' turn de tray roun' and pray for de North to win.'

"After de war dere was a lot of excitement 'mong de niggers. Dey was rejoicin' and singin'. Some of 'em looked puzzled, sorter skeered like. But dey danced and had a big jamboree.

"Lots of 'em stayed and worked on de halves. Others hired out. I went to work in a grocery store and he paid me $1.50 a week. I give my mother de dollar and keeped de half. Den I got married and farmed for awhile. Den I come to Fort Worth and I been yere since.

United States.Work Project Administration

SARAH ALLEN

SARAH ALLEN was born a slave of John and Sally Goodren, in the Blue Ridge Mountains of Virginia. Before the Civil War, her owners came to Texas, locating near a small town then called Freedom. She lives at 3322 Frutas St., El Paso, Texas.

"I was birthed in time of bondage. You know, some people are ashamed to tell it, but I thank God I was 'llowed to see them times as well as now. It's a pretty hard story, how cruel some of the marsters was, but I had the luck to be with good white people. But some I knew were put on the block and sold. I 'member when they'd come to John Goodren's place to buy, but he not sell any. They'd have certain days when they'd sell off the block and they took chillen 'way from mothers, screamin' for dere chillen.

"I was birthed in ole Virginia in de Blue Ridge Mountains. When de white people come to Texas, de cullud people come with them. Dat's been a long time.

"My maw was named Charlotte, my paw Parks Adams. He's a white man. I guess I'm about eighty some years ole.

"You know, in slavery times when dey had bad marsters dey'd run away, but we didn' want to. My missus would see her people had something good to eat every Sunday mornin'. You had to mind your missus and marster and you be treated well. I think I was about twelve when dey freed us and we stayed with marster 'bout a year, then went to John Ecols' place and rented some lan'. We made two bales of cotton and it was the first money we ever saw.

"Back when we lived with Marster Goodren we had big candy pullin's. Invite everybody and play. We had good times. De worst thing, we didn' never have no schoolin' till after I married. Den I went to school two weeks. My husban' was teacher. He never was a slave. His father bought freedom through a blacksmith shop, some way.

"I had a nice weddin'. My dress was white and trimmed with blue ribbon. My second day dress was white with red dots. I had a beautiful veil and a wreath and 'bout two, three waiters for table dat day.

"My mother was nearly white. Brighter than me. We lef' my father in Virginia. I was jus' as white as de chillen I played with. I used to be plum bright, but here lately I'm gettin' awful dark.

"My husban' was of a mixture, like you call bright ginger-cake color. I don' know where he got his learnin'. I feel so bad since he's gone to Glory.

"Now I'm ole, de Lord has taken care of me. He put that spirit in people to look after ole folks and now my chillen look after me. I've two sons, one name James Allen, one R.M. Both live in El Paso.

"After we go to sleep, de people will know these things, 'cause if freedom hadn' come, it would have been so miserable.

ANDY ANDERSON

ANDY ANDERSON, 94, was born a slave of Jack Haley, who owned a plantation in Williamson Co., Texas. During the Civil War, Andy was sold to W.T. House, of Blanco County, who in less than a year sold Andy to his brother, John House. Andy now lives with his third wife and eight of his children at 301 Armour St., Fort Worth, Texas.

"My name am Andy J. Anderson, and I's born on Massa Jack Haley's plantation in Williamson County, Texas, and Massa Haley owned my folks and 'bout twelve other families of niggers. I's born in 1843 and that makes me 94 year old and 18 year when de war starts. I's had 'speriences durin' dat time.

"Massa Haley am kind to his cullud folks, and him am kind to everybody, and all de folks likes him. De other white folks called we'uns de petted niggers. There am 'bout 30 old and young niggers and 'bout 20 piccaninnies too little to work, and de nuss cares for dem while dey mammies works.

"I's gwine 'splain how it am managed on Massa Haley's plantation. It am sort of like de small town, 'cause everything we uses am made right there. There am de shoemaker and he is de tanner and make de leather from de hides. Den massa has 'bout a thousand sheep and he gits de wool, and de niggers cards and spins and weaves it, and dat makes all de clothes. Den massa have cattle and sich purvide de milk and de butter and beef meat for eatin'. Den massa have de turkeys and chickens and de hawgs and de bees. With all that, us never was hongry.

"De plantation am planted in cotton, mostly, with de corn

and de wheat a little, 'cause massa don't need much of dem. He never sell nothin' but de cotton.

"De livin' for de cullud folks am good. De quarters am built from logs like deys all in dem days. De floor am de dirt but we has de benches and what is made on de place. And we has de big fireplace for to cook and we has plenty to cook in dat fireplace, 'cause massa allus 'lows plenty good rations, but he watch close for de wastin' of de food.

"De war breaks and dat make de big change on de massas place. He jines de army and hires a man call' Delbridge for overseer. After dat, de hell start to pop, 'cause de first thing Delbridge do is cut de rations. He weighs out de meat, three pound for de week, and he measure a peck of meal. And 'twarn't enough. He half starve us niggers and he want mo' work and he start de whippin's. I guesses he starts to edumacate 'em. I guess dat Delbridge go to hell when he died, but I don't see how de debbil could stand him.

"We'uns am not use' to sich and some runs off. When dey am cotched there am a whippin' at de stake. But dat Delbridge, he sold me to Massa House, in Blanco County. I's sho' glad when I's sold, but it am short gladness, 'cause here am another man what hell am too good for. He gives me de whippin' and de scars am still on my arms and my back, too. I'll carry dem to my grave. He sends me for firewood and when I gits it loaded, de wheel hits a stump and de team jerks and dat breaks de whippletree. So he ties me to de stake and every half hour for four hours, dey lays ta lashes on my back. For de first couple hours de pain am awful. I's never forgot it. Den I's stood so much pain I not feel so much and when dey takes me loose, I's jus' 'bout half dead. I lays in de bunk two days, gittin' over dat whippin', gittin' over it in de body but not de heart. No, suh, I has dat in de heart till dis day.

"After dat whippin' I doesn't have de heart to work for de massa. If I seed de cattle in de cornfield, I turns de back, 'stead of chasin' 'em out. I guess dat de reason de massa sold me to his brother, Massa John. And he am good like my first massa, he never whipped me.

"Den surrender am 'nounced and massa tells us we's free. When dat takes place, it am 'bout one hour by sun. I says to myself, 'I won't be here long.' But I's not realise what I's in for till after I's started, but I couldn't turn back. For dat means de whippin' or danger from de patter rollers. Dere I was and I kep' on gwine. No nigger am sposed to be off de massa's place without de pass, so I travels at night and hides durin' de daylight. I stays in de bresh and gits water from de creeks, but not much to eat. Twice I's sho' dem patter rollers am passin' while I's hidin'.

"I's 21 year old den, but it am de first time I's gone any place, 'cept to de neighbors, so I's worried 'bout de right way to Massa Haley's place. But de mornin' of de third day I comes to he place and I's so hongry and tired and scairt for fear Massa Haley not home from de army yit. So I finds my pappy and he hides me in he cabin till a week and den luck comes to me when Massa Haley come home. He come at night and de next mornin' dat Delbridge am shunt off de place, 'cause Massa Haley seed he niggers was all gaunt and lots am ran off and de fields am not plowed right, and only half de sheep and everything left. So massa say to dat Delbridge, 'Dere am no words can 'splain what yous done. Git off my place 'fore I smashes you.'

"Den I kin come out from my pappy's cabin and de old massa was glad to see me, and he let me stay till freedom am ordered. Dat's de happies' time in my life, when I gits back to Massa Haley.

United States.Work Project Administration

Slave Narratives

WASH ANDERSON

Dibble, Fred, P.W., Beehler, Rheba, P.W., Beaumont, Jefferson, Dist. #3.

A frail sick man, neatly clad in white pajamas lying patiently in a clean bed awaiting the end which does not seem far away. Although we protested against his talking, because of his weakness, he told a brief story of his life in a whisper, his breath very short and every word was spoken with great effort. His light skin and his features denote no characteristic of his race, has a bald head with a bit of gray hair around the crown and a slight growth of gray whiskers about his face, is medium in height and build. WASH ANDERSON, although born in Charleston, S.C., has spent practically all of his life in Texas [Handwritten Note: (Beaumont, Texas—]

"Mos' folks call me Wash Anderson, but dey uster call me George. My whole name' George Washington Anderson. I was bo'n in Charleston, Sou'f Ca'lina in 1855. Bill Anderson was my ol' marster. Dey was two boy' and two gal' in his family. We all lef' Charleston and come to Orange, Texas, befo' freedom come. I was fo' year' ol' when dey mek dat trip."

"I don' 'member nuttin 'bout Charleston. You see where I was bo'n was 'bout two mile' from de city. I went back one time in 1917, but I didn' stay dere long."

"My pa was Irvin' Anderson and my mommer was name' Eliza. Ol' marster was pretty rough on his niggers. Dey tell me he had my gran'daddy beat to death. Dey never did beat me."

"Dey made de trip from Charleston 'cross de country and settle' in Duncan's Wood' down here in Orange county. Dey had a big plantation dere. I dunno if ol' marster had money back in Charleston, but I t'ink he must have. He had 'bout 25 or 30 slaves on de place."

"Ol' man Anderson he had a big two-story house. It was buil' out of logs but it was a big fine house. De slaves jis' had little log huts. Dere warn't no flo's to 'em, nuthin' but de groun'. Dem little huts jis' had one room in 'em. Dey was one family to de house, 'cep'n' sometime dey put two or t'ree family' to a house. Dey jis' herd de slaves in dere like a bunch of pigs."

"Dey uster raise cotton, and co'n, and sugar cane, and sich like, but dey didn' uster raise no rice. Dey uster sen' stuff to Terry on a railroad to sen' it to market. Sometime dey hitch up dey teams and sen' it to Orange and Beaumont in wagons. De ol' marster he had a boat, too, and sometime he sen' a boatload of his stuff to Beaumont."

"My work was to drive de surrey for de family and look atter de hosses and de harness and sich. I jis' have de bes' hosses on de place to see atter."

"I saw lots of sojers durin' de war. I see 'em marchin' by, goin' to Sabine Pass 'bout de time of dat battle."

"Back in slavery time dey uster have a white preacher to come 'roun' and preach to de cullud folks. But I don't 'member much 'bout de songs what dey uster sing."

"I play 'roun' right smart when I was little. Dey uster have lots of fun playin' 'hide and seek,' and 'hide de switch.' We uster ride stick hosses and play 'roun' at all dem t'ings what chillun play at."

"Dey had plenty of hosses and mules and cows on de ol' plantation. I had to look atter some of de hosses, but dem what I hatter look atter was s'pose to be de bes' hosses in de bunch. Like I say, I drive de surrey and dey allus have de bes' hosses to pull dat surrey. Dey had a log stable. Dey kep' de harness in dere, too. Eb'ryt'ing what de stock eat dey raise on de plantation, all de co'n and fodder and sich like."

"Atter freedom come I went 'roun' doin' dif'rent kind of work. I uster work on steamboats, and on de railroad and at sawmillin'. I was a sawyer for a long, long time. I work 'roun' in Lou'sana and Arkansas, and Oklahoma, as well as in Texas. When I wasn't doin' dem kinds of work, I uster work 'roun' at anyt'ing what come to han'. I 'member one time I was workin' for de Burr Lumber Company at Fort Townsend up dere in Arkansas."

"When I was 'bout 36 year' ol' I git marry. I been married twice. My fus' wife was name' Hannah and Reverend George Childress was de preacher dat marry us. He was a cullud preacher. Atter Hannah been dead some time I marry my secon' wife. Her name was Tempie Perkins. Later on, us sep'rate. Us sep'rate on 'count of money matters."

"I b'longs to de Baptis' Chu'ch. Sometime' de preacher come 'roun' and see me. He was here a few days ago dis week."

United States.Work Project Administration

Slave Narratives

"UNCLE WILLIS ANDERSON"

REFERENCES

1. Coronado's Children—J. Frank Dobie, Pub. 1929, Austin, Tex.

2. Leon County News—Centerville, Texas—Thursday May 21, 1936.

3. Consultant—Uncle Willis Anderson, resident of Centerville, Tex, born April 15, 1844.

An interesting character at Centerville, Texas, is "Uncle Willis" Anderson, an ex-slave, born April 15, 1844, 6 miles west of Centerville on the old McDaniels plantation near what is now known as Hopewell Settlement. It is generally said that "Uncle Willis" is one of the oldest living citizens in the County, black or white. He is referred to generally for information concerning days gone by and for the history of that County, especially in the immediate vicinity of Centerville.

"Uncle Willis" is an interesting figure. He may be found sitting on the porches of the stores facing Federal Highway No. 75, nodding or conversing with small groups of white or colored people that gather around him telling of the days gone by. He also likes to watch the busses and automobiles that pass through the small town musing and commenting on the swiftness of things today. Uncle Willis still cultivates a small patch five miles out from the town.

"Uncle Willis" is a tall dark, brown-skinned man having a large head covered with mixed gray wooly hair. He has lost very few teeth considering his age. When sitting on the porches of the stores the soles of his farm-shoes may be seen tied together with pieces of wire. He supports himself with a cane made from the Elm tree. At present he wears a tall white Texas Centennial hat which makes him appear more unique than ever.

"Uncle Willis'" memory is vivid. He is familiar with the older figures in the history of the County. He tells tales of having travelled by oxen to West Texas for flour and being gone for six months at a time. He remembers the Keechi and the Kickapoo Indians and also claims that he can point out a tree where the Americans hung an Indian Chief. He says that he has plowed up arrows, pots and flints on the Reubens Bains place and on the McDaniel farms. He can tell of the early lawlessness in the County. His face lights up when he recalls how the Yankee soldiers came through Centerville telling the slave owners to free their slaves. He also talks very low when he mentions the name of Jeff Davis because he says, "Wha' man eavesdrops the niggers houses in slavery time and if yer' sed' that Jeff Davis was a good man, they barbecued a hog for you, but if yer' sed' that Abe Lincoln was a good man, yer' had to fight or go to the woods."

Among the most interesting tales told by "Uncle Willis" is the tale of the "Lead mine." "Uncle Willis" says that some where along Boggy Creek near a large hickory tree and a red oak tree, near Patrick's Lake, he and his master, Auss McDaniels, would dig lead out of the ground which they used to make pistol and rifle balls for the old Mississippi rifles during slavery time. Uncle Willis claims that they would dig slags of lead out of the ground some 12 and 15 inches long, and others as large as a man's fist. They would carry this ore back to the big house and melt it down to get the trash out of it, then they would pour it into molds and make rifle balls and pistol balls from it. In this way they kept plenty of amunition on hand. In recent years the land has changed ownership, and the present owners live in Dallas. Learning of the tale of the "lead mine" on their property they went to Centerville in an attempt to locate it and were referred to "Uncle Willis." Uncle Willis says they offered him two hundred dollars if he could locate the mine. Being so sure that he knew its exact location, said that the $200 was his meat. However, Uncle Willis was unable to locate the spot where they dug the lead and the mine remains a mystery.[C]

Recently a group of citizens of Leon County including W.D. Lacey, Joe McDaniel, Debbs Brown, W.H. Hill and Judge Lacey cross questioned Uncle Willis about the lead mine. Judge Lacey did the questioning while them others formed an audience. The conversation went as follows:

"Which way would you go when you went to the mine?" Judge Lacey asked.

"Out tow'hd Normangee."

"How long would it take you to get there?"

"Two or three hours."

"Was it on a creek?"

"Yessuh."

"But you cant go to it now?"

"Nosuh, I just can't recollect exactly where 'tis.[B]

J. Frank Dobie mentions many tales of lost lead mines throughout Texas in Coronado's Children, a publication of the Texas Folk-Lore Society. Lead in the early days of the Republic and the State was very valuable, as it was the source of protection from the Indians and also the means of supplying food.[A]

United States.Work Project Administration

MARY ARMSTRONG

MARY ARMSTRONG, 91, lives at 3326 Pierce Ave., Houston, Texas. She was born on a farm near St. Louis, Missouri, a slave of William Cleveland. Her father, Sam Adams, belonged to a "nigger trader," who had a farm adjoining the Cleveland place.

"I's Aunt Mary, all right, but you all has to 'scuse me if I don't talk so good, 'cause I's been feelin' poorly for a spell and I ain't so young no more. Law me, when I think back what I used to do, and now it's all I can do to hobble 'round a little. Why, Miss Olivia, my mistress, used to put a glass plumb full of water on my head and then have me waltz 'round the room, and I'd dance so smoothlike, I don't spill nary drap.

"That was in St. Louis, where I's born. You see, my mamma belong to old William Cleveland and old Polly Cleveland, and they was the meanest two white folks what ever lived, 'cause they was allus beatin' on their slaves. I know, 'cause mamma told me, and I hears about it other places, and besides, old Polly, she was a Polly devil if there ever was one, and she whipped my little sister what was only nine months old and jes' a baby to death. She come and took the diaper offen my little sister and whipped till the blood jes' ran—jes' 'cause she cry like all babies do, and it kilt my sister. I never forgot that, but I sot some even with that old Polly devil and it's this-a-way.

"You see, I's 'bout 10 year old and I belongs to Miss Olivia, what was that old Polly's daughter, and one day old Polly devil comes to where Miss Olivia lives after she marries, and trys to give me a lick out in the yard, and I picks up a rock 'bout as big as half your fist and hits her right in the eye and busted the eyeball, and tells her that's for whippin' my baby sister to death. You could hear her holler for five miles, but Miss Olivia, when I tells her, says, 'Well, I guess mamma has larnt her lesson at last.' But that old Polly was mean like her husban', old Cleveland, till she die, and I hopes they is burnin' in torment now.

"I don't 'member 'bout the start of things so much, 'cept what Miss Olivia and my mamma, her name was Siby, tells me. Course, it's powerful cold in winter times and the farms was lots different from down here. They calls 'em plantations down here but up at St. Louis they was jes' called farms, and that's what they was, 'cause we raises wheat and barley and rye and oats and corn and fruit.

"The houses was builded with brick and heavy wood, too, 'cause it's cold up there, and we has to wear the warm clothes and they's wove on the place, and we works at it in the evenin's.

"Old Cleveland takes a lot of his slaves what was in 'custom' and brings 'em to Texas to sell. You know, he wasn't sposed to do that, 'cause when you's in 'custom', that's 'cause he borrowed money on you, and you's not sposed to leave the place till he paid up. Course, old Cleveland jes' tells the one he owed the money to, you had run off, or squirmed out some way, he was that mean.

"Mamma say she was in one bunch and me in 'nother. Mamma had been put 'fore this with my papa, Sam Adams, but that makes no diff'rence to Old Cleveland. He's so mean he never would sell the man and woman and chillen to the same one. He'd sell the man here and the woman there and if they's chillen, he'd sell them some place else. Oh, old Satan in torment couldn't be no meaner than what he and Old Polly was to they slaves. He'd chain a nigger up to whip 'em and rub salt and pepper on him, like he said, 'to season him up.' And when he'd sell a slave, he'd grease their mouth all up to make it look like they'd been fed good and was strong and healthy.

"Well mamma say they hadn't no more'n got to Shreveport 'fore some law man cotch old Cleveland and takes 'em all back to St. Louis. Then my little sister's born, the one old Polly devil kilt, and I's 'bout four year old then.

"Miss Olivia takes a likin' to me and, though her papa and mama so mean, she's kind to everyone, and they jes' love her. She marries to Mr. Will Adams what was a fine man, and has 'bout five farms and 500 slaves, and he buys me for her from old Cleveland and pays him $2,500.00, and gives him George Henry, a nigger, to boot. Lawsy, I's sho' happy to be with Miss Olivia and away from old Cleveland and Old Polly, 'cause they kilt my little sister.

"We lives in St. Louis, on Chinquapin Hill, and I's housegirl, and when the babies starts to come I nusses 'em and spins thread for clothes on the loom. I spins six cuts of thread a week, but I has plenty of time for myself and that's where I larns to dance so good. Law, I sho' jes' crazy 'bout dancin'. If I's settin' eatin' my victuals and hears a fiddle play, I gets up and dances.

"Mr. Will and Miss Olivia sho' is good to me, and I never calls Mr. Will 'massa' neither, but when they's company I calls him Mr. Will and 'round the house by ourselves I calls them 'pappy' and 'mammy', 'cause they raises me up from the little girl. I hears old Cleveland done took my mamma to Texas 'gain but I couldn't do nothin', 'cause Miss Olivia wouldn't have much truck with her folks. Once in a while old Polly comes over, but Miss Olivia tells her not to touch me or the others. Old Polly trys to buy me back from Miss Olivia, and if they had they'd kilt me sho'. But Miss Olivia say, 'I'd wade in blood as deep as Hell 'fore I'd let you have Mary.' That's jes' the very words she told 'em.

"Then I hears my papa is sold some place I don't know where. 'Course, I didn't know him so well, jes' what mamma done told me, so that didn't worry me like mamma being took so far away.

"One day Mr. Will say, 'Mary, you want to go to the river and see the boat race?' Law me, I never won't forget that. Where we live it ain't far to the Miss'sippi River and pretty soon here they comes, the Natchez and the Eclipse, with smoke and fire jes' pourin' out of they smokestacks. That old captain on the 'Clipse starts puttin' in bacon meat in the boiler and the grease jes' comes out a-blazin' and it beat the Natchez to pieces.

"I stays with Miss Olivia till '63 when Mr. Will set us all free. I was 'bout 17 year old then or more. I say I goin' find my mamma. Mr. Will fixes me up two papers, one 'bout a yard long and the other some smaller, but both has big, gold seals what he says is the seal of the State of Missouri. He gives me money and buys my fare ticket to Texas and tells me they is still slave times down here and to put the papers in my bosom but to do whatever the white folks tells me, even if they wants to sell me. But he say, 'Fore you gets off the block, jes' pull out the papers, but jes' hold 'em up to let folks see and don't let 'em out of your hands, and when they sees them they has to let you alone.'

"Miss Olivia cry and carry on and say be careful of myself 'cause it sho' rough in Texas. She give me a big basket what had so much to eat in it I couldn't hardly heft it and 'nother with clothes in it. They puts me in the back end a the boat where the big, old wheel what run the boat was and I goes to New Orleans, and the captain puts me on 'nother boat and I comes to Galveston, and that captain puts me on 'nother boat and I comes up this here Buffalo Bayou to Houston.

"I looks 'round Houston, but not long. It sho' was a dumpy little place then and I gets the stagecoach to Austin. It takes us two days to get there and I thinks my back busted sho' 'nough, it was sich rough ridin'. Then I has trouble sho'. A man asks me where I goin' and says to come 'long and he takes me to a Mr. Charley Crosby. They takes me to the block what they sells slaves on. I gets right up like they tells me, 'cause I 'lects what Mr. Will done told me to do, and they starts biddin' on me. And when they cried off and this Mr. Crosby comes up to get me, I jes' pulled out my papers and helt 'em up high and when he sees 'em, he say, 'Let me see them.' But I says, 'You jes' look at it up here,' and he squints up and say, 'This gal am free and has papers,' and tells me he a legislature man and takes me and lets me stay with his slaves. He is a good man.

"He tells me there's a slave refugee camp in Wharton

County but I didn't have no money left, but he pays me some for workin' and when the war's over I starts to hunt mamma 'gain, and finds her in Wharton County near where Wharton is. Law me, talk 'bout cryin' and singin' and cryin' some more, we sure done it. I stays with mamma till I gets married in 1871 to John Armstrong, and then we all comes to Houston.

"I gets me a job nussin' for Dr. Rellaford and was all through the yellow fever epidemic. I 'lects in '75 people die jes' like sheep with the rots. I's seen folks with the fever jump from their bed with death on 'em and grab other folks. The doctor saved lots of folks, white and black, 'cause he sweat it out of 'em. He mixed up hot water and vinegar and mustard and some else in it.

"But, law me, so much is gone out of my mind, 'cause I's 91 year old now and my mind jes' like my legs, jes' kinda hobble 'round a bit.

STERLIN ARNWINE

STEARLIN ARNWINE, 94, was born a slave to Albertus Arnwine, near Jacksonville, Texas, who died when Stearlin was seven or eight. He was bought by John Moseley, of Rusk, Texas, who made Stearlin a houseboy, and was very kind to him. He now lives about six miles west of Jacksonville.

"I was bo'n 'fore de war, in 1853, right near this here town, on Gum Creek. My mammy belonged to Massa Albertus Arnwine, and he wasn' ever married. He owned four women, my mammy, Ann, my grandmother, Gracie, and my Aunt Winnie and Aunt Mary. He didn' own any nigger men, 'cept the chillen of these women. Grandma lived in de house with

Massa Arnwine and the rest of us lived in cabins in de ya'd. My mammy come from Memphis but I don' know whar my pappy come from. He was Ike Lane. I has three half brothers, and their names is Joe and Will and John Schot, and two sisters called Polly and Rosie.

"Massa Arnwine died 'fore de war and he made a will and it gave all he owned to the women he owned, and Jedge Jowell promised massa on his deathbed he would take us to de free country, but he didn'. He took us to his place to work for him for 'bout two years and the women never did get that 900 acres of land Massa Arnwine willed to'em. I don' know who got it, but they didn'. I knows I still has a share in that land, but it takes money to git it in cou't.

"When war broke I fell into the han's of Massa John Moseley at Rusk. They brought the dogs to roun' us up from the fiel's whar we was workin'. I was the only one of my fam'ly to go to Massa John.

"I never did wo'k in the fiel's at Massa John's place. He said I mus' be his houseboy and houseboy I was. Massa was sho' good to me and I did love to be with him and follow him 'roun'.

"The kitchen was out in de ya'd and I had to carry the victuals to the big dinin'-room. When dinner was over, Massa John tuk a nap and I had to fan him, and Lawsy me, I'd git so sleepy. I kin hear him now, for he'd wake up and say, 'Go get me a drink outta the northeast corner of de well.'

"We had straw and grass beds, we put it in sacks on de groun' and slep' on de sacks. I don' 'member how much land Massa John had but it was a big place and he had lots of slaves. We chillun had supper early in de evenin' and mostly cornbread and hawg meat and milk. We all ate from a big pot. I larned to spin and weave and knit and made lots of socks.

"Massa John had two step-daughters, Miss Mollie and

Miss Laura, and they wen' to school at Rusk. It was my job to take 'em thar ev'ry Monday mornin' on horses and go back after 'em Friday afternoon.

"I never earnt no money 'fore freedom come, but once my brother-in-law give me five dollars. I was so proud of it I showed it to de ladies and one of 'em said, 'You don' need dat,' and she give me two sticks of candy and tuk de money. But I didn' know any better then.

"I seed slaves for sale on de auction block. They sol' 'em 'cordin' to strengt' and muscles. They was stripped to de wais'. I seed the women and little chillun cryin' and beggin' not to be separated, but it didn' do no good. They had to go.

"The only chu'ch I knowed 'bout was when we'd git together in de night and have prayer meetin' and singin.' We use' to go way out in de woods so de white folks wouldn' hear nothin'. Sometimes we'd stay nearly all night on Saturday, 'cause we didn' have to work Sunday.

"'Bout the only thing we could play was stick hosses. I made miles and miles on the stick hosses. After the War Massa John have his chillun a big roll of Confederate money and they give us some of it to trade and buy stick hosses with.

"When Massa John tol' us we was free, he didn' seem to min', but Miss Em, she bawled and squalled, say her prop'ty taken 'way from her. After dat, my mammy gathers us togedder and tuk us to the Dr. Middleton place, out from Jacksonville. From thar to de Ragsdale place whar I's been ever since.

"I wore my first pants when I was fourteen years ole, and they stung 'till I was mis'ble. The cloth was store bought but mammy made the pants at home. It was what we called dog-hair cloth. Mammy made my first shoes, we called 'em 'red rippers'.

United States.Work Project Administration

SARAH ASHLEY

SARAH ASHLEY, 93, was born in Mississippi. She recalls her experiences when sold on the block in New Orleans, and on a cotton plantation in Texas. She now lives at Goodrich, Texas.

"I ain't able to do nothin' no more. I's jus' plumb give out and I stays here by myself. My daughter, Georgia Grime, she used to live with me but she's been dead four year.

"I was born in Miss'ippi and Massa Henry Thomas buy us and bring us here. He a spec'lator and buys up lots of niggers and sells 'em. Us family was sep'rated. My two sisters and my papa was sold to a man in Georgia. Den dey put me on a block and bid me off. Dat in New Orleans and I scairt and cry, but dey put me up dere anyway. First dey takes me to Georgia and dey didn't sell me for a long spell. Massa Thomas he travel round and buy and sell niggers. Us stay in de spec'lators drove de long time.

"After 'while Massa Mose Davis come from Cold Spring, in Texas, and buys us. He was buyin' up little chillen for he chillen. Dat 'bout four year befo' da first war. I was 19 year old when de burst of freedom come in June and I git turn loose.

"I was workin' in de field den. Jus' befo' dat de old Massa he go off and buy more niggers. He go east. He on a boat what git stove up and he die and never come back no more. Us never see him no more.

"I used to have to pick cotton and sometime I pick 300 pound and tote it a mile to de cotton house. Some pick 300 to 800 pound cotton and have to tote de bag de whole mile to de gin. Iffen dey didn't do dey work dey git whip till dey have blister on 'em. Den iffen dey didn't do it, de man on a hoss goes down de rows and whip with a paddle make with holes in it and bus' de blisters. I never git whip, 'cause I allus git my 300 pound. Us have to go early to do dat, when de horn goes early, befo' daylight. Us have to take de victuals in de bucket to de field.

"Massa have de log house and us live in little houses, strowed in long rows. Dere wasn't no meetin's 'lowed in de quarters and iffen dey have prayer meetin' de boss man whip dem. Sometime us run off at night and go to camp meetin'. I takes de white chillen to church sometime, but dey couldn't larn me to sing no songs 'cause I didn' have no spirit.

"Us never got 'nough to eat, so us keeps stealin' stuff. Us has to. Dey give us de peck of meal to last de week and two, three pound bacon in chunk. Us never have flour or sugar, jus' cornmeal and de meat and 'taters. De niggers has de big box under de fireplace, where dey kep' all de pig and chickens what dey steal, down in salt.

"I seed a man run away and de white men got de dogs and dey kotch him and put him in de front room and he jump through de big window and break de glass all up. Dey sho' whips him when dey kotches him.

"De way dey whip de niggers was to strip 'em off naked and whip 'em till dey make blisters and bus' de blisters. Den dey take de salt and red pepper and put in de wounds. After dey wash and grease dem and put somethin' on dem, to keep dem from bleed to death.

"When de boss man told us freedom was come he didn't like it, but he give all us de bale of cotton and some corn. He ask us to stay and he'p with de crop but we'uns so glad to git 'way dat nobody stays. I got 'bout fifty dollars for de cotton and den I lends it to a nigger what never pays me back yit. Den I got no place to go, so I cooks for a white man name' Dick Cole. He sposen give me $5.00 de month but he never paid me no money. He'd give me eats and clothes, 'cause he has de little store.

"Now, I's all alone and thinks of dem old times what was so bad, and I's ready for de Lawd to call me."

United States.Work Project Administration

AGATHA BABINO

AGATHA BABINO, born a slave of Ogis Guidry, near Carenco, Louisiana, now lives in a cottage on the property of the Blessed Sacrament Church, in Beaumont, Texas. She says she is at least eighty-seven and probably much older.

"Old Marse was Ogis Guidry. Old Miss was Laurentine. Dey had four chillen, Placid, Alphonse and Mary and Alexandrine, and live in a big, one-story house with a gallery and brick pillars. Dey had a big place. I 'spect a mile 'cross it, and fifty slaves.

"My mama name was Clarice Richard. She come from South Carolina. Papa was Dick Richard. He come from North Carolina. He was slave of old Placid Guilbeau. He live near Old Marse. My brothers was Joe and Nicholas and Oui and Albert and Maurice, and sisters was Maud and Celestine and Pauline.

"Us slaves lived in shabby houses. Dey builded of logs and have dirt floor. We have a four foot bench. We pull it to a table and set on it. De bed a platform with planks and moss.

"We had Sunday off. Christmas was off, too. Dey give us chicken and flour den. But most holidays de white folks has company. Dat mean more work for us.

"Old Marse bad. He beat us till we bleed. He rub salt and pepper in. One time I sweep de yard. Young miss come home from college. She slap my face. She want to beat me. Mama say to beat her, so dey did. She took de beatin' for me.

"My aunt run off 'cause dey beat her so much. Dey brung her back and beat her some more.

"We have dance outdoors sometime. Somebody play fiddle and banjo. We dance de reel and quadrille and buck dance. De men dance dat. If we go to dance on 'nother plantation we have to have pass. De patterrollers come and make us show de slip. If dey ain't no slip, we git beat.

"I see plenty sojers. Dey fight at Pines and we hear ball go 'zing—zing.' Young marse have blue coat. He put it on and climb a tree to see. De sojers come and think he a Yankee. Dey take his gun. Dey turn him loose when dey find out he ain't no Yankee.

"When de real Yankees come dey take corn and gooses and hosses. Dey don't ask for nothin'. Dey take what dey wants.

"Some masters have chillen by slaves. Some sold dere own chillen. Some sot dem free.

"When freedom come we have to sign up to work for money for a year. We couldn't go work for nobody else. After de year some stays, but not long.

"De Ku Klux kill niggers. Dey come to take my uncle. He open de door. Dey don't take him but tell him to vote Democrat next day or dey will. Dey kilt some niggers what wouldn't vote Democrat.

"Dey kill my old uncle Davis. He won't vote Democrat. Dey shoot him. Den dey stand him up and let him fall down. Dey tie him by de feet. Dey drag him through de bresh. Dey dare his wife to cry.

"When I thirty I marry Tesisfor Babino. Pere Abadie marry us at Grand Coteau. We have dinner with wine. Den come big dance. We have twelve chillen. We works in de field in Opelousas. We come here twenty-five year ago. He die in

1917. Dey let's me live here. It nice to be near de church. I can go to prayers when I wants to.

United States.Work Project Administration

MRS. JOHN BARCLAY

MRS. JOHN BARCLAY (nee Sarah Sanders) Brownwood, Texas was born in Komo, Mississippi, September 1, 1853. She was born a slave at the North Slades' place. Mr. and Mrs. North Slade were the only owners she ever had. She served as nurse-maid for her marster's children and did general housework. She, with her mother and father and family stayed with the Slades until the end of the year after the Civil War. They then moved to themselves, hiring out to "White Folks."

"My marster and mistress was good to all de slaves dat worked for dem. But our over-seer, Jimmy Shearer, was sho' mean. One day he done git mad at me for some little somethin' and when I take de ashes to de garden he catches me and churns me up and down on de groun'. One day he got mad at my brother and kicked him end over end, jes' like a stick of wood. He would whip us 'til we was raw and then put pepper and salt in de sores. If he thought we was too slow in doin' anything he would kick us off de groun' and churn us up and down. Our punishment depended on de mood of de over-seer. I never did see no slaves sold. When we was sick dey give us medicine out of drug stores. De over-seer would git some coarse cotton cloth to make our work clothes out of and den he would make dem so narrow we couldn' hardly' walk.

"There was 1800 acres in Marster Slade's plantation, we got up at 5:00 o'clock in de mornin' and de field workers would quit after sun-down. We didn' have no jails for slaves. We went to church with de white folks and there was a place in de back of de church for us to sit.

"I was jes' a child den and us chilluns would gather in de back yard and sing songs and play games and dance jigs. Song I 'member most is 'The Day is Past and Gone.'

"One time marster found out the over-seer was so mean to me, so he discharged him and released me from duty for awhile.

"We never did wear shoes through de week but on Sunday we would dress up in our white cotton dresses and put on shoes.

"We wasn't taught to read or write. Our owner didn't think anything about it. We had to work if there was work to be done. When we got caught up den we could have time off. If any of us got sick our mistress would 'tend to us herself. If she thought we was sick enough she would call de white doctor.

"When de marster done told us we was free we jumped up and down and slapped our hands and shouted 'Glory to God!' Lord, child dat was one happy bunch of niggers. Awhile after dat some of de slaves told marster dey wanted to stay on with him like dey had been but he told 'em no dey couldn't, 'cause dey was free. He said he could use some of 'em but dey would have to buy what dey got and he would have to pay 'em like men.

"When I was 'bout 18 years old I married John Barclay. I's had ten chillun and four gran'-chillun and now I lives by myself."

JOHN BARKER

JOHN BARKER, age 84, Houston.

5 photographs marked Green Cumby have been assigned to this manuscript—the 'Green Cumby' photos are attached to the proper manuscript and the five referred to above are probably pictures of John Barker.

JOHN BARKER, age 84, was born near Cincinnati, Ohio, the property of the Barker family, who moved to Missouri and later to Texas. He and his wife live in a neat cottage in Houston, Texas.

"I was born a slave. I'm a Malagasser (Madagascar) nigger. I 'member all 'bout dem times, even up in Ohio, though de Barkers brought me to Texas later on. My mother and father was call Goodman, but dey died when I was little and Missy Barker raised me on de plantation down near Houston. Dey was plenty of work and plenty of room.

"I 'member my grandma and grandpa. In dem days de horned toads runs over de world and my grandpa would gather 'em and lay 'em in de fireplace till dey dried and roll 'em with bottles till dey like ashes and den rub it on de shoe bottoms. You see, when dey wants to run away, dat stuff don't stick all on de shoes, it stick to de track. Den dey carries some of dat powder and throws it as far as dey could jump and den jump over it, and do dat again till dey use all de powder. Dat throwed de common hounds off de trail altogether. But dey have de bloodhounds, hell hounds, we calls 'em, and dey could pick up dat trail. Dey run my grandpa over 100 mile and three or four days and nights and found him under a bridge.

What dey put on him was enough! I seen 'em whip runaway niggers till de blood run down dere backs and den put salt in de places.

"I 'spect dere was 'bout 40 or 50 acres in de plantation. Dey worked and worked and didn't have no dances or church. Dances nothin'!

"My massa and missus house was nice, but it was a log house. They had big fireplaces what took great big chunks of wood and kep' fire all night. We lives in de back in a little bitty house like a chicken house. We makes beds out of posts and slats across 'em and fills tow sacks with shucks in 'em for mattress and pillows.

"I seed slaves sold and they was yoked like steers and sold by pairs sometimes. Dey wasn't 'lowed to marry, 'cause they could be sold and it wasn't no use, but you could live with 'em.

"We used to eat possums and dese old-fashioned coons and ducks. Sometimes we'd eat goats, too. We has plenty cornmeal and 'lasses and we gets milk sometimes, but we has no fine food, 'cept on Christmas, we gits some cake, maybe.

"My grandma says one day dat we all is free, but we stayed with Massa Barker quite a while. Dey pays us for workin' but it ain't much pay, 'cause de war done took dere money and all. But they was good to us, so we stayed.

"I was 'bout 20 when I marries de fust time. It was a big blow-out and I was scared de whole time. First time I ever tackled marryin'. Dey had a big paper sack of rice and throwed it all over her and I, enough rice to last three or four days, throwed away jus' for nothin'. I had on a black, alpaca suit with frock tail coat and, if I ain't mistaken, a right white shirt. My wife have a great train on her dress and one dem things you call a wreath. I wore de loudest shoes we could find, what you call patent leather.

"Dis here my third wife. We marries in Eagle Pass and comes up to de Seminole Reservation and works for de army till we goes to work for de Pattersons, and we been here 23 years now.

"Ghosties? I was takin' care of a white man when he died and I seed something 'bout three feet high and black. I reckon I must have fainted 'cause they has de doctor for me. And on dark nights I seed ghosties what has no head. Dey looks like dey wild and dey is all in different performance. When I goin' down de road and feel a hot steam and look over my shoulder I can see 'em plain as you standin' dere. I seed 'em when my wife was with me, but she can't see 'em, 'cause some people ain't gifted to see 'em.

United States.Work Project Administration

JOE BARNES

JOE BARNES, 89, was born in Tyler Co., Texas, on Jim Sapp's plantation. He is very feeble, but keeps his great grandchildren in line while their mother works. They live in Beaumont. Joe is tall, slight, and has gray hair and a stubby gray mustache. In his kind, gentle voice he relates his experiences in slavery days.

"Dey calls me Paul Barnes, but my name ain't Paul, it am Joe. My massa was Jim Sapp, up here in Tyler County, and missus' name was Ann. De Sapp place was big and dey raise' a sight of cotton and corn. Old massa Jim he have 'bout 25 or 30 slaves.

"My mammy's name was Artimisi, but dey call her Emily, and pa's name Jerry Wooten, 'cause he live on de Wooten place. My steppa named Barnes and I taken dat name. My parents, dey have de broomstick weddin'.

"When I's a chile us play marbles and run rabbits and ride de stick hoss and de like. When I gits more bigger, us play ball, sort of like baseball. One time my brudder go git de hosses and dey lots of rain and de creek swoll up high. De water so fast it wash him off he hoss and I ain't seed him since. Dey never find de body. He's 'bout ten year old den.

"Massa live in de big box house and de quarters am in a row in de back. Some of dem box and some of dem log. Dey have two rooms. Every day de big, old cowhorn blow for dinner and us have de little tin cup what us git potlicker in and meat and cornbread and salt bacon. Us gits greens, too. De chimneys 'bout four feet wide and dey cooks everything in de fireplace. Dey have pots and ovens and put fire below and 'bove 'em.

"I used to wear what I calls a one-button cutaway. It was jis' a shirt make out of homespun with pleats down front. Dey make dey own cloth dem time.

"Massa marry de folks in de broomstick style. Us don' have de party but sometime us sing and play games, like de round dance.

"Dey give de little ones bacon to suck and tie de string to de bacon and de other round dey wrists, so dey won't swallow or lose de bacon. For de little bits of ones dey rings de bell for dey mommers to come from de field and nuss 'em.

"After freedom come us stay a year and den move to Beaumont and us work in de sawmill for Mr. Jim Long. De fust money I git I give to my mammy. Me and mammy and stepdaddy stays in Beaumont two years den moves to Tyler and plants de crop. But de next year us move back to Beaumont on de Langham place and mammy work for de Longs till she die.

"When I git marry I marry Dicey Allen and she die and I never marry no more. I worked in sawmillin' and on de log pond and allus gits by pretty good. I ain't done no work much de last ten year, I's too old.

"I sort a looks after my grandchillen and I sho' loves dem. I sits 'round and hurts all de time. It am rheumatism in de feets, I reckon. I got six grandchillen and three great-grandchillen and dat one you hears cryin', dat de baby I's raisin' in dere.

"I's feared I didn't tell you so much 'bout things way back, but da truth am, I can't 'member like I used to.

ARMSTEAD BARRETT

ARMSTEAD BARRETT, born in 1847, was a slave of Stafford Barrett, who lived in Huntsville, Texas. He is the husband of Harriett Barrett. Armstead has a very poor memory and can tell little about early days. He and Harriet receive old age pensions.

"I's really owned by Massa Stafford Barrett, but my mammy 'longed to Massa Ben Walker and was 'lowed to keep me with her. So after we'uns got free, I lives with my daddy and mammy and goes by de name of Barrett. Daddy's name was Henry Barrett and he's brung to Texas from Richmond, in Virginny, and mammy come from Kentucky. Us all lived in Huntsville. I waited on Miss Ann and mammy was cook.

"Old massa have doctor for us when us sick. We's too val'ble. Jus' like to de fat beef, massa am good to us. Massa go to other states and git men and women and chile slaves and bring dem back to sell, 'cause he spec'lator. He make dem wash up good and den sell dem.

"Mos' time we'uns went naked. Jus' have on one shirt or no shirt a-tall.

"I know when peace 'clared dey all shoutin'. One woman hollerin' and a white man with de high-steppin' hoss ride clost to her and I see him git out and open he knife and cut her wide 'cross de stomach. Den he put he hat inside he shirt and rid off like lightnin'. De woman put in wagon and I never heered no more 'bout her.

"I didn't git nothin' when us freed. Only some cast-off clothes. Long time after I rents de place on halves and farms most my life. Now I's too old to work and gits a pension to live on.

"I seems to think us have more freedom when us slaves, 'cause we have no 'sponsibility for sickness den. We have to take care all dat now and de white man, he beats de nigger out what he makes. Back in de old days, de white men am hones'. All the nigger knowed was hard work. I think de cullud folks ought to be 'lowed more privileges in votin' now, 'cause dey have de same 'sponsibility as white men and day more and more educated and brighter and brighter.

"I think our young folks pretty sorry. They wont do right, but I 'lieve iffen dey could git fair wages dey'd do better. Dey git beat out of what dey does, anyway.

"I 'member a owner had some slaves and de overseer had it in for two of dem. He'd whip dem near every day and dey does all could be did to please him. So one day he come to de field and calls one dem slaves and dat slave draps he hoe and goes over and grabs dat overseer. Den de other slave cut dat overseer's head right slap off and throwed it down one of de rows. De owner he fools 'round and sells dem two slaves for $800.00 each and dat all de punishment dem two slaves ever got.

HARRIET BARRETT

HARRIET BARRETT, 86, was born in Walker Co., Texas, in 1851, a slave of Steve Glass. She now lives in Palestine, Texas.

"Massa Steve Glass, he own my pappy and mammy and me, until the war freed us. Pappy's borned in Africy and mammy in Virginy, and brung to Texas 'fore de war, and I's borned in Texas in 1851. I's heered my grandpa was wild and dey didn't know 'bout marryin' in Africy. My brother name Steve Glass and I dunno iffen I had sisters or not.

"Dey put me to cookin' when I's a li'l kid and people says now dat Aunt Harriet am de bes' cook in Madisonville. Massa have great big garden and plenty to eat. I's cook big skillet plumb full corn at de time and us all have plenty meat. Massa, he step out and kill big deer and put in de great big pot and cook it. Then us have cornbread and syrup.

"Us have log quarters with stick posts for bed and deerskin stretch over it. Den us pull moss and throw over dat. I have de good massa, bless he soul. Missy, she plumb good. She sick all de time and dey never have white chillen. Dey live in big, log house, four rooms in it and de great hall both ways through it.

"Massa, he have big bunch slaves and work dem long as dey could see and den lock 'em up in de quarters at night to keep 'em from runnin' off. De patterrollers come and go through de quarters to see if all de niggers dere. Dey walk right over us when us sleeps.

"Some slave run off, gwine to de north, and massa he

cotch him and give him thirty-nine licks with rawhide and lock dem up at night, too, and keep chain on him in daytime.

"I have de good massa, bless he soul, and missy she plumb good. I'll never forgit dem. Massa 'low us have holiday Saturday night and go to nigger dance if it on 'nother plantation. Boy, oh boy, de tin pan beatin' and de banjo pickin' and de dance all night long.

"When de war start, white missy die, and massa have de preacher. She was white angel. Den massa marry Missy Alice Long and she de bad woman with us niggers. She hard on us, not like old missy.

"I larned lots of remedies for sick people. Charcoal and onions and honey for de li'l baby am good, and camphor for de chills and fever and teeth cuttin'. I's boil red oak bark and make tea for fever and make cactus weed root tea for fever and chills and colic. De best remedy for chills and fever am to git rabbit foot tie on string 'round de neck.

"Massa, he carry me to war with him, 'cause I's de good cook. In dat New Orleans battle he wounded and guns roarin' everywhere. Dey brung massa in and I's jus' as white as he am den. Dem Yankees done shoot de roof off de house. I nuss de sick and wounded clean through de war and seed dem dyin' on every side of me.

"I's most scared to death when de war end. Us still in New Orleans and all de shoutin' dat took place 'cause us free! Dey crowds on de streets and was in a stir jus' as thick as flies on de dog. Massa say I's free as him, but iffen I wants to cook for him and missy I gits $2.50 de month, so I cooks for him till I marries Armstead Barrett, and then us farm for de livin'. Us have big church weddin' and I has white loyal dress and black brogan shoes. Us been married 51 years now.

JOHN BATES

JOHN BATES, 84, was born in Little Rock, Arkansas, a slave of Mock Bateman. When still very young, John moved with his mother, a slave of Harry Hogan, to Limestone Co., Texas. John now lives in Corsicana, supported by his children and an old age pension.

"My pappy was Ike Bateman, 'cause his massa's name am Mock Bateman, and mammy's name was Francis. They come from Tennessee and I had four brothers and six sisters. We jes' left de last part of de name off and call it Bates and dat's how I got my name. Mammy 'longed to Massa Harry Hogan and while I's small us move to Texas, to Limestone County, and I don't 'member much 'bout pappy, 'cause I ain't never seed him since.

"Massa Hogan was a purty good sort of fellow, but us went hongry de fust winter in Texas. He lived in de big log house with de hallway clean through and a gallery clean 'cross de front. De chimney was big 'nough to burn logs in and it sho' throwed out de heat. It was a good, big place and young massa come out early and holler for us to git up and be in de field.

"Missy Hogan was de good woman and try her dead level best to teach me to read and write, but my head jes' too thick, I jes' couldn't larn. My Uncle Ben he could read de Bible and he allus tell us some day us be free and Massa Harry laugh, haw, haw, haw, and he say, 'Hell, no, yous never be free, yous ain't got sense 'nough to make de livin' if yous was free.' Den he takes de Bible 'way from Uncle Ben and say it put de bad ideas in he head, but Uncle gits 'nother Bible and hides it and massa never finds it out.

"We'uns goes to de big baptisin' one time and it's at de big sawmill tank and 50 is baptise' and I's in dat bunch myself. But dey didn't have no funerals for de slaves, but jes' bury dem like a cow or a hoss, jes' dig de hole and roll 'em in it and cover 'em up.

"War come and durin' dem times jes' like today nearly everybody knows what gwine on, news travels purty fast, and iffen de slaves couldn't git it with de pass dey slips out after dark and go in another plantation by de back way. Course, iffen dem patterrollers cotch dem it jus' too bad and dey gits whip.

"When de news comes in dat us free, Massa Harry never call us up like everybody else did the slaves, us has to go up and ask him 'bout it. He come out on de front gallery and says we is free and turns 'round and goes in de house without 'nother word. We all sho' feels sorry for him the way he acts and hates to leave him, but we wants to go. We knowed he wasn't able to give us nothin' so begins to scatter and 'bout ten or fifteen days Massa Harry dies. I think he jes' grieve himself to death, all he trouble comin' on him to once.

"Us worked on diff'rent farms till I marries and my fust wife am Emma Williams and a cullud preacher marries us at her house. Us picked cotton after dat and den I rents a place on de halvers for five year and after sev'ral years I buys eighty acres of land. Fin'ly us done paid dat out and done some repairs and den us sep'rate after livin' twenty-three year together. So I gives dat place to her and de six chillen and I walks out ready to start all over 'gain.

"Then I meets Sarah Jones and us marries, but she gives me de divorcement. All dis time I works on a farm for de day wages, den I rents 'nother farm on de halvers on de black land and stays dere sev'ral year. Fin'ly I gits de job workin' at de cotton oil mill in Corsicana and stays at dat job till dey says I's too old. I done buy dis li'l home here and now has a place to live. Sarah done come back to me and us has seven chillen. One of de boys works at de cotton oil mill and two works at de compress right here in Corsicana and one works at de beer place in Dallas.

"Us raises a li'l on dese two lots and de chillen brings some from de farm, I mean my fust wife's chillen, and with de pension check us manage to live a li'l longer. Us boys pays de taxes and de insurance for us.

United States.Work Project Administration

HARRISON BECKETT

HARRISON BECKETT, born a slave of I.D. Thomas of San Augustine, Texas, now lives in Beaumont. A great-grandson climbed into Harrison's lap during the interview, and his genial face lit up with a smile. He chuckled as he told of his own boyhood days, and appeared to enjoy reminiscing. At times he uses big words, some of his own coining.

"I's 'mong de culls now, like a hoss what am too old. I's purty small yit when 'mancipation comes and didn't have no hard work. Old Massa have me and de other li'l niggers keep de stock out de fields. Us li'l boogers have to run and keep de cows out de corn and de cotton patch. Dat ought to been 'nough to keep us out of debbilment.

"It come to pass my mammy work in de field. Her name Cynthia Thomas and daddy's name Isaac Thomas. But after freedom he goes back to Florida and find out he people and git he real name, and dat am Beckett. Dat 'bout ten years after 'mancipation he go back to he old home in Florida. Mammy's people was de Polkses, in Georgia. Mammy come in from de field at nine or ten o'clock at night and she be all wore out and too tired to cook lots of times. But she have to git some food for us. We all had a tin pan and git round de table and dat like a feast. But lots of times she's so tired she go to bed without eatin' nothin' herself.

"My sisters was Ellen and Sani and Georgy-Ann and Cindy and Sidi-Ann. Dey's all big 'nough to work in de field. My brudders name Matthew and Ed and Henry and Harry, what am me, and de oldes' one am General Thomas.

"Dey more'n a hundred head of black folks on Massa Thomas' two farms, and 'bout a hundred fifty acres in each farm. One de farms in iron ore, what am red land, and de other in gray land, half sand and half black dirt.

"Us slaves live in pole houses and some in split log houses, with two rooms, one for to sleep in and one for to cook in. Day ain't no glass windows, jus' holes in de walls. Dere was jack beds to sleep on, made out of poles. Dey has four legs and ain't nail to de walls.

"Old Massa he care for he hands purty well, considerin' everything. In ginnin' time he 'low de women to pick up cotton from de ground and make mattresses and quilts. He make some cloth and buy some. A woman weave all de time and when de shickle jump out on de floor I picks it up. I used to could knit socks and I was jes' a li'l boy then, but I keep everything in 'membrance.

"Dey have some school and de chillen larnt readin' and writin', and manners and behaviour, too. Sometime dey git de broke-down white man to be teacher. But us didn't know much and it taken ten years or more after freedom to git de black men de qualification way he could handle things.

"One time us boys git some watermillions out in de bresh and hit 'em or drap 'em to break 'em open. Dere come massa and cotch us not workin', but eatin' he watermillions. He tell my daddy to whip me. But lots of times when us sposed to mind de calves, us am out eatin' watermillions in de bresh. Den de calves git out and massa see dem run and cotch us.

"Old massa was kind and good, though. He have partiality 'bout him, and wouldn't whip nobody without de cause. He whip with de long, keen switch and it didn't bruise de back, but sho' did sting. When he git real mad, he pull up you shirt and whip on de bare hide. One time he whippin' me and I busts de button off my shirt what he holdin' on to, and runs away. I tries to outrun him, and dat tickle him. I sho' give de ground fits with my feets. But dem whippin's done me good. Dey break me up from thievin' and make de man of me.

"De way dey dress us li'l nigger boys den, dey give us a shirt what come way down 'tween de knees and ankles. When de weather am too cold, dey sometimes give us pants.

"De white preachers come round and preach. Dey have de tabernacle like a arbor and cullud folks come from all round to hear de Gospel 'spounded. Most every farm have de cullud man larnin' to preach. I used to 'long to de Methodists but now I 'longs to de Church of Christ.

"Massa Thomas, he de wholesale merchant and git kilt in New Orleans. A big box of freight goods fall on him, a box 'bout a yard square on de end and six yards long. He's carryin' back some good for to make exchangement and dey pullin' up de box with pulley and rope and it fall on him. De New Orleans folks say it am de accidentment, but de rest say de rope am cut. One of massa's old friends was Lawyer Brooks. He used to firmanize de word.

"Massa have two boys, Mr. Jimmie and Li'l Ide and dey both goes to de war. Li'l Ide, he go up in Arkansas and dey say when dat first cannon busts at Li'l Rock, he starts runnin' and never stops till he gits back home. I don't see how he could do dat, 'cause Li'l Rock am way far off, but dat what dey say. Den de men comes to git 'serters and dey gits Li'l Ide and takes him back. Mr. Jimmie, he didn't break de ranks. He stood he ground.

"Mammy and dem tell me when war am over de boss and he wife, dey calls de slaves up in de bunch and tells 'em, 'You's free as I is. Keep on or quit, if you wants. You don't have to stay no further, you's free today.' Dat near June 19th, and all of 'em stays. Massa say, 'Go 'head and finish de crop and I feed you and pay you.' Dey all knowed when he kilt de hawgs us git plenty of meat. Dat young massa say all dat, 'cause old massa done git kilt.

"It's at Panola County where I first hears of de Klux. Dey call dem White Caps den. Dey move over in Panola County and ranges at de place call Big Creek Merval by McFaddin Creek. Dey's purty rough. De landowners tell dey niggers not to kill de White Caps but to scare dem 'way. At night dey come knock and if you don't open it dey pry it open and run you out in de field. Dey run de niggers from Merryville round Longview. Dey some good men in de Klux and some bad men. But us work hard and go home and dey ain't bother us none.

"Dey used to be a nigger round dere, call Bandy Joe. He git kilt at Nacogdoches fin'ly. He could turn into anything. De jedge of he parish was Massa Lee and he say dey ought let Bandy Joe live, so dey could larn he art. Dey done try cotch him de long time, and maybe be holdin' him and first thing they know he gone and dey left holdin' he coat. Dey shoot at him and not hurt him. He tell he wife dey ain't no kind bullet can hurt him but de silver bullet.

"Dat Bandy Joe, he say he a spirit and a human both. Iffen he didn't want you to see him you jus' couldn't see him. Lots of folks liked him. De jedge say he wish he could'a been brung to town, so he could 'zamine him 'bout he gifts. De jedge knowed Bandy Joe could dis'pear jus' like nothin', and he like to hear he quotation how he git out he skin. I'd like to know dat myself.

"I 'magines I seed ghosties two, three times. I used to range round at nighttime. I rides through a old slavery field and de folks tell me, 'Harry, you better be careful gwine 'cross dat old field. They's things dere what makes mules run 'way. One night it am late and my mule run 'way. I make my mind I go back and see what he run from and somethin' am by de fence like de bear stand up straight. It stand dere 'bout fifteen minutes while I draws my best 'pinion of it. I didn't get any nearer dan to see it. A man down de road tell me de place am hanted and he dunno how many wagons and mules git pull by dat thing at dat place.

"One time I's livin' 'nother place and it am 'twixt sundown and dusk. I had a li'l boy 'hind me and I seed a big sow with no head comin' over de fence. My ma, she allus say what I see might be 'magination and to turn my head and look 'gain and I does dat. But it still dere. Den I seed a hoss goin' down de road and he drag a chain, and cross de bridge and turn down de side road. But when I git to de side road I ain't seed no hoss or nothin'. I didn't say nothin' to de li'l boy 'hind me on de mule till I gits most home, den asks him did he see anythin'. He say no. I wouldn't tell him 'fore dat, 'cause I 'fraid he light out and outrun me and I didn't want to be by myself with dem things. When I gits home and tell everybody, dey say dat a man name McCoy, what was kilt dere and I seed he spirit.

"I's 'bout twenty-one when I marries Mandy Green. Us has twelve chillen, and a world of grandchillen. I travels all over Louisiana and Texas in my time, and come here three year ago. My son he work in de box fact'ry here, and he git a bodily injurement while he workin' and die, and I come here to de burial and I been here ever since.

United States.Work Project Administration

Slave Narratives

FRANK BELL

FRANK BELL, 86, was a slave of Johnson Bell, who ran a saloon in New Orleans. Frank lives in Madisonville, Texas.

"I was owned by Johnson Bell and born in New Orleans, in Louisiana. 'Cordin' to the bill of sale, I'm eighty-six years old, and my master was a Frenchman and was real mean to me. He run saloon and kept bad women. I don't know nothing 'bout my folks, if I even had any, 'cept mama. They done tell me she was a bad woman and a French Creole.

"I worked 'round master's saloon, kep' everything cleaned up after they'd have all night drinkin' parties, men and women. I earned nickels to tip off where to go, so's they could sow wild oats. I buried the nickels under rocks. If master done cotch me with money, he'd take it and beat me nearly to death. All I had to eat was old stuff those people left, all scraps what was left.

"One time some bad men come to master's and gits in a shootin' scrape and they was two men kilt. I sho' did run. But master cotch me and make me take them men to the river and tie a weight on them, so they'd sink and the law wouldn't git him.

"The clothes I wore was some master's old ones. They allus had holes in them. Master he stay drunk nearly all time and was mean to his slave. I'm the only one he had, and didn't cost him nothing. He have bill of sale made, 'cause the law say he done stole me when I'm small child. Master kept me in chains sometimes. He shot several men.

"I didn't have no quarters but stays 'round the place and

throw old sack down and lay there and sleep. I'm 'fraid to run, 'cause master say he'd hunt me and kill nigger.

"When I's 'bout seventeen I marries a gal while master on drunk spell. Master he run her off, and I slips off at night to see her, but he finds it out. He takes a big, long knife and cuts her head plumb off, and ties a great, heavy weight to her and makes me throw her in the river. Then he puts me in chains and every night he come give me a whippin', for long time.

"When war come, master swear he not gwine fight, but the Yankees they captures New Orleans and throws master in a pen and guards him. He gets a chance and 'scapes.

"When war am over he won't free me, says I'm valuable to him in his trade. He say, 'Nigger, you's suppose to be free but I'll pay you a dollar a week and iffen you runs off I'll kill you.' So he makes me do like befo' the war, but give me 'bout a dollar a month, 'stead week.

"He say I cost more'n I'm worth, but he won't let me go. Times I don't know why I didn't die befo' I'm growed, sleepin' on the ground, winter and summer, rain and snow. But not much snow there.

"Master helt me long years after the war. If anybody git after him, he told them I stay 'cause I wants to stay, but told me if I left he'd kill him 'nother nigger. I stayed till he gits in a drunk brawl one night with men and women and they gits to shootin' and some kilt. Master got kilt. Then I'm left to live or die, so I wanders from place to place. I nearly starved to death befo' I'd leave New Orleans, 'cause I couldn't think master am dead and I'm 'fraid. Finally I gits up nerve to leave town, and stays the first night in white man's barn. I never slep'. Every time I hears something, I jumps up and master be standin' there, lookin' at me, but soon's I git up he'd leave. Next night I slep' out in a hay field, and master he git right top of a tree and start hollerin at me. I never stays in that place. I gits gone from that place. I gits back to town fast as my legs carry me.

"Then I gits locked up in jail. I don't know what for, never did know. One the men says to me to come with him and takes me to the woods and gives me an ax. I cuts rails till I nearly falls, all with chain locked 'round feet, so I couldn't run off. He turns me loose and I wanders 'gain. Never had a home. Works for men long 'nough to git fifty, sixty cents, then starts roamin' 'gain, like a stray dog like.

"After long time I marries Feline Graham. Then I has a home and we has a white preacher marry us. We has one boy and he farms and I lives with him. I worked at sawmill and farms all my life, but never could make much money.

"You know, the nigger was wild till the white man made what he has out of the nigger. He done ed'cate them real smart.

United States.Work Project Administration

AUNT VIRGINIA BELL

Aunt VIRGINIA BELL, 1205 Ruthven St., Houston, was born a slave near Opelousas, Louisiana, on the plantation of Thomas Lewis. Although she remembers being told she was born on Christmas Day, she does not know the year, but says she guesses she is about 88 years old.

"Well, suh, the fus' question you ask me, 'bout how old I is, I don' know 'zactly. You see it ain't like things is today. The young folks can tell you their 'zact age and everything, but in those days we didn' pay much 'tention to such things. But I knows I was bo'n in slavery times and my pappy tol' me I was bo'n on a Christmas Day, but didn' 'member jus' what year.

"We was owned by Massa Lewis. Thomas Lewis was his name, and he was a United States lawyer. I ain't gwineter talk 'gainst my white folks like some cullud folks do, 'cause Massa Lewis was a mighty fine man and so was Miss Mary, and they treated us mighty good.

"Massa had a big plantation near Opelousas and I was bo'n there. I 'member the neighbor folks used to bring their cotton to the gin on his farm for ginnin' and balin'. My mother's name was Della. That was all, jus' Della. My pappy's name was Jim Blair. Both of them was from Virginny, but from diff'rent places, and was brought to Louisiana by nigger traders and sold to Massa Lewis. I know my pappy was lots older than my mother and he had a wife and five chillen back in Virginny and had been sold away from them out here. Then he and my mother started a family out here. I don' know what become of his family back in Virginny, 'cause when we was freed he stayed with us.

"When I got old enough I was housegirl and used to carry notes for Miss Mary to the neighbors and bring back answers. Miss Mary would say, 'Now, Virginny, you take this note to sech and sech place and be sure and be back in sech and sech time,' and I allus was.

"Massa Lewis had four or five families of us slaves, but we used to have some fun after work and us young folks would skip rope and play ring games. Durin' week days the field hands would work till the sun was jus' goin' down and then the overseer would holler 'all right' and that was the signal to quit. All hands knocked off Sat'day noon.

"We didn' have no schoolin' or preachin'. Only the white folks had them, but sometimes on Sundays we'd go up to the house and listen to the white folks singin'.

"Iffen any of the slave hands wanted to git married, Massa Lewis would git them up to the house after supper time, have the man and woman jine hands and then read to them outen a book. I guess it was the Scriptures. Then he'd tell 'em they was married but to be ready for work in the mornin'. Massa Lewis married us 'cordin' to Gospel.

"Massa used to feed us good, too, and we had plenty clothes. Iffen we got took sick, we had doctor treatment, too. Iffen a hand took sick in the field with a misery, they was carried to their quarters and Massa or Miss Mary would give them a dose of epecac and make them vomit and would sen' for the doctor. They wouldn' fool none iffen one of us took sick, but would clean us out and take care of us till we was well.

"There was mighty little whippin' goin' on at our place, 'cause Massa Lewis and Miss Mary treated us good. They wasn't no overseer goin' to whip, 'cause Massa wouldn' 'low him to. Le's see, I don' rec'lec' more than two whippin's I see anyone git from Massa, and that has been so long ago I don' rec'lec' what they was for.

"When the War done come 'long it sho' changed things, and we heerd this and that, but we didn' know much what it was about. Then one day Massa Lewis had all the wagons loaded with food and chairs and beds and other things from the house and our quarters, and I heerd him say we was movin' to Polk County, way over in Texas. I know it took us a long time to git there, and when we did I never see so much woods. It sho' was diff'rent from the plantation.

"I had to work in the fields, same as the res', and we stayed there three years and made three crops of cotton, but not so much as on our old place, 'cause there wasn't so much clearin'. Then one day Massa Lewis tol' us we was free, jus' as free as he was—jus' like you take the bridle offen a hoss and turn him loose. We jus' looked 'roun as iffen we hadn' good sense. We didn' have nothin' nor nowhere to go, and Massa Lewis say iffen we finish makin' de crop, he would take us back to Opelousas and give us a place to stay and feed us. So after pickin' we goes back and when we git there we sees where those rascal Yankees 'stroyed everything—houses burned, sugar kettles broke up. It looked mighty bad.

"Massa Lewis hadn' no money, but he fixed us up a place to stay and give us what he could to eat, but things was mighty hard for a while. I know pappy used to catch rabbits and take them to town and sell them or trade them for somethin' to eat, and you know that wasn't much, 'cause you can't git much for a little ol' rabbit.

"Then the Provo' Marshal, that was his name, give us a order for things to put in a crop with and to live till we made the crop. 'Course, I guess we wasn' as bad off as some, 'cause white folks knew we was Massa Lewis' folks and didn' bother us none.

Then I got married to John Bell, and it was a scripture weddin', too. He died 28 years ago, but I has stayed married to him ever since. We had thirteen chillen, but they is all dead now 'cept four, but they was raised up right and they is mighty good to they ol' mammy.

EDGAR AND MINERVA BENDY

EDGAR BENDY, 90 odd years, was the slave of Henry Bendy, of Woodville, Texas, has to make an effort to remember and is forced to seek aid from his wife, Minerva, at certain points in his story. Edgar has lived in Woodville all his life.

"I's a good size' boy when de war gwine on and I seed de soldiers come right here in Woodville. A big bunch of dem come through and dey have cannons with dem. My marster he didn't go to war, 'cause he too old, I guess.

"I's born right here and done live hereabouts every since. Old man Henry Bendy, he my marster and he run de store here in Woodville and have de farm, too. I didn't do nothin' 'cept nuss babies. I jes' jump dem up and down and de old marster hire me out to nuss other white folks chillen, big and little.

"My daddy name' Jack Crews and my mammy was Winnie. Both of dem worked on de farm and I never seed dem much. I didn't have no house of my own, 'cause de marster, he give me de room in he house. He have lots of slaves and 'bout 100 acres in cult'vation. He gave dem plenty to eat and good homespun clothes to wear. He was mighty good.

"Marster have de plank house and all de things in it was home-made. De cook was a old cullud woman and I eat at de kitchen table and have de same what de white folks eats. Us has lots of meat, deer meat and possum and coon and sich, and us sets traps for birds.

"Dey ain't nothin' better dat go in de wood dan de big, fat possum. Dey git fat on black haws and acorns and chinquapin and sich. Chinquapin is good for people to eat and to roast. I used to be plumb give up to be de best hunter in Tyler and in de whole country. I kilt more deer dan any other man in de county and I been guide for all de big men what comes here to hunt. My wife, Minerva, she used to go huntin' with me.

"I kep' on huntin' and huntin' till de Jack-a-my-lanterns git after me. Dat a light you sees all 'round you. Dey follow all 'long and dey stop you still. Den one time it git all over me. Come like de wind, blow, blow, and come jes' like fire all on my arm and my clothes and things. When dat git after me I quit huntin' at nighttime and ain't been huntin' since.

"One time I fishin' on de creek and I ain't got no gun, and I look up and dere a big, wild cat. He never pay me no mind, no more dan nothin', but dat ain't made no diff'rence to me. I jes' flew in dat creek!

"I used to belong to de lodge but when I git so old I couldn't pay my jews, I git unfinancial and I ain't a member no more.

MINERVA BENDY

MINERVA BENDY, 83, was born a slave to Lazarus Goolsby, Henry Co. Alabama, who brought her to Texas when she was five. They settled near Woodville, where Minerva still lives.

"My earlies' 'membrance was de big, white sandy road what lead 'way from de house. It was clean and white and us chillen love to walk in de soft, hot sand. Dat in Henry County, Alabama, where I's born and my old marster was Lazarus Goolsby and he have de big plantation with lots of nigger folks. I 'member jus' as good as yesterday wigglin' my toes in dat sandy road and runnin' 'way to de grits mill where dey grind de meal. Dat have de big water wheel dat sing and squeak as it go 'round.

"Aunt Mary, she make all us little chillen sleep in de heat of de day under de big, spreadin' oak tree in de yard. My mama have 17 chillen. Her name Dollie and my daddy name Herd.

"I's jus' a little chile in dem days and I stay in de house with de white folks. Dey raise me a pet in de family. Missus Goolsby, she have two gals and dey give me to de oldest. When she die dey put me in de bed with her but iffen I knowed she dyin' dey wouldn't been able to cotch me. She rub my head and tell her papa and mama, 'I's gwine 'way but I wants you promise you ain't never whip my little nigger.' Dey never did.

"I's jus' 'bout five year old when us make de trip to Texas. Us come right near Woodville and make de plantation. It a big place and dey raise corn and cotton and cane. We makes our own sugar and has many as six kettle on de furnace at one time. Dey raise dey tobacco, too. I's sick and a old man he say he make me tobacco medicine and dey dry de leafs and make dem sweet like sugar and feed me like candy.

"I 'member old marster say war broke out and Capt. Collier's men was a-drillin' right dere south of Woodville. All de wives and chillen watch dem drill. Dey was lots of dem, but I couldn't count. De whole shebang from de town go watch dem.

"Four of the Goolsby boys goes to dat war and dey call John and Ziby and Zabud and Addison. Zabud, he git wounded, no he git kilt, and Addison he git wounded. I worry den, 'cause I ain't see no reason for dem to have to die.

"After us free dey turn us loose in de woods and dat de bad time, 'cause most us didn't know where to turn. I wasn't raise to do nothin' and I didn't know how. Dey didn't even give us a hoecake or a slice of bacon.

"I's a June bride 59 year ago when I git married. De old white Baptist preacher name Blacksheer put me and dat nigger over dere, Edgar Bendy, togedder and us been togedder ever since. Us never have chick or chile. I's such a good nuss I guess de Lawd didn't want me to have none of my own, so's I could nuss all de others and I 'spect I's nussed most de white chillen and cullud, too, here in Woodville.

SARAH BENJAMIN

SARAH BENJAMIN, 82, was born a slave of the Gilbert family, in Clavin Parish, Louisiana. In 1867 she married Cal Benjamin and they settled in Corsicana, Texas, where Sarah now lives.

"I is Sarah Benjamin and is 82 year old, 'cause my mammy told me I's born in 1855 in Clavin Parish in Louisiana. Her name was Fannie and my pappy's name Jack Callahan. There was jus' three of us chillen and I's de oldest.

"Marse Gilbert was tol'able good to we'uns, and give us plenty to eat. He had a smokehouse big as a church and it was full, and in de big kitchen we all et, chillen and all. De grown folks et first and den de chillen. Did we have plenty of possums and fish by de barrels full! All dis was cooked in de racks over de fireplace and it were good.

"Our clothes was all homespun and de shoes made by de shoemaker. Old marse wanted all us to go to church and if dey didn't have shoes dey have something like de moccasin.

"I don't know how many slaves there was, but it was a lot, maybe 60 or 70. Dey worked hard every day 'cept Sunday. Iffen they was bad they might git whuppin's, but not too hard, not to de blood. Iffen dey was still bad, dey puts chains on dem and puts dem in de stocks, 'cause there wasn't no jail there.

"Once when I's little, marse stripped me stark modern naked and puts me on de block, but he wouldn't sell me, 'cause he was bid only $350.00 and he say no, 'cause I was good and fat.

"Dey didn't larn us nothin' and iffen you did larn to write, you better keep it to yourse'f, 'cause some slaves got de thumb or finger cut off for larnin' to write. When de slaves come in from de fields dey didn't larn nothin', they jus' go to bed, 'lessen de moonshine nights come and dey could work in de tobacco patch. De marster give each one de little tobacco patch and iffen he raised more'n he could use he could sell it.

"On Christmas we all has de week vacation and maybe de dance. We allus have de gran' dinner on dat day, and no whuppin's. But dey couldn't leave de plantation without de pass, even on Christmas.

"De women had to run de gin in de daytime and de man at night. Dey fed de old gin from baskets and my mammy fed from dose baskets all day with de high fever and died dat night. She wouldn't tell de marster she sick, fer fear she have to take de quinine.

"De day we was freed, de slaves jus' scattered, 'cepting me. Missy Gilbert says I wasn't no slave no more but I had to stay and he'p her for my board 'till I's grown. I stayed 'till I was 'bout 16, den I runs away and marries Cal Benjamin, and we comes to Texas. Cal and me has six chillen, but he died 'fore dey was grown.

JACK BESS

JACK BESS was born near Goliad, Texas in 1854, a slave of Steve Bess who was a rancher. He worked with stock as a very young boy and this was his duty during and after the Civil War, as he remained with his boss for three years after emancipation. He then came to old Ben Ficklin four miles south of the present San Angelo, Texas, when it was the county seat of Tom Green County and before there was a San Angelo. He continued his work on ranches here and has never done any other kind of work. For the past several years he has been very feeble and has made his home with a daughter in San Angelo, Texas.

Jack who was assisted out of bed and dressed by his grandson, hobbled in on his cane and said, "I was jes' a small boy workin' on de ranch when I hear talk 'bout conscription' de men for de war what was agoin' to set de slaves free. We didn' know hardly what dey was a talkin' 'bout 'cause we knowed dat would be too good to be true. I jes' keeps on workin' wid my hosses and my cattle (dere wasn't no sheep den) jes' like dere wasn't no war, 'cause dat was all I ever knowed how to do.

"Our ole marster, he wasn't so very mean to us, course he whips us once and awhile but dat wasn't like de slave holders what had dem colored drivers. Dey sho' was rough on de slaves. I's been told lots 'bout de chains and de diffe'nt punishments but our treatment wasn't so bad. Our beds was pretty good when we uses dem. Lots of de time we jes' sleeps on de groun', 'specially in summer.

"Our log huts was comfortable and we had some kind of floors in all of dem. Some was plank and some was poles but dat was better den de dirt floors some cabins have.

"De eats we have was jes' good eats, lots of meats and vegetables and de like; 'possum and coon and beef and pork all cooked good. Our clothes was jes' home spun like all de others.

"We didn' have such a big ranch and not many slaves but we all gits along. We learns a little 'bout readin' and writin'.

"I don't 'member any camp meetin's 'til after de war. We had a few den and on Christmas times we jes' tears up de country. Lawdy! Lawd! Dat fiddlin' went on all night, and we dance awhile den lay down and sleeps, den gits up and dances some mo'e. We would have big cakes and everything good to eat.

"When we gits sick dey jes' gives us some kind of tea, mostly made from weeds. Mos' of de time we gits well.

"When de news comes dat we was free our boss, he say, 'You free now.' Course we was glad but we didn' know nothin' to do but jes' stay on dere, and we did 'bout three years and de boss pays us a little by de month for our work.

"I's lef' dere den and comes to old Ben Ficklin to work on a ranch. Dat was before dere was any San Angelo, Texas. I's been here ever since, jes' a workin' from one ranch to another long as I was able. Now I's jes' stayin' 'round wid my chillun and dey takes good care of me."

United States.Work Project Administration

ELLEN BETTS

ELLEN BETTS, 118 N. Live Oak St., Houston, Texas, is 84. All of her people and their masters came from Virginia and settled in Louisiana about 1853. Her grandparents belonged to the Green family and her parents, Charity and William Green, belonged to Tolas Parsons. Ellen lives with friends who support her. Her sole belonging is an old trunk and she carries the key on a string around her neck.

"I got borned on de Bayou Teche, clost to Opelousas. Dat in St. Mary's Parish, in Louisiana, and I belonged to Tolas Parsons, what had 'bout 500 slaves, countin' de big ones and de little ones, and he had God know what else. When my eyes jes' barely fresh open, Marse Tolas die and will de hull lot of us to he brother, William Tolas. And I tells you dat Marse William am de greates' man what ever walk dis earth. Dat's de truth. I can't lie on him when de pore man's in he grave.

"When a whuppin' got to be done, old Marse do it heself. He don't 'low no overseer to throw he gals down and pull up dere dress and whup on dere bottoms like I hear tell some of 'em do. Was he still livin' I 'spect one part of he hands be with him today. I knows I would.

"When us niggers go down de road folks say, 'Dem's Parson's niggers. Don't hit one dem niggers for God's sake, or Parsons sho' eat your jacket up.'

"Aunt Rachel what cook in de big house for Miss Cornelia had four young'uns and dem chillen fat and slick as I ever seen. All de niggers have to stoop to Aunt Rachel jes' like dey curtsy to Missy. I mind de time her husband, Uncle Jim, git mad and hit her over de head with de poker. A big knot raise up on Aunt Rachel's head and when Marse 'quire 'bout it, she say she done bump de head. She dassn't tell on Uncle Jim or Marse sho' beat him. Marse sho' proud dem black, slick chillen of Rachels. You couldn't find a yaller chile on he place. He sho' got no use for mixin' black and white.

"Marse William have de pretties' place up and down dat bayou, with de fine house and fine trees and sech. From where we live it's five mile to Centerville one way and five mile to Patterson t'other. Dey hauls de lumber from one place or t'other to make wood houses for de slaves. Sometime Marse buy de furniture and sometime de carpenter make it.

"Miss Sidney was Marse's first wife and he had six boys by her. Den he marry de widow Cornelius and she give him four boys. With ten chillen springin' up quick like dat and all de cullud chillen comin' 'long fast as pig litters, I don't do nothin' all my days, but nuss, nuss, nuss. I nuss so many chillen it done went and stunted my growth and dat's why I ain't nothin' but bones to dis day.

"When de cullud women has to cut cane all day till midnight come and after, I has to nuss de babies for dem and tend de white chillen, too. Some dem babies so fat and big I had to tote de feet while 'nother gal tote de head. I was sech a li'l one, 'bout seven or eight year old. De big folks leave some toddy for colic and cryin' and sech and I done drink de toddy and let de chillen have de milk. I don't know no better. Lawsy me, it a wonder I ain't de bigges' drunker in dis here country, countin' all de toddy I done put in my young belly!

"When late of night come, iffen dem babies wake up and bawl, I set up a screech and out-screech dem till dey shut dere mouth. De louder day bawl de louder I bawl. Sometime when Marse hear de babies cry, he come down and say, 'Why de chillen cry like dat, Ellen?' I say, 'Marse, I git so hongry and tired I done drink de milk up.' When I talk sassy like dat, Marse jes' shake he finger at me, 'cause he knowed I's a good one and don't let no little mite starve.

"Nobody ever hit me a lick. Marse allus say bein' mean to de young'uns make dem mean when dey grows up and nobody gwineter buy a mean nigger. Marse don't even let de chillen go to de big cane patch. He plant little bitty patches close to de house and each li'l nigger have a patch and he work it till it got growed. Marse have de house girls make popcorn for 'em and candy.

"I nuss de sick folks too. Sometime I dose with Blue Mass pills and sometime Dr. Fawcett leave rhubarb and ipicac and calomel and castor oil and sech. Two year after de war, I git marry and git chillen of my own and den I turn into de wet nuss. I wet nuss de white chillen and black chillen, like dey all de same color. Sometime I have a white'un pullin' de one side and a black one de other.

"I wanted to git de papers for midwifin' but, law, I don't never have no time for larnin' in slave time. If Marse cotch a paper in you hand he sho' whop you. He don't 'low no bright niggers 'round, he sell 'em quick. He allus say, 'Book larnin' don't raise no good sugar cane.' De only larnin' he 'low was when dey larn de cullud chillen de Methodist catechism. De only writin' a nigger ever git, am when he git born or marry or die, den Marse put de name in de big book.

Law, I 'lect de time Marse marry Miss Cornelia. He went on de mail boat and brung her from New Orleans. She de pretties' woman in de world almost, 'ceptin' she have de bigges' mouth I nearly ever seed. He brung her up to de house and all de niggers and boys and girls and cats and dogs and sech come and salute her. Dere she stand on de gallery, with a purty white dress on with red stripes runnin' up and down. Marse say to her, 'Honey, see all de black folks, dey 'longs to you now.' She wave to us and smile on us and nex' day she give her weddin' dress to my ma. Dat de fines' dress I ever seen. It was purple and green silk and all de nigger gals wear dat dress when dey git marry. My sister Sidney wore it and Sary and Mary.

"Miss Cornelia was de fines' woman in de world. Come Sunday mornin' she done put a bucket of dimes on de front gallery and stand dere and throw dimes to de nigger chillen jes' like feedin' chickens. I sho' right here to test'fy, 'cause I's right dere helpin' grab. Sometime she done put da washtub of buttermilk on de back gallery and us chillen bring us gourds and dip up dat good, old buttermilk till it all git drunk up. Sometime she fotch bread and butter to de back gallery and pass it out when it don't even come mealtime.

"Miss Cornelia set my ma to cuttin' patterns and sewin' right away. She give all de women a bolt or linsey to make clothes and ma cut de pattern. Us all have de fine drawers down to de ankle, buttoned with pretty white buttons on de bottom. Lawsy, ma sho' cut a mite of drawers, with sewin' for her eleven gals and four boys, too. In de summertime we all git a bolt of blue cloth and white tape for trimmin', to make Sunday dresses. For de field, all de niggers git homespun what you make jumpers out of. I 'lect how Marse say, 'Don't go into de field dirty Monday mornin'. Scrub youself and put on de clean jumper.'

"Marse sho' good to dem gals and bucks what cuttin' de cane. When dey git done makin' sugar, he give a drink call 'Peach 'n Honey' to de women folk and whiskey and brandy to de men. And of all de dancin' and caperin' you ever seen! My pa was fiddler and we'd cut de pigeon wing and cut de buck and every other kind of dance. Sometime pa git tired and say he ain't gwineter play no more and us gals git busy and pop him corn and make candy, so to 'tice him to play more.

"Marse sho' turn over in he grave did he know 'bout some dat 'lasses. Dem black boys don't care. I seen 'em pull rats out de sugar barrel and dey taste de sugar and say, 'Ain't nothin' wrong with dat sugar. It still sweet.' One day a pert one pull a dead scorpion out de syrup kettle and he jes' laugh and say, 'Marse don't want waste none dis syrup,' and he lick de syrup right off dat scorpion's body and legs.

"Lawsy me, I seen thousands and thousands sugar barrels and kettles of syrup in my day. Lawd knows how much cane old Marse have. To dem cuttin' de cane it don't seem so much, but to dem what work hour in, hour out, dem sugar cane fields sho' stretch from one end de earth to de other. Marse ship hogs and hogs of sugar down de bayou. I seen de river boats go down with big signs what say, 'Buy dis here 'lasses' on de side. And he raise a world of rice and 'taters and corn and peanuts, too.

"When de work slight, us black folks sho have de balls and dinners and sech. We git all day to barbecue meat down on de bayou and de white folks come down and eat long side de cullud.

"When a black gal marry, Marse marry her hisself in de big house. He marry 'em Saturday, so dey git Sunday off, too. One time de river boat come bearin' de license for niggers to git marry with. Marse chase 'em off and say, 'Don't you come truckin' no no-count papers roun' my niggers. When I marry 'em, dey marry as good as if de Lawd God hisself marry 'em and it don't take no paper to bind de tie.' Marse don't stand no messin' 'round, neither. A gal have to be of age and ask her pa and ma and Marse and Missy, and if dey 'gree, dey go ahead and git marry. Marse have de marry book to put de name down.

"One time Marse take me 'long to help tote some chillen. He done write up to Virginny for to buy fresh hands. Dey a old man dat hobble 'long de road and de chillen start to throw rocks and de old man turn 'round to one prissy one and say, 'Go on, young'un, you'll be where dogs can't bark at you tomorrow. Nex' mornin' us cookin' in de kitchen and all a sudden dat li'l boy jes' crumple up dead on de floor. Law, we's scairt. Nobody ever bother dat old man no more, for he sho' lay de evil finger on you.

"Marse's brother, Conrad, what was a widdyman, come to live on de plantation and he had a li'l gal 'bout eight year old. One day she in de plum orchard playin' with a rattlesnake and Marse Conrad have de fit. De li'l gal won't let nobody hurt dat snake and she play with him. He won't bite her. She keeps him 'bout three year, and she'd rub and grease him. One day he got sick and dey give him some brandy, but he die and old Doc pickle him in de bottle of brandy. Dat gal git so full of grief dey take her to de infirm'ry in New Orleans and den one day she up and die.

"Dat snake ain't all what Doc Fawcett pickle. A slave woman give birth to a baby gal what have two faces with a strip of hair runnin' 'tween. Old Doc Fawcett pickle it in de jar of brandy. Old doc start to court Miss Cornelia when Marse die, but she don't have none of him and he done went straight 'way and kill hisself.

"One day a li'l man come ridin' by on a li'l dun hoss so fast you couldn't see dat hoss tail a-switchin'. He whoopin' and hollerin'. Us niggers 'gun whoop and holler, too. Den first thing you know de Yanks and de Democrats 'gun to fight right dere. Dey a high old mountain front Marse's house and de

Yanks 'gun pepper cannon ball down from de top dat hill. De war met right dere and dem Yanks and Democrats fit for twenty-four hours straight runnin'.

"When de bullets starts rainin' down, Marse call us and slip us way back into de woods, where it so black and deep. Next day, when de fight over, Marse come out with great big wagons piles full of mess-poke for us to eat. Dat what us call hog meat. Us sho' glad to 'scape from de Yankees.

"When us driv back to de plantation, sech a sight I never seen. Law, de things I can tell. Dem Yanks have kilt men and women. I seed babies pick up from de road with dere brains bust right out. One old man am drawin' water and a cannon ball shoots him right in de well. Dey draws him up with de fishin' line. Dey's a old sugar boat out on de bayou with blood and sugar runnin' long side de busted barrels. 'Lasses run in de bayou and blood run in de ditches. Marse have de great big orchard on de road and it wipe clean as de whistle. Bullets wipe up everythin' and bust dat sugar cane all to pieces. De house sot far back and 'scape de bullets, but, law, de time dey have!

"Dey's awful, awful times after dat. A old cotton dress cost five dollars and a pound of coffee cost five dollars and a pint cup flour cost six bits. De Yanks 'round all de time and one day they comes right in de house where Miss Cornelia eatin' her dinner. Dey march 'round de table, jes' scoopin' up meat and 'taters and grabbin' cornpone right and left. Miss Cornelia don't say a word, jes' smile sweet as honey-cake. I reckon dem sojers might a took de silver and sech only she charm 'em by bein' so quiet and ladylike. First thing you know dem sojers curtsy to Missy and take dereself right out de door and don't come back.

"Den it seem like Marse have all de trouble in de world. He boy, Ned, die in de war and William, what name for he pa, drink bad all de time. And after de war dem Ku Kluxers what wear de false faces try to tinker with Marse's niggers. One day Uncle Dave start to town and a Kluxer ask him where am he pass. Dat Kluxer clout him but Uncle Dave outrun him in de cane. Marse grab de hoss and go 'rest dat man and Marse a jedge and he make dat man pay de fine for hittin' Uncle Dave. After dey hears of dat, dem old poky faces sho' scairt of old Marse and dey git out from Opelousas and stays out. When me and my husband, John, come to Texas de folks say dat Louisiana masters de meanes' in de world and I say right back at 'em dat dey is good and mean in every spot of de earth. What more, de Louisiana masters free dere niggers a year befo' any Texas nigger git free.

"When 'mancipation come, Marse git on de big block and say, 'You all is as free as I is, standin' right here. Does you want to stay with me, you can, and I'll pay you for de work.' All de niggers cheer and say dey want to stay, but Marse die not long after and all us niggers scatter.

"I sho' 'lect dat day old Marse die. He won't die till ma gits there. He keep sayin', "Where's Charity, tell Charity to come." Dey fotch ma from de cane patch and she hold Marse's hand till he die. Us niggers went to de graveyard and us sho' cry over old Marse.

"Marse's brother, Goldham, carries all he hands back to de free country to turn 'em loose. He say de free country am de ones what's yellin' 'bout slave times, so dey could jes' take care of de niggers. Marse Goldham so big dat when he stand in de door you couldn't git by him, 'thout he stand sideways.

"Law, times ain't like dey was in slave days. All my ten chillen is dead and my old man gone, and now I reckon my time 'bout 'rive. All I got to do now am pray de Lawd to keep me straight, den when de great day come, I can march de road to glory.

United States.Work Project Administration

CHARLOTTE BEVERLEY

CHARLOTTE BEVERLY was born a slave to Captain Pankey's wife, in Montgomery County, Texas. She has lived most of her life within a radius of 60 miles from Houston, and now lives with one of her children in a little house on the highway between Cleveland and Shepherd, Texas. She does not know her age, but appears to be about ninety.

"I's born in Montgomery County and I's the mudder of eleven chillen, four gals and seven boys. My grandma come from Alabama and my daddy was Strawder Green and he belong to Col. Hughes. My maw named Phyllis and she belong to Capt. Pankey.

"There was 'bout forty niggers, big and little, on the plantation. Lawd, they was good to us. Us didn' know nothin' 'bout bad times and cutting and whipping and slashing. I had to work in the house and I 'member one thing I has to do was scrub Mistus' gol' snuffbox twict a week. She kep' sweet, Scotch snuff and sometimes I takes a pinch out.

"We used to go to the white folks church and if us couldn' git in we'd stand round by the door and sing. Mistus wouldn' 'low us dance on the place but they give us pass to go to dance on nex' plantation, where my daddy live.

"Every year they have big Christmas dinner and ham and turkey and allus feed us good. Us have Christmas party and sing songs. That was sweet music.

"Marster have a lovely house, all ceiled and plastered. It was a log house but it was make all beautiful inside with mirrors and on the board was lots of silver and china and silver spoons with the gol' linin's and part of my job was to keep 'em sparklin'.

"Folks in them times cooks in the fireplace and my auntie, she cook. She make 'simmon bread and 'tater pone and the like. She mash up 'simmons with butter and pour sweet milk and flour in it. That make good 'simmon bread. We has skillets what was flat and deep and set on three legs.

"The slaves lived in little log houses and sleep on wood beds. The beds was make three-legged. They make augur hole in side of the house and put in pieces of wood to make the bed frame, and they put straw and cotton mattress on them bed.

"Old marster used to let he slaves have a extry cotton patch to theyselves and they work it by the moonlight. They could sell that cotton and have the money for theyselves.

"My white mistus was a Christian and she'd own her God anywhere. She used to shout, jus' sit and clap her hands and say, 'Hallalujah.' Once I seed her shout in church and I thinks something ail her and I run down the aisle and goes to fannin' her.

"One of the slaves was a sort-a preacher and sometimes marster 'lowed him to preach to the niggers, but he have to preach with a tub over his head, 'cause he git so happy he talk too loud. Somebody from the big house liable to come down and make him quit 'cause he makin' 'sturbance.

"I brings water from the well and they have what they call piggins, and they was little tubs with two handles. Mistus wouldn' 'low me to do any heavy work.

"I see sojers and knits socks for 'em by moonshine. Me and my husban' was married by a Yankee sojer. I was dress in white Tarleyton weddin' dress and I didn' wear no hoop skirt. I had a pretty wreath of little white flowers, little bitty, little dainty ones, the pretties' little things. When I marry, my sister marry too and our husban's was brudders. My husban' dress in suit of white linen. He sho' look handsome. He give me a gol' ring and a cup and saucer for weddin' gif'. We git married in Huntsville and us didn' go no weddin' journey trip. We was so poor we couldn' go round the house! I's 'bout twenty some year when I marries, but I don' know jus' how old. We has a big dance that night and the white folks come, 'cause they likes to see the niggers dance.

"The white folks had interes' in they cullud people where I live. Sometimes they's as many as fifty cradle with little nigger babies in 'em and the mistus, she look after them and take care of them, too. She turn them and dry them herself. She had a little gal git water and help. She never had no chillen of her own. I'd blow the horn for the mudders of the little babies to come in from the fields and nurse 'em, in mornin' and afternoon. Mistus feed them what was old enough to eat victuals. Sometimes, they mammies take them to the field and fix pallet on ground for them to lay on.

"The las' word my old Mistus Pankey say when she die was, 'You take care of Charlette.'

United States.Work Project Administration

FRANCIS BLACK

FRANCIS BLACK was born at Grand Bluff, Mississippi, about 1850, on the Jim Carlton plantation. When five years old, she was stolen and taken to the slave market in New Orleans. Failing to sell her there, the slave traders took her to Jefferson, Texas, and sold her to Bill Tumlin. Francis stayed with him five years after she was freed, then married and moved to Cass County, Texas. She became blind a year ago, and now lives at the Bagland Old Folks Home, 313 Elm St., Texarkana, Texas.

"My name am Francis Black, and I don't know jes' how old I is, but 'members lots 'bout them slave days. I was a big gal, washin' and ironin', when they sot the darkies free. From that, I cal'late I'm in my eighties.

"I was born in Grand Bluff, in Mississippi, on Old Man Carlton's plantation, and I was stole from my folks when I was a li'l gal and never seed them no more. Us kids played in the big road there in Mississippi, and one day me and 'nother gal is playin' up and down the road and three white men come 'long in a wagon. They grabs us up and puts us in the wagon and covers us with quilts. I hollers and yells and one the men say, 'Shet up, you nigger, or I'll kill you.' I told him, 'Kill me if you wants to—you stole me from my folks.'

"Them men took us to New Orleans to the big slave market. I had long hair and they cut it off like a boy and tried to sell me, but I told them men what looks at me, the men cut my hair off and stole me. The man what cut my hair off cursed me and said if I didn't hush he'd kill me, but he couldn't sell us at New Orleans and took us to Jefferson.

"I never knowed what they done with the other gal, but they sold me to Marse Bill Tumlin, what run a big livery stable in Jefferson, and I 'longed to him till surrender. I lived in the house with them, 'cause they had a boy and gal and I did for them. They bought me clothes and took good care of me but I never seed no money till surrender. I et what they et, after they got through. Missy say she didn't 'lieve in feedin' the darkies scraps, like some folks.

"I played with them two chillen all day, then sot the table. I was so small I'd git in a chair to reach the dishes out of the safe. I had to pull a long flybrush over the table whilst the white folks et.

"Marse Tumlin had a farm 'bout four mile from town, and a overseer, and I seed him buckle the niggers crost a log and whip them. Marse lived in Jefferson, heself, and when he'd go to the farm he allus took his boy with him. We'd be playin' in the barn and Marse call from the house, 'Come on, Jimmie, we're gwine to the farm.' Jimmie allus say to me, 'Come on, nigger, let's ride round the farm.' I'd say, 'I ain't no nigger.' He'd say, 'Yes, you is, my pa paid $200 for you. He bought you for to play with me.'

"Jefferson was a good town till it burned up. I 'members the big fire what looked like the whole town gwineter burn up. Marse Bill lost his livery stable in the fire.

"The Yankee soldiers, all dressed in blue, come to run the town after the war. Marse Tumlin done told me I'm free, but I stays on till I'm most growed. Then I works round town and marries Dave Black, and we moved to Cass County. I raises six chillun but my old man done git so triflin' and mean I quit him and worked for myself. I come to Texarkana to work, and allus could earn my own livin' till 'bout a year ago I lost my seein', and Albert Ragland done took me in his home for the old folks. They gives me a $10 a month pension now. They is good to me here and feeds us good.

United States.Work Project Administration

OLIVIER BLANCHARD

OLIVIER BLANCHARD, 95 years old, was a slave of Clairville La San, who owned a large plantation in Martinville Parish, Louisiana. His father was a Frenchman and Olivier speaks rather haltingly, as though it is difficult for him to express his thoughts in English, for he has talked a species of French all his life. He lives in Beaumont, Texas.

"I was plowing and hoeing before the freedom and I talk more of the French 'cause I comes from St. Martinville Parish. I was born there in Louisiana and my mama was Angeline Jean Pierre and she was slave born. My papa was Olivier Blanchard and he white man carpenter on old plantation. We belong to Clairville La San and all live on that place. My papa just plain carpenter but could draw patterns for houses. I don't know where he larn that work.

"I was count freeborn and still have one white half sister alive. When freedom come my mama and papa split up and mama get marry.

"I pick cotton and mama cook. She make koosh-koosh and cyayah—that last plain clabber. Mama cook lots of gaspergou and carp and the poisson ami fish, with the long snout—what they call gar now. I think it eel fish they strip the skin off and wrap round the hair and make it curly.

"The Bayou Teche, it run close by and the women do all the clothes with a big paddle with holes in it to clean them in the bayou. They paddle them clean on the rocks and then wash them in the water.

"One time one big bayou 'gator come up and bite a woman's arm off. She my sister in law. But they keep on washing the clothes in the bayou just the same.

"We have plenty to eat and peaches and muscadines and pecans, 'cause there right smart woods and swamp there. We play in the woods and most time in the bayou on boats with planks what would float. We had the good time and had a little pet coon. You know, the coon like sweet things and he steal our syrup and when we chase him with the switch he hide under the bed.

"My old missus was good Catholic and she have us christened and make the first communion. That not registered, 'cause it before the freedom, but it were in old St. Martin's church, same old church what stand now. There was a statue of Pere Jean, the old priest, in front the church and one of St. Martin, too.

"Plenty men from St. Martinville go to the war and Archie DeBlieu, he go to Virginia and fight. The first one to pass our place was John Well Banks and he was a Yankee going up the Red River.

"The yellow fever came durin' that war and kill lots. All the big plantation have the graveyard for the cullud people. That fever so bad they get the coffin ready before they dead and they so scared that some weren't dead but they think they are and bury them. There was a white girl call Colene Sonnier what was to marry Sunday and she take sick Friday before. She say not to bury her in the ground but they put her there while they got the tomb ready. When they open the ground grave to put her in the tomb they find she buried alive and she eat all her own shoulder and hand away. Her sweetheart, Gart Berrild, he see that corpse, and he go home and get took with yellow fever and die.

"They was the old lady what die. She was a terrible soul. One time after she die I go to get water out of her rain barrel and I had a lamp in one hand. That old lady's ghost blowed out the lamp and slapped the pitcher out my hand. After she first die her husband put black dress on her and tie up the jaw with a rag and my girl look in the room and there that old lady, Liza Lee, sittin' by the fire. My girl tell her mama and after three day she go back, and Liza Lee buried but my wife see her sittin' by the fire. Then she sorry she whip the chile for sayin' she saw Liza Lee. That old lady, Liza Lee, was a tart and she stay a tart for a long time.

"I marry 72 year ago in the Catholic Church in St. Martinville. My wife call Adeline Chretien and she dead 37 year. We have seven children but four live now. Frank my only boy live now, in Iowa, in Louisiana, and my two girls live, Enziede De Querive and Rose Baptiste.

United States.Work Project Administration

JULIA BLANKS

JULIA BLANKS was born of a slave mother and a three-quarter Indian father, in San Antonio, in the second year of the Civil War. Her mother, part French and part Negro, was owned by Mrs. John G. Wilcox, formerly a Miss Donaldson, who had lived at the White House, and who gave Julia to her daughter. After the slaves were freed, Julia continued to live with her mother in San Antonio until, at fifteen, she married Henry Hall. Five years later her second marriage took place, at Leon Springs, Texas, where she lived until moving to the Adams ranch, on the Frio River. Here she raised her family. After leaving the Adams ranch, Julia and Henry bought two sections of state land, but after four years they let it go back because of Henry's ill health, and moved to Uvalde.

"I was born in San Antonio, in 1862. My mother's name was Rachael Miller. I don't know if she was born in Tennessee or Mississippi. I heard her talk of both places. I don't know nothing about my father, because he run off when I was about three months old. He was three-quarter Cherokee Indian. They were lots of Indians then, and my husband's people come from Savannah, Georgia, and he said they was lots of Indians there. I had two sisters and one brother and the sisters are dead but my brother lives somewhere in Arizona. My mother's master's name was John. G. Wilcox.

"When we was small chillen, they hired my sisters out, but not me. My grandfather bought my grandmother's time and they run a laundry house. They hired my mother out, too.

"You see, my grandmother was free born, but they stole

her and sold her to Miss Donaldson. She was half French. She looked jes' like a French woman. She wasn't a slave, but she and her brother were stolen and sold. She said the stage coach used to pass her aunt's house, and one day she and her brother went down to town to buy some buns, and when they were comin' back, the stage stopped and asked 'em to ride. She wanted to ride, but her brother didn't. But they kep' coaxin' 'em till they got 'em in. They set her down between the two women that was in there and set her brother between two men, and when they got close to the house, they threw cloaks over their heads and told the driver to drive as fast as he could, and he sure drove. They taken 'em to Washin'ton, to the White House, and made her a present to Mary Wilcox (Miss Donaldson) and her brother to somebody else. Then this woman married John C. Wilcox and they come to Texas.

"She saw a cousin of hers when they got to Washin'ton, and she knew, after that, he had somethin' to do with her and her brother bein' stolen. One day she found a piece of yellow money and took it to her cousin and he told her it wasn't no good and gave her a dime to go get her some candy. After that, she saw gold money and knew what it was.

"She said she had a good time, though, when she was growing up. They were pretty good to her, but after they came to San Antonio, Mrs. Wilcox began bein' mean. She kep' my mother hired out all the time and gave me to her daughter and my sister to her son. My mother was kep' hired out all the time, cooking; and after freedom, she just took to washin' and ironin'. My grandfather bought his time and my grandmother's time out. They didn't stay with her.

"I've heard my mother talk about coffee. They roasted beans and made coffee. She says, out on the plantation, they would take bran and put it in a tub and have 'em stir it up with water in it and let all the white go to the bottom and dip it off and strain it and make starch. I have made starch out of flour over and often, myself. I had four or five little girls; and I had to keep 'em like pins. In them days they wore little calico dresses, wide and full and standin' out, and a bonnet to match every dress.

"I used to hear my grandmother tell about the good times they used to have. They would go from one plantation to another and have quiltin's and corn huskin's. And they would dance. They didn't have dances then like they do now. The white people would give them things to eat. They would have to hoof it five or six miles and didn't mind it.

"They had what they called patros, and if you didn't have a pass they would whip you and put you in jail. Old Man Burns was hired at the courthouse, and if the marsters had slaves that they didn't want to whip, they would send them to the courthouse to be whipped. Some of the marsters was good and some wasn't. There was a woman, oh, she was the meanest thing! I don't know if she had a husband—I never did hear anything about him. When she would get mad at one of her slave women, she would make the men tie her down, and she had what they called cat-o'-nine-tails, and after she got the blood to come, she would dip it in salt and pepper and whip her again. Oh, she was mean! My mother's marster was good; he wouldn't whip any of his slaves. But his wife wasn't good. If she got mad at the women, when he would come home she would say: 'John, I want you to whip Liza.' Or Martha. And he would say, 'Them are your slaves. You whip them.' He was good and she was mean.

"When my aunt would go to clean house, she (Mrs. Wilcox) would turn all the pictures in the house but one, the meanest looking one—you know how it always looks like a picture is watching you everywhere you go—and she would tell her if she touched a thing or left a bit of dirt or if she didn't do it good, this picture would tell. And she believed it.

"My grandmother told a tale one time. You know in slave time they had an old woman to cook for the chillen. One day they were going to have company. This woman that was the boss of the place where the chillen was kept told the old cullud woman to take a piece of bacon and grease the mouths of all the chillen. Then she told a boy to bring them up to these people, and the woman said: 'Oh, you must feed these chillen good, just look at their mouths!' And the woman said, 'Oh, that's the way they eat.' They didn't get meat often. That was just to make them believe they had lots to eat.

"No. They were cut off from education. The way my stepfather got his learning was a cullud blacksmith would teach school at night, and us chillen taught our mother. She didn't know how to spell or read or nothin'. She didn't know B from bull's foot. Some of them were allowed to have church and some didn't. Mighty few read the Bible 'cause they couldn't read. As my mother used to say, they were raised up as green as cucumbers. That old blacksmith was the onlyist man that knew how to read and write in slavery time that I knew of. My grandmother or none of them knew how to read; they could count, but that was all. That's what makes me mad. I tell my grandchillen they ought to learn all they can 'cause the old people never had a chance. My husband never did have any schooling, but he sure could figger. Now, if you want me to get tangled up, just give me a pencil and paper and I don't know nothing." She tapped her skull. "I figger in my head! The chillen, today, ought to appreciate an education.

"Oh, yes, they were good to the slaves when they were sick. They would have the doctor come out and wait on them. Most plantations had what they called an old granny cullud woman that treated the chillen with herbs and such things.

"Games? I don't know. We used to play rap jacket. We would get switches and whip one another. You know, after you was hit several times it didn't hurt much. I've played a many time. In slave time the men used to go huntin' at night, and hunt 'possums and 'coons. They would have a dog or two along. They used to go six or seven miles afoot to corn huskin's and quiltin's. And those off the other plantations would come over and join in the work. And they would nearly always have a good dinner. Sometimes some of the owners would give 'em a hog or somethin' nice to eat, but some of 'em didn't.

"No'm, I don't know if they run off to the North, but some of them runned off and stayed in the swamps, and they was mean. They called them runaways. If they saw you, they would tell you to bring them something to eat. And if you didn't do it, if they ever got you they sure would fix you.

"I don't know when my mother was set free. My husband's marster's name was King. He was from Savannah, Georgia, but at the time was living close to Boerne. My husband's father was killed in the war. When my husband was about ten years old, his marster hadn't told them they was free. You know some of them didn't tell the slaves they was free until they had to. After freedom was declared, lots of people didn't tell the slaves they were free. One morning, my husband said, he happenned to look out and he saw a big bunch of men coming down the road, and he thought he never saw such pretty men in his life on them horses. They had so many brass buttons on their clothes it looked like gold. So he run and told his mama, and she looked and saw it was soldiers, and some of 'em told the boss, and he looked and saw them soldiers comin' in the big gate and he called 'em in quick, and told them they were free. So when the soldiers come, they asked him if he had told his slaves they were free, and he said yes. They asked the Negroes if they lived there, and they said yes.

One said, 'He just told us we was free.' The soldiers asked him why he had just told them, and he said they wasn't all there and he was waiting for them all to be there.

"My husband said he thought them was the prettiest bunch of men he ever saw, and the prettiest horses. Of course, he hadn't never saw any soldiers before. I know it looked pretty to me when I used to see the soldiers at the barracks and hear the band playin' and see them drillin' and ever'thing. You see, we lived on a little cross-street right back of St. Mary's Church in San Antonio. I don't know how that place is now. Where the post office is now, there used to be a blacksmith shop and my father worked there. I went back to San Antonio about fifteen years ago and jes' took it afoot and looked at the changes.

"I was fifteen years old the first time I married. It was almost a run-a-way marriage. I was married in San Antonio. My first husband's name was Henry Hall. My first wedding dress was as wide as a wagon sheet. It was white lawn, full of tucks, and had a big ruffle at the bottom. I had a wreath and a veil, too. The veil had lace all around it. We danced and had a supper. We danced all the dances they danced then; the waltz, square, quadrille, polka, and the gallopade—and that's what it was, all right; you shore galloped. You'd start from one end of the hall and run clear to the other end. In those days, the women with all them long trains—the man would hold it over his arm. No, Lord! Honeymoons wasn't thought of then. No'm, I never worked out a day in my life." Jokingly, "I guess they thought I was too good looking. I was about twenty years old when I married the second time. I was married in Leon Springs the second time.

"Before we come out to this country from Leon Springs, they was wild grapes, dewberries, plums and agaritas, black haws, red haws. M-m-m! Them dewberries, I dearly love 'em!

I never did see wild cherries out here. I didn't like the cherries much, but they make fine wine. We used to gather mustang grapes and make a barrel of wine.

"After I married the second time, we lived on the Adams ranch on the Frio and stayed on that ranch fifteen years. We raised all our chillen right on that ranch. I am taken for a Mexkin very often. I jes' talk Mexkin back to 'em. I learned to talk it on the ranch. As long as I have lived at this place, I have never had a cross word about the chillen. All my neighbors here is Mexkins. They used to laugh at me when I tried to talk to the hands on the ranch, but I learned to talk like 'em.

"We used to have big round-ups out on the Adams ranch. They had fences then. The neighbors would all come over and get out and gather the cattle and bring 'em in. Up at Leon Springs at that time they didn't have any fences, and they would have big round-ups there. But after we come out here, it was different. He would notify his neighbors they were goin' to gather cattle on a certain day. The chuck wagon was right there at the ranch, that is, I was the chuck wagon. But if they were goin' to take the cattle off, they would have a chuck wagon. They would round up a pasture at a time and come in to the ranch for their meals. Now on the Wallace ranch, they would always take a chuck wagon. When they were gettin' ready to start brandin' at the ranch, my husband always kep' his brandin' irons all in the house, hangin' up right where he could get his hands on 'em. Whenever they would go off to other ranches to gather cattle, you would see ever' man with his beddin' tied up behind him on his horse. He'd have jes' a small roll. They would always have a slicker if nothin' else. That slicker answered for ever'thing sometimes. My husband slep' many a night with his saddle under his head.

"He used to carry mail from San Antonio to Dog Town, horseback. That was the town they used to call Lodi (Lodo), but I don't know how to spell it, and don't know what it means. It was a pretty tough town. The jail house was made out of 'dobe and pickets. They had a big picket fence all around it. They had a ferry that went right across the San Antonio River from Floresville to Dog Town. I know he told me he come to a place and they had a big sign that said, 'Nigga, don't let the sun go down on you here.' They was awful bad down in there. He would leave Dog Town in the evenin' and he would get to a certain place up toward San Antonio to camp, and once he stopped before he got to the place he always camped at. He said he didn't know what made 'im stop there that time, but he stopped and took the saddle off his horse and let 'im graze while he lay down. After a while, he saw two cigarette fires in the dark right up the road a little piece, and he heard a Mexkin say, 'I don't see why he's so late tonight. He always gets here before night and camps right there.' He knew they was waylayin' 'im, so he picked his saddle up right easy and carried it fu'ther back down the road in the brush and then come got his horse and took him out there and saddled 'im up and went away 'round them Mexkins. He went on in to San Antonio and didn't go back any more. A white man took the mail to carry then and the first trip he made, he never come back. He went down with the mail and they found the mail scattered somewhere on the road, but they never found the man, or the horse, either.

"On the Adams ranch, in the early days, we used to have to pack water up the bank. You might not believe it, but one of these sixty-pound lard cans full of water, I've a-carried it on my head many a time. We had steps cut into the bank, and it was a good ways down to the water, and I'd pack that can up to the first level and go back and get a couple a buckets of water, and carry a bucket in each hand and the can on my head up the next little slantin' hill before I got to level ground.

I carried water that way till my chillen got big enough to carry water, then they took it up. When I was carryin' water in them big cans my head would sound like new leather—you know how it squeaks, and that was the way it sounded in my head. But, it never did hurt me. You see, the Mexkins carry loads on their heads, but they fix a rag around their heads some way to help balance it. But I never did. I jes' set it up on my head and carried it that way. Oh, we used to carry water! My goodness! My mother said it was the Indian in me—the way I could carry water.

"When we were first married and moved to the Adams ranch, we used to come here to Uvalde to dances. They had square dances then. They hadn't commenced all these frolicky dances they have now. They would have a supper, but they had it to sell. Every fellow would have to treat his girl he danced with.

"I can remember when my grandfather lived in a house with a dirt floor, and they had a fireplace. And I can remember just as well how he used to bake hoecakes for us kids. He would rake back the coals and ashes real smooth and put a wet paper down on that and then lay his hoecake down on the paper and put another paper on top of that and the ashes on top. I used to think that was the best bread I ever ate. I tried it a few times, but I made such a mess I didn't try it any more. One thing I have seen 'em make, especially on the ranch. You take and clean a stick and you put on a piece of meat and piece of fat till you take and use up the heart and liver and sweetbread and other meat and put it on the stick and wrap it around with leaf fat and then put the milk gut, or marrow gut, around the whole thing. They call that macho (mule), and I tell you, it's good. They make it out of a goat and sheep, mostly.

"Another thing, we used to have big round-ups, and I have cooked great pans of steak and mountain orshters.

Generally, at the brandin' and markin', I cooked up many a big pan of mountain orshters. I wish I had a nickel for ever' one I've cooked, and ate too! People from up North have come down there, and, when they were brandin' and cuttin' calves there, they sure did eat and enjoy that dinner.

"The men used to go up to the lake, fishin', and catch big trout, or bass, they call 'em now; and we'd take big buckets of butter—we didn't take a saucer of butter or a pound; we taken butter up there in buckets, for we sure had plenty of it—and we'd take lard too, and cook our fish up there, and had corn bread or hoe cakes and plenty of butter for ever'thing, and it sure was good. I tell you—like my husband used to say—we was livin' ten days in the week, then.

"When we killed hogs, the meat from last winter was hung outside and then new meat, salted down and then smoked, put in there, and we would cook the old bacon for the dogs. We always kep' some good dogs there, and anybody'll tell you they was always fat. We had lots of wild turkeys and I raised turkeys, too, till I got sick of cookin' turkeys. Don't talk about deer! You know, it wasn't then like it is now. You could go kill venison any time you wanted to. But I don't blame 'em for passin' that law, for people used to go kill 'em and jes' take out the hams and tenderloin and leave the other layin' there. I have saved many a sack of dried meat to keep it from spoilin'.

"We would raise watermelons, too. We had a big field three mile from the house and a ninety-acre field right in the house. We used to go get loads of melons for the hogs and they got to where they didn't eat anything but the heart.

"I used to leave my babies at the house with the older girl and go out horseback with my husband. My oldest girl used to take the place of a cowboy, and put her hair up in her hat. And ride! My goodness, she loved to ride! They thought she was a boy. She wore pants and leggin's. And maybe you think she couldn't ride!

"After we left that ranch, we took up some state land. I couldn't tell you how big that place was. We had 640 in one place and 640 in another place; it was a good big place. After my husband got sick, we had to let it go back. We couldn't pay it out. We only lived on it about four years.

"My husband has been dead about nineteen years. I had a pen full and a half of chillen. I have four livin' chillen, two girls and two boys. I have a girl, Carrie, in California, workin' in the fruit all the time; one boy, George, in Arizona, workin' in the mines; and a girl in Arizona, Lavinia, washes and irons and cooks and ever'thing else she can get at. And I have one boy here. I have ten grandchillen and I've got five great grandchillen.

"I belong to the Methodist Church. I joined about twenty-five years ago. My husband joined with me. But here, of late years, when I go to church, it makes me mad to see how the people do the preacher up there trying to do all the good he can do and them settin' back there laughin' and talkin'. I was baptized. There was about five or six of us baptized in the Leona down here.

"People tell that I've got plenty and don't need help. Even the Mexkins here and ever'body say I've got money. Jes' because we had that farm down there they think I come out with money. But what in the world would I want with money if I didn't use it? I can't take it with me when I die and I could be gettin' the use of it now while I need it. I could have what I want to eat, anyway. I'm gettin' a little pension, but it ain't near enough to keep us. I've got these two grandchillen here, and things is so high, too, so I don't have enough of anything without skimpin' all the time.

United States.Work Project Administration

ELVIRA BOLES

ELVIRA BOLES, 94, has outlived nine of her ten children. She lives at 3109 Manzana St., El Paso, Texas, with her daughter, Minnie. She was born a slave of the Levi Ray family near Lexington, Mississippi, and was sold as a child to Elihn Boles, a neighboring plantation owner. During the last year of the Civil War she was brought to Texas, with other refugee slaves.

"I jus' 'member my first marster and missus, 'cause she don' want me there. I'se a child of the marster. Dey didn' tell me how old I was when dey sold me to Boles. My missus sold me to Boles. Dey tuk us to where dere was a heap of white folks down by the court house and we'd be there in lots and den de whites 'ud bid for us. I don' know how old I was, but I washed dishes and den dey put me to work in de fields. We don' git a nickel in slavery.

"Marster Boles didn' have many slaves on de farm, but lots in brickyard. I toted brick back and put 'em down where dey had to be. Six bricks each load all day. That's de reason I ain't no 'count, I'se worked to death. I fired de furnace for three years. Stan'in' front wid hot fire on my face. Hard work, but God was wid me. We'd work 'till dark, quit awhile after sundown. Marster was good to slaves, didn' believe in jus' lashin' 'em. He'd not be brutal but he'd kill 'em dead right on the spot. Overseers 'ud git after 'em and whop 'em down.

"I'se seventeen, maybe, when I married to slave of Boles. Married on Saturday night. Dey give me a dress and dey had things to eat, let me have something like what you call a party. We just had common clothes on. And then I had to work every day. I'd leave my baby cryin' in de yard and he'd be cryin', but I couldn' stay. Done everything but split rails. I've cut timber and ploughed. Done everything a man could do. I couldn' notice de time, but I'd be glad to git back to my baby.

"Log cabins had dirt floor, sometimes plankin' down. I worked late and made pretty quilts. Sometimes dey'd let us have a party. Saturday nights, de white people give us meat and stuff. Give us syrup and we'd make candy, out in de yard. We'd ask our frien's and dance all night. Den go to work next day. We'd clean off de yard and dance out dere. Christmas come, dey give us a big eggnog and give us cake. Our white folks did. White folks chillen had bought candy. We didn' git any, but dey let us play wid de white chillen. We'd play smut. Whoever beat wid de cards, he'd git to smut you. Take de smut from fireplace and rub on your face.

"Doctor take care of us iffen we sick, so's git us well to git us to work.

"Iffen dey had a pretty girl dey would take 'em, and I'se one of 'em, and my oldest child, he boy by Boles, almost white.

"We had to steal away at night to have church on de ditch bank, and crawl home on de belly. Once overseers heered us prayin', give us one day each 100 lashes.

"Den when de Yankees come through, dey 'ud be good to de slaves, to keep 'em from tellin' on 'em. Freedom was give Jan. 1, 1865, but de slaves didn' know it 'till June 19. We'se refugees. Boles, our marster, sent us out and we come from Holmes County to Cherokee County in a wagon. We was a dodgin' in and out, runnin' from de Yankees. Marster said dey was runnin' us from de Yankees to keep us, but we was free and didn' know it. I lost my baby, its buried somewhere on dat road. Died at Red River and we left it. De white folks go out and buy food 'long de road and hide us. Dey say we'd never be free iffen dey could git to Texas wid us, but de people in Texas tol' us we's free. Den marster turn us loose in de world, without a penny. Oh, dey was awful times. We jus' worked from place to place after freedom.

"When we started from Mississippi, dey tol' us de Yankees 'ud kill us iffen dey foun' us, and dey say, 'You ain't got no time to take nothin' to whar you goin'. Take your little bundle and leave all you has in your house.' So when we got to Texas I jus' had one dress, what I had on. Dat's de way all de cullud people was after freedom, never had nothin' but what had on de back. Some of dem had right smart in dere cabins, but they was skeered and dey lef' everything. Bed clothes and all you had was lef'. We didn' know any better den."

United States.Work Project Administration

BETTY BORMER (BONNER)

BETTY BORMER, 80, was born a slave to Col. M.T. Johnson, who farmed at Johnson Station in Tarrant County. He owned Betty's parents, five sisters and four brothers, in addition to about 75 other slaves. After the family was freed, they moved with the other slaves to a piece of land Col. Johnson allowed them the use of until his death. Betty lives in a negro settlement at Stop Six, a suburb of Fort Worth.

"I'se bo'n April 4th, in 1857, at Johnson Station. It was named after my marster. He had a big farm, I'se don' know how many acres. He had seven chillen; three boys, Ben, Tom and Mart, and four girls, Elizabeth, Sally, Roddy and Veanna.

"Marster Johnson was good to us cullud folks and he feeds us good. He kep' lots of hawgs, dat makes de meat. In de smokehouse am hung up meat enough for to feed de army, it looks like. We'uns have all de clothes we need and dey was made on de place. My mammy am de sewing woman and my pappy am de shoemaker. My work, for to nuss de small chillen of de marster.

"On Sat'day we's let off work and lots de time some of us come to Fort Worth wid de marster and he gives us a nickel or a dime for to buy candy.

"Dey whips de niggers sometimes, but 'twarn't hard. You know, de nigger gits de devilment in de head, like folks do, sometimes, and de marster have to larn 'em better. He done dat hisself and he have no overseer. No nigger tried run away, 'cause each family have a cabin wid bunks for to sleep on and we'uns all live in de quarters. Sich nigger as wants to larn read and write, de marster's girls and boys larns 'em. De girls larned my auntie how to play de piano.

"Dere am lots of music on dat place; fiddle, banjo and de piano. Singin', we had lots of dat, songs like Ole Black Joe and 'ligious songs and sich. Often de marster have we'uns come in his house and clears de dinin' room for de dance. Dat am big time, on special occasion. Dey not calls it 'dance' dem days, dey calls it de 'ball.'

"Sho', we'uns goes to church and de preacher's name, it was Jack Ditto.

"Durin' de war, I notices de vittles am 'bout de same. De soldiers come dere and dey driv' off over de hill some of de cattle for to kill for to eat. Once dey took some hosses and I hears marster say dem was de Quantrell mens. Dey comes several times and de marster don' like it, but he cain't help it.

"When freedom come marster tells all us to come to front of de house. He am standin' on de porch. Him 'splains 'bout freedom and says, 'You is now free and can go whar you pleases.' Den he tells us he have larned us not to steal and to be good and we'uns should 'member dat and if we'uns gets in trouble to come to him and he will help us. He sho' do dat, too, 'cause de niggers goes to him lots of times and he always helps.

"Marster says dat he needs help on de place and sich dat stays, he'd pay 'em for de work. Lots of dem stayed, but some left. To dem dat leaves, marster gives a mule, or cow and sich for de start. To my folks, marster gives some land. He doesn't give us de deed, but de right to stay till he dies.

"Sho', I seen de Klux after de war but I has no 'sperience wid 'em. My uncle, he gits whipped by 'em, what for I don' know 'zactly, but I think it was 'bout a hoss. Marster sho' rave 'bout dat, 'cause my uncle weren't to blame.

"When de Klux come de no 'count nigger sho make de scatterment. Some climb up de chimney or jump out de winder and hide in de dugout and sich.

"De marster dies 'bout seven years after freedom and everybody sorry den. I never seen such a fun'ral and lots of big men from Austin comes. He was de blessed man!

"I married de second year after de T.P. railroad come to Fort Worth, to Sam Jones and he work on de Burk Burnett stock ranch. I'se divorseted from him after five years and den after 12 more years I marries Rubbin Felps. My las' husban's named Joe Borner, but I'se never married to the father of my only chile. His name am George Pace.

"I allus gits long fair, 'cause after freedom I keeps on workin' doin' de nussin'. Now I'se gittin' 'leven dollars from de state for pension, and gits it every month so now I'se sho' of somethin' to eat and dat makes me happy.

United States.Work Project Administration

HARRISON BOYD

H ARRISON BOYD, 87, was born in Rusk County, Texas, a slave of Wash Trammel. Boyd remained with his master for four years after emancipation, then moved to Harrison County, where he now lives. His memory is poor, but he managed to recall a few incidents.

"I was fifteen years when they says we're free. That's the age my Old Missy done give me when the war stopped. She had all us niggers' ages in a book, and told me I was born near Henderson. My Old Marse was Wash Trammel and he brunged me and my mama and papa from Alabama. Mama was named Juliet and papa, Amos. Marse Trammel owned my grandpa and grandma, too, and they was named Jeanette and Josh.

"The plantation was two made into one, and plenty big, and more'n a hundred slaves to work it. Marse lived in a hewed log house, weather-boarded out and in, and the quarters was good, log houses with bed railin's hewed out of logs. We raised everything we et, 'cept sugar, and Marse bought that in big hogsheads. We got our week's rations every Sunday, and when we went to eat, everybody's part was put out to them on a tin plate.

"Marse Trammel give a big cornshucking every fall. He had two bottom fields in corn. First we'd gather peas and cushaws and pumpkins out the corn field, then get the corn and pile it front the cribs. They was two big cribs for the corn we kep' to use and five big cribs for sale corn. My uncle stayed round the sale corn cribs all spring, till ginnin' time, 'cause folks come for miles after corn. Marse had five wheat cribs and one rye crib. We went ten mile to Tatum to git our meal and flour ground.

"The patterrollers darsn't come 'bout our place or bother us niggers. Marse Wash allus say, 'I'll patteroller my own place.' Marse was good to us and only once a overseer beat a woman up a trifle, and Marse Trammel fired him that same day.

"The sojers 'fiscated lots of corn from Marse and some more owners in Rusk County piled corn up in a big heap and made me go mind it till the rest the sojers got there. I was settin' top that corn pile, me and my big bulldog, and the General rode up. My dog growled and I made him hush. The General man say to me, 'Boy, you is 'scused now, go on home.' I got to a fence and looked back, and that General was hewin' him a hoss trough out a log. The sojers come in droves and set up they camp. I sot on a stump and watched them pass. They stayed three, four days till the corn was all fed up.

"While they's camped there they'd cotch chickens. They had a fishin' pole and line and hook. They'd put a grain of corn on the hook and ride on they hoss and pitch the hook out 'mong the chickens. When a chicken swallowed the corn they'd jerk up the line with that chicken and ride off.

"Marse had six hundred bales cotton in the Shreveport warehouse when war was over. He got word them Yankees done take it on a boat. He got his brother to take him to Shreveport and say, 'I'll follow that cotton to Hell and back.' He followed his cotton to Alabama and got it back, but he died and was buried there in Alabama 'fore Old Missy knowed it.

"I stayed with her four years after surrender and then went to farmin' with my folks, for $10.00 a month. After a year or two I went to railroadin', helping cut the right-of-way for the T.& P. Railroad, from Marshall to Longview. They paid us $1.50 the day and three drinks of whiskey a day.

"I marries four times but had only one child, but I never done nothin' 'citin'. I lives by myself now, and gits $11.00 pension to eat on.

United States.Work Project Administration

ISSABELLA BOYD

ISSABELLA BOYD was born a slave of Gus Wood, in Richmond, Va., who moved to Texas by boat before the Civil War. Isabella still lives in Beaumont.

"Lemme see, I come from Richmond, Virginy, to Texas. Massa Gus Wood was my owner and I kin recollect my white folks. I's born in dat country and dey brought me over to Richmond and my papa and mama, too. I was jus' 'bout big 'nough to begin to 'member.

"I come from Richmond yere on de boat, sometime de steamboat, sometime de big boat. When we left New Orleans dat evenin' we struck a big storm. Us git on dat boat in Richmond and went floatin' down to de big boat dat mornin'. Looks like it jus' fun for us, but every time we look back and think 'bout home it make us sad.

"I had a dear, good mistus and my boss man, he furnish a house for he servants, a purty good house. And dey had a place for de Sunday School. Dem was good times. De mistus cook dinner and send it down for de old folks and chillen to have plenty.

"My mistus kep' me right in de house, right by her, sewing. I could sew so fast I git my task over 'fore de others git started good.

"Lots of times when de gals wants to go to de dance I he'p make de dresses. I 'member de pretties' one like yesterday. It have tucks from de waist to de hem and had diamonds cut all in de skirt.

"Our boss man was 'ticular 'bout us being tended to and we was well took care of. He brung us to Beaumont when it was de plumb mud hole, and he settle down and try to build up and make it a go.

"Massa Wood he allus takes de paper and one night they set up da long time and do dey readin'. Next mornin' de old cook woman, she say, 'Well, dey have de big war, and lots of dem wounded.' Befo' long us has to take care of some dem wounded soldiers, and dey has de camp place near us. Dey all camp 'round dere and I don't know which was de Yankees and de 'federates.

"When we all gits free, dey's de long time lettin' us know. Dey wants to git through with de corn and de cotton befo' dey let's de hands loose. Dey was people from other plantations say. 'Niggers, you's free and yere you workin'.' Us say, 'No, de gov'ment tell us when we's free.' We workin' one day when somebody from Massa Grissom place come by and tell us we's free, and us stop workin'. Dey tell us to go on workin' and de boss man he come up and he say he gwine knock us off de fence if we don't go to work. Mistus come out and say, 'Ain't you gwine make dem niggers go to work?' He send her back in de house and he call for de carriage and say he goin' to town for to see what de gov'ment goin' do. Nex' day he come back and say, 'Well, you's jus' as free as I is.'

"He say to me I could stay and cook for dem, and he give me five dollar a month and a house to stay in and all I kin eat. I stays de month to do dere work.

"After dat I wishes sometimes dat old times is back 'gain. I likes to be free, but I wasn't used to it and it was hard to know how to do. I 'members de dances we has in de old times, when we makes de music with banjo and other things. Some de good massas 'lowed de niggers dance in de back yard and if we goes over dere without de pass de patterroles gits us maybe. One time my papa he runnin' from dem patterroles and he run slap into de young massa and he say, 'Oh, you ain't no nigger, I kin tell by de smell.'

"Dat mind me of de ghost story dey used to tell 'bout de ghosties what live in de big bridge down in de hollow. De niggers day say dat ghostie make too much noise, with all he hollerin' and he rattlin' dem chain. So dat night one us niggers what dey call Charlie, he say he ain't 'fraid and he gwineter git him a ghostie, sho' 'nough. Us didn't believe him but purty soon us hears right smart wrastlin' with de chains and hollerin' down by de bridge and after 'while he come and say he git de best of dat ghostie, 'cause he ain't got strength like de man.

"Me and my old man us have twelve chillens altogedder. My husban' he come from South Car'lina whar dey eats cottonseed. I used to joke him 'bout it. I allus say Virginny de best, 'cause I come from dere.

United States.Work Project Administration

JAMES BOYD

JAMES BOYD was born in Phantom Valley, Indian Territory, in an Indian hut. A man named Sanford Wooldrige stole him and brought him to Texas, somewhere near Waco. James does not know his age, but thinks he is a hundred years or more old. He now lives in Itasca, Texas.

"I's born in dat Phantom Valley, in de Indian Territory, what am now call Oklahoma. Us live in a Indian hut. My pappy Blue Bull Bird and mammy Nancy Will. She come to de Indian Territory with Santa Anna, from Mississippi, and pappy raise in de Territory. I don' 'member much 'bout my folks, 'cause I stole from dem when I a real li'l feller. I's a-fishin' in de Cherokee River and a man name Sanford Wooldrige come by. You see, de white folks and de Indians have de fight 'bout dat day. I's on de river and I heared yellin' and shootin' and folkses runnin' and I slips into some bresh right near. Den come de white man and he say, 'Everybody kilt, nigger, and dem Indians gwine kill you iffen day cotch you. Come with me and I ain't 'low dem hurt you.' So I goes with him.

"He brung me to Texas, but I don't know jus' where, 'cause I didn't know nothin' 'bout dat place. Massa Sanford good to us, but look out for he missus, she sho' tough on niggers. Dere 'bout 1,600 acres in de plantation and de big house am nice. When de niggers wouldn't work dey whup 'em. Us work all week and sometime Sunday, iffen de crops in a rush. Massa not much on presents or money but us have warm clothes and plenty to eat and de dry place to live, and dat more'n lots of niggers has now.

"Sometime us have de corn huskin' and dere a dollar for de one what shuck de mos' corn. Us have de big dance 'bout twict a year, on Christmas and sometime in de summer. When de white folks have dere big balls us niggers cook and watch dem dance. Us have fun den.

"I likes to think of dem times when us fish all de hot day or hunts or jus' lazed 'round when de crops am laid by. I likes to shet de eyes and be back in old times and hear 'em sing, "Swing, low, Sweet Chariot." I can't sing, now you knows can't no old man sing what ain't got no teef or hair. I used to like to swing dat 'Ginia Reel and I's spry and young den.

"Dere's lots I can't 'member, 'cause my mem'ry done gone weak like de res' of me, but I 'member when us free us throw de hats in de air and holler. Old massa say, 'How you gwine eat and git clothes and sech?' Den us sho' scairt and stays with us white folks long as us can. But 'bout a year after dat I gits de job punchin' cattle on a ranch in South Texas. I druv cattle into Kansas, over what de white folks calls de Chissum Trail. I worked lots of cattle and is what dey call a top hand. I's workin' for Massa Boyd den, and he gits me to drive some cattle to Mexico. He say he ain't well no more and for me to sell de cattle and send him de money and git de job down dere. I goes on down to Mexico and do what he say. I marries a gal name Martina in 1869, down in Matamoras. Us have four chillen and she die. Dat break me up and I drifts back to Huntsville.

"I done change my name from Scott Bird, what it am up in de Territory, and make it James Boyd, 'cause I done work for Massa Boyd. I's gwine be 'bout 108 year old in next January, iffen de Lawd spare me dat long.

"After I been in Huntsville awhile, I marries Emma Smith but us only stay together 'bout a year and a half. Wasn't no chillen. Den I drifts to Fort Bend County and dere I marries Mary McDowd and us have two chillen. She die with de yellow fever and off I goes for Burleson County. Dere I marries Sally McDave and she quits me after us have three chillen. Down in old Washington County I marries Frances Williams and us lived together till 1900. Dere am no chillen dere. Den I goes to Austin after she die and marries Eliza Bunton in 1903. Us have eight chillen and she die in 1911. Den I comes to Hill County and marries Mittie Cahee in 1916. She quit me. In 1924 I marries Hegar Price clost to Milford. Us live together now, in Itasca. Us didn't have no chillen, but dat don't matter, 'cause I's de daddy of 'bout twenty already.

"I mos' allus wore de black suit when I marries. Jes' seemed more dressed up like. Some my wives wear white and some colors, didn't make much diff'rence, so dey a likely lookin' gal for me. Sometime it am a preacher and sometime it am Jestice of Peace, but de fust time it am Catholic and priest and all.

"Talkin' 'bout all dis marryin', I mos' forgit to show you my scar. I fit in dat freedom war 'long side Massa Sanford and got shot. Dat bullet go through de breast and out de back and keep me six months in de bed. De fust battle I's in am at Halifax, in North Car'lina. Us git de news of freedom when us at Vicksburg, in Mississippi. Mos' us niggers 'fraid say much. De new niggers 'spect de gov'ment give dem de span of mules and dey be rich and not work. But dey done larn a lot dese past years. Us am sho' slaves now to hard work, and lucky iffen us git work. Lots dem niggers figgers dey'd git dere massa's land, but dey didn't. Dey oughta of knowed dey wouldn't. Warn't no plantation ever divided I knowed of, but some de massas give de oldest slaves a li'l piece land.

"After de cattle days done gone, I farms in Hill County. I works twelve year for Massa Claude Wakefield, right near Milford, too. De old man ain't due to live nowhere long and I's gittin' 'bout ready to cross de river. I's seed a heap of dis here earth and de people in it, but I tells you it am sho' hard time now. Us is old and cripple' and iffen de white folks don't holp us I don't know what us gwine do.

"Some dese young niggers gone plumb wild with dere cigars and cars and truckin' and jazzin' and sech. Some go to school and larn like white folks and teach and be real helpful. But talk 'bout workin' in slave time—'twarn't so hard as now. Den you fuss 'cause dere's work, now you fuss 'cause dere ain't no work. But den us have somethin' to eat and wear and a place to sleep, and now us don't know one day what gwine fill us tomorrow, or nothin'.

"I'd sho' like to shake Massa Boyd's hand again and hear him come singin' down de lane. Us hear him sing or whistle long 'fore he git dere and it mighty good to see him. De slaves allus say, 'I's gwine 'way tomorrow,' and I guess I's gwine 'way pretty soon tomorrow.

JERRY BOYKINS

JERRY BOYKINS, spry and jolly at the age of 92, lived with his aged wife in their own cabin at 1015 Plum St., Abilene, Texas. He was born a slave to John Thomas Boykin, Troupe Co., Georgia, 80 miles from Lagrange, Ga. His master was a very wealthy plantation owner, working 1,000 slaves.

"I been well taken care of durin' my life. When I was young I lived right in de big house with my marster. I was houseboy. My mother's name was Betsy Ann Boykin and she was cook for Old Missus. My grandpa was blacksmith. I slept on a pallet in de kitchen and in winter time on cold nights I 'members how cold I would get. I'd wake up and slip in by marsters bed and den I'd say, 'Marster John, I's about to freeze.' He'd say, 'You ought to freeze, you little black devil. What you standin' dere for?' I'd say, 'Please, marster John, jes' let me crawl in by your feet.' He'd say, 'Well, I will dis one time,' and dat's de way I'd do every cold night.

"I was full of mischief and I'd tu'n de mules out of de lot, jus' to see de stableboy git a lickin'. One time I wanted a fiddle a white man named Cocoanut Harper kep' tryin' to sell me for $7.50. I didn' never have any money, 'cept a little the missie give me, so I kep' teasin' her to buy de fiddle for me. She was allus on my side, so she tol' me to take some co'n from de crib and trade in for de fiddle. In de night I slips out and hitch up de mules and fetched de co'n to old Harper's house and traded for dat fiddle. Den I hides out and play it, so's marster wouldn' fin' out, but he did and he whip all de daylight outta me. When de missie try to whip me, I jes' wrop up in her big skirts and she never could hurt me much.

"I allus ate my meals in de house at de white folks table, after dey done et. Iffen I couldn' sit in de marster's chair, I'd swell up like a toad.

"De marster done all de whippin', 'cause dey had been two overseers killed on de plantation for whippin' slaves till de blood run out dey body.

"Was I bovered with haints and spooks? I been meetin' up with 'em all my life. When I was younger I was such an old scratch I'd meet 'em right in de road, some without heads. I'd take to my heels and then I'd stop and look 'round and they'd be gone.

"I wore home-weaved shirts till I was grown, then I had some pants and dey was homemade, too. The women gathered womack leaves to dye de goods black.

"I well rec'lects when my marster went to war. He called all us in de kitchen and telled us he had to go over dere and whip those sons-of-bitches and would be back 'fore breakfast. He didn' return for two years. I says, 'Marster, we sho' would have waited breakfast on you a long time.' He said, 'Yes; deys de hardes' sons-of-bitches to whip I ever had dealins' with.'

"When war was over, he called us together and tol' us we were free. He said, 'Now, I'm goin' to give you a big day and after that you can stay and work for pay or you can go.' So he rolled out two barrels of whiskey and killed hogs and spread a big day.

"I wants to tell you 'bout how we killed hogs in my day. We digged a deep pit in de groun' and heated big rocks red hot and filled up de pit with water and dropped dem hot rocks in and got de water hot; den we stuck de hogs and rolled 'em in dat pit.

"Soon after I's free a man come for me from Louisville to

hire me as foreman in his cotton mule barn. So I went there and I worked in Kentucky for 18 year. Fifty-one years ago I married my ol' woman, Rachel Taylor, at Corsicana, Texas, and I think she's jes' as fine as the day I married her. We has six chillen and all works hard for a livin' and we got one lil' grandbaby 10 years ol'. She lives here at our house and we're educatin' her.

"I knows I's goin' to live to be over 100 years ol', 'cause my marster done tol' me so."

United States.Work Project Administration

Slave Narratives

MONROE BRACKINS

MONROE BRACKINS, born in Monroe Co., Mississippi, in 1853, was the property of George Reedes. He was brought to Medina County, Texas, when two years old. Monroe learned to snare and break mustangs and became a cowpuncher. He lives in Hondo, Texas. He has an air of pride and self-respect, and explained that he used little dialect because he learned to talk from the "white folks" as he was growing up.

"I was bo'n in Mississippi, Monroe County. I'm 84 years old. My master, George Reedes, brought me, my father and mother and my two sisters to Texas when I was two years old. My father was Nelson Brackins and my mother was Rosanna.

"My master settled here at a place called Malone, on the Hondo River. He went into the stock business. Our house there was a little, old picket house with a grass roof over it out of the sage grass. The bed was made with a tick of shucks and the children slept on the floor. The boss had just a little lumber house. Later on he taken us about 20 miles fu'ther down on the Hondo, the Old Adams Ranch, and he had a rock house.

"I was about six years old then. I had some shoes, to keep the thorns outa my feet, and I had rawhide leggin's. We just had such clothes as we could get, old patched-up clothes. They just had that jeans cloth, homemade clothes.

"I was with George Reedes 10 or 12 years. It was my first trainin' learnin' the stock business and horse breakin'. He was tol'able good to us, to be slaves as we was. His brother had a hired man that whipped me once, with a quirt. I've heard my father and mother tell how they whipped 'em. They'd tie 'em down on a log or up to a post and whip 'em till the blisters rose, then take a paddle and open 'em up and pour salt in 'em. Yes'm, they whipped the women. The most I remember about that, my father and sister was in the barn shuckin' co'n and the master come in there and whipped my sister with a cowhide whip. My father caught a lick in the face and he told the master to keep his whip offen him. So the master started on my father and he run away. When he finally come in he was so wild his master had to call him to get orders for work, and finally the boss shot at him, but they didn't whip him any more. Of course, some of 'em whipped with more mercy. They had a whippin' post and when they strapped 'em down on a log they called it a 'stroppin' log.'

"I remember they tasked the cotton pickers in Mississippi. They had to bring in so many pounds in the evenin' and if they didn't they got a whippin' for it. My sister there, she had to bring in 900 pounds a day. Well, cotton was heavier there. Most any of 'em could pick 900 pounds. It was heavier and fluffier. We left the cotton country in Mississippi, but nobody knew anything about cotton out here that I knew of.

"I've heard my parents say too, them men that had plantations and a great lot of slaves, they would speculate with 'em and would have a chain that run from the front ones to the back ones. Sometimes they would have 15 or 20 miles to make to get them to the sale place, but they couldn't make a break. Where they expected to make a sale, they kept 'em in corrals and they had a block there to put 'em up on and bid 'em off. The average price was about $500, but some that had good practice, like a blacksmith, brought a good price, as high as $1,500.

"I heard my mother and father say they would go 15 or 20 miles to a dance, walkin', and get back before daylight, before the 'padderollers' got 'em. The slaves would go off when they had no permission and them that would ketch 'em and whip 'em was the 'padderollers.' Sometimes they would have an awful race.

"If they happened to be a slave on the plantation that could jes' read a little print, they would get rid of him right now. He would ruin the niggers, they would get too smart. The' was no such thing as school here for culluds in early days. The white folks we was raised up with had pretty good education. That's why I don't talk like most cullud folks. I was about grown and the' was an English family settled close, about half a mile, I guess. They had a little boy, his name was Arthur Ederle, and he come over and learned me how to spell 'cat' and 'dog' and 'hen' and such like. I was right around about 20 years old. I couldn't sign my name when I was 18 years old.

"I can remember one time when I was young, I saw something I couldn't 'magine what it was, like a billygoat reared up on a tree. But I knew the' wasn't a billygoat round there near, nor no other kinds of goats. It was in the daytime and I was out in a horse pasture, I was jes' walkin' along, huntin', when I saw that sight. I guess I got within 50 steps of it, then I turned around and got away. I never did think much about a ghost, but I think it could be possible.

"I don't remember scarcely anything about the war because I was so little and times was so different; the country wasn't settled up and everything was wild, no people, hardly. Of course, my life was in the woods, you might say, didn't hardly know when Sunday come.

"The northern soldiers never did get down in here that I know of. I know once, when they was enlisting men to go to battle a whole lot of 'em didn't want to fight and would run away and dodge out, and they would follow 'em and try to make 'em fight. They had a battle up here on the Nueces once and killed some of 'em. I know my boss was in the bunch that followed 'em and he got scared for fear this old case would be brought up after the war. The company that followed these men was called Old Duff Company. I think somewhere around 40 was in the bunch that they followed, but I don't know how many was killed. They was a big bluff and a big water hole and they said they was throwed in that big water hole.

"We had possums and 'coons to eat sometimes. My father, he gen'rally cooked the 'coons, he would dress 'em and stew 'em and then bake 'em. My mother wouldn't eat them. There was plenty of rabbits, too. Sometimes when they had potatoes they cooked 'em with 'em. I remember one time they had just a little patch of blackhead sugar cane. After the freedom, my mother had a kind of garden and she planted snap beans and watermelons pretty much every year.

"The master fed us tol'bly well. Everything was wild, beef was free, just had to bring one in and kill it. Once in awhile, of a Sunday mornin', we'd get biscuit flour bread to eat. It was a treat to us. They measured the flour out and it had to pan out just like they measured. He give us a little somethin' ever' Christmas and somethin' good to eat. I heard my people say coffee was high, at times, and I know we didn't get no flour, only Sunday mornin'. We lived on co'nbread, mostly, and beef and game outta the woods. That was durin' the war and after the war, too.

"I was around about 6 or 7 years old when we was freed. We worked for George Reedes awhile, then drifted on down to the Frio river and stayed there about a year, then we come to Medina County and settled here close to where I was raised. We didn't think it hard times at all right after the war. The country was wild and unsettled, with ranches 15 or 20 miles apart. You never did see anybody and we didn't know really what was goin' on in the rest of the country. Sometimes something could happen in 5 miles of us and we didn't know it for a month.

"I was on the Adams Ranch on the Hondo when my master come out and told us we were as free as he was. He said we could stay on and work or could go if we wanted to. He gave my mother and father 50 cents apiece and 25 cents for the children. We stayed awhile and then went west to the Frio.

"I used to be along with old man Big-foot Wallace in my early days. He was a mighty fine man. I worked for the people that was gathering stock together there. Big Foot raised nice horses, old reg'lar Texas horses, and they was better than the reg'lar old Spanish bronco. I used to go to his camp down on the San Miguel. He lived in one part and his chickens in the rest of his house. His friends liked to hear him talk about his travels. He used to run stock horses and had a figger 7 on the left shoulder for his brand and the tip of each ear split was his earmark.

"The last man I broke horses for was Wilson Bailey. I was there about 12 years. He raised just cavi-yard—we called it a cavi-yard of horses, just the same thing as a remuda. We called 'em that later, but we got that from the Spanish. We would get up in a tree with our loop till the horse come under and drop it down on him. When they were so spoilt, we got 'em in a sort of cavi-yard and drove 'em under trees and caught 'em in a snare. We had lots of wild horses, just this side of Pearsall. 'Bout the only way I'd get throwed was to get careless. We'd ketch 'im up, hackamore 'im up, saddle 'im up and get on 'im and let 'im go. Sometimes he'd be too wild to pitch, he'd break and run and you had to let 'im run himself down. I used to rather ketch up a wild horse and break 'im than to eat breakfast.

"When I first started farmin' I taken up some state land, about 80 acres, down on Black Creek, in Medina County. I stayed there ten or twelve years. Cotton hadn't got in this country and I raised some corn, sugar cane and watermelons. I commenced with horses, but 'long 'way down the line I used oxen some, too. I used one of those old walking plows.

"I sold that place and moved to a place on the Tywaukney Creek (Tonkawa). I come up to church and met my wife then. Her name was Ida Bradley and I was 38 years old. We lived down on the Tywaukney right about 23 years and raised our children there. We jes' had a little home weddin'. I wore a suit, dark suit. We got married about 8 o'clock in the evenin' and we had barbecue, cake and ice cream. You see, in them times I wasn't taught anything about years and dates, but I judge it was about 25 years after the war before I settled on the Tywaukney."

United States.Work Project Administration

GUS BRADSHAW

GUS BRADSHAW was born about 1845, at Keecheye, Alabama, a slave of David Cavin. He recalls being brought to Texas in the 1850's, when the Cavin family settled near old Port Caddo. Gus remained with his master for ten years after emancipation. He now lives alone on a fifty acre farm seven miles northeast of Marshall, which he bought in 1877. Gus receives an $11.00 per month pension.

"I was born at Keecheye, Alabama, and belonged to old man David Cavin. The only statement I can make 'bout my age is I knows I was 'bout twenty years old when us slaves was freed. I never knowed my daddy, but my mammy was Amelia Cavin. I's heard her say she's born in Alabama more times than I got fingers and toes. Our old master brung us to Texas when I's a good sized kid. I 'members like it am yesterday, how we camped more'n a week in New Orleans. I seed 'em sell niggers off the block there jus' like they was cattle. Then we came to old Port Caddo on Caddo Lake and master settles a big farm close to where the boats run. Port Caddo was a big shipping place then, and Dud and John Perry run the first store there. The folks hauled cotton there from miles away.

"Mammy's folks was named Maria and Joe Gloster and they come to Texas with the Cavins. My grandma say to me, 'Gus, don't run you mouth too much and allus have manners to whites and blacks.' Chillen was raise right then, but now they come up any way. I seed young niggers turn the dipper up and drink 'fore old folks. I wouldn't dare do that when I's comin' up.

"Maria say to me one day, 'Son, I's here when the stars fell.' She tell me they fell like a sheet and spread over the ground. Ike Hood, the old blacksmith on our place, he told me, too. I says, 'Ike, how old was you when the stars fell?' He say, 'I's thirty-two.'

"Massa David had big quarters for us niggers, with chimneys and fireplaces. They use to go round and pick up old hawg or cow bones to bile with greens and cabbage. They was plenty of wild game, and deer and wolves howlin' right through this country, but you can't even find the track of one now.

"The first work I done was pickin' cotton. Every fellow was out at daylight pickin' cotton or hoein' or plowin'. They was one overseer and two nigger drivers. But at night you could hear us laughin' and talkin' and singin' and prayin', and hear them fiddles and things playin'. It look like darkies git 'long more better then than now. Some folks says niggers oughtn't to be slaves, but I says they ought, 'cause they jus' won't do right onless they is made to do it.

"Massa David allus give us eggnog and plenty good whiskey at Christmas. We had all day to eat and drink and sing and dance. We didn't git no presents, but we had a good time.

"I don't know much 'bout the war, only Massa Bob Perry come over one day and say to Grandma Maria, 'They is surrender, Maria, you is free.' She say to him, 'I don't care, I gwine stay with my white folks.'

"The Klu Klux done lots of cuttin' up round there. Two of 'em come to Dr. Taylor's house. He had two niggers what run off from the Klux and they want to whip 'em, but Dr. Taylor wouldn't 'low 'em. I knowed old Col. Alford, one of the Klux leaders, and he was a sight. He told me once, 'Gus, they done send me to the pen for Kluxing.' I say, 'Massa Alford, didn't they make a gentleman of you?' He say, 'Hell, no!'

"I knowed old Col. Haggerdy, too. He marries a widow of a rich old Indian chief, name McIntosh. He broke a treaty with his people and had to hide out in a cave a long time, and his wife brung food to him. One time when she went to the cave he was gone. She knowed then the Indians done git him and kilt him for vi'latin' the treaty. So she marries old Col. Haggerdy.

"The only time I votes was against whiskey. I voted for it. Some white folks done say they'd whip me if I voted for it, but Mr. Joe Strickland done told me they jus' tryin' scare me, so I voted for it. I don't think niggers ought to vote. If some niggers had things in hand 'stead of white folks, I couldn't stay here. These eddicated niggers am causin' the devilment. The young niggers ain't got no 'spect for old age.

"I bought and paid for fifty acres land here in Harrison County and I has lived on it sixty years. I lived with my wife fifty years 'fore she died and done raise two chillen. These young niggers don't stay married fifty days, sometimes. I don't mess with 'em, but if I needs help I goes to the white folks. If you 'have youself, they allus help you if you needs it.

United States.Work Project Administration

WES BRADY

WES BRADY, 88, was born a slave of John Jeems, who had a farm five miles north of Marshall. Wes has farmed in Harrison County all his life. He now lives with friends on the Long's Camp Road, and draws a $11.00 monthly pension.

"I was born and raised in Harrison County, and I was eighty-eight years old this July past and has wore myself out here in this county. I was born on Massa John Jeem's place, on the old Jefferson Road, and my father was Peter Calloway, and he was born in Alabama and his whole fam'ly brought to Texas by nigger traders. My mother was Harriet Ellis and I had two brothers named George and Andrew, and four sisters, Lula and Judy and Mary and Sallie. My old Grandpa Phil told me how he helped run the Indians off the land.

"Grandpa Phil told me 'bout meetin' his massa. Massa Jeems had three or four places and grandpa hadn't seed him and he went to one of the other farms and meets a man goin' down the road. The man say, 'Who you belong to?' Grandpa Phil say, 'Massa Jeems.' The man say, 'Is he a mean man?' Grandpa say, 'I don't know him, but they say he's purty tight.' It was Massa Jeems talkin' and he laughs and gives Grandpa Phil five dollars.

"We niggers lived in log houses and slep' on hay mattress with lowell covers, and et fat pork and cornbread and 'lasses and all kinds garden stuff. If we et flour bread, our women folks had to slip the flour siftin's from missy's kitchen and darsn't let the white folks know it. We wore one riggin' lowell clothes a year and I never had shoes on till after surrender come. I run all over the place till I was a big chap in jes' a long shirt with a string tied round the bottom for a belt. I went with my young massa that way when he hunted in the woods, and toted squirrels for him.

"Some white folks might want to put me back in slavery if I tells how we was used in slavery time, but you asks me for the truth. The overseer was 'straddle his big horse at three o'clock in the mornin', roustin' the hands off to the field. He got them all lined up and then come back to the house for breakfas'. The rows was a mile long and no matter how much grass was in them, if you leaves one sprig on your row they beats you nearly to death. Lots of times they weighed cotton by candlelight. All the hands took dinner to the field in buckets and the overseer give them fifteen minutes to git dinner. He'd start cuffin' some of them over the head when it was time to stop eatin' and go back to work. He'd go to the house and eat his dinner and then he'd come back and look in all the buckets and if a piece of anything that was there when he left was et, he'd say you was losin' time and had to be whipped. He'd drive four stakes in the ground and tie a nigger down and beat him till he's raw. Then he'd take a brick and grind it up in a powder and mix it with lard and put it all over him and roll him in a sheet. It'd be two days or more 'fore that nigger could work 'gain. I seed one nigger done that way for stealin' a meat bone from the meathouse. That nigger got fifteen hundred lashes. The li'l chaps would pick up egg shells and play with them and if the overseer seed them he'd say you was stealin' eggs and give you a beatin'. I seed long lines of slaves chained together driv by a white man on a hoss, down the Jefferson road.

"The first work I done was drappin' corn, and then cow-pen boy and sheep herder. All us house chaps had to shell a half bushel corn every night for to feed the sheep. Many times I has walked through the quarters when I was a little chap, cryin' for my mother. We mos'ly only saw her on Sunday. Us chillen was in bed when the folks went to the field and come back. I 'members wakin' up at night lots of times and seein' her make a little mush on the coals in the fireplace, but she allus made sho' that overseer was asleep 'fore she done that.

"One time the stock got in the field and the overseer 'cuses a old man and jumps on him and breaks his neck. When he seed the old man dead, he run off to the woods, but massa sent some nigger after him and say for him to come back, the old man jus' got overhet and died.

"We went to church on the place and you ought to heared that preachin'. Obey your massa and missy, don't steal chickens and eggs and meat, but nary a word 'bout havin' a soul to save.

"We had parties Saturday nights and massa come out and showed us new steps. He allus had a extra job for us on Sunday, but he gave us Christmas Day and all the meat we wanted. But if you had money you'd better hide it, 'cause he'd git it.

"The fightin' was did off from us. My father went to war to wait on Josh Calloway. My father never come back. Massa Jeems cussed and 'bused us niggers more'n ever, but he took sick and died and stepped off to Hell 'bout six months 'fore we got free. When we was free, they beat drums in Marshall. I stayed on 'bout seven months and then my mother and me went to farmin' for ourselves.

"I wore myself out right in this county and now I'm too old to work. These folks I lives with takes good care of me and the gov'ment gives me $11.00 a month what I is proud to git.

United States.Work Project Administration

JACOB BRANCH

JACOB BRANCH, about 86, was a slave of the Van Loos family, in Louisiana, who sold him when a baby to Elisha Stevenson, of Double Bayou, Texas. Jacob helps his son, Enrichs, farm, and is unusually agile for his age. They live in the Double Bayou settlement, near Beaumont, Texas.

"I's bought and fotched here to Double Bayou when I's jes' three year old. I and my half-brother, Eleck, he de baby, was both born in Louisiana on de Van Loos place, but I go by de name of Branch, 'cause my daddy name Branch. My mama name Renee. Dey split up us family and Elisha Stevenson buy my mama and de two chillen. I ain't never see my daddy no more and don't 'member him at all.

"Old 'Lisha Stevenson he a great one for to raise pigs. He sell sometime 500 hawgs at one time. He take he dogs and drive dem hawgs 'cross de Neches River all by hisself, to sell dem. Dat how he git money to buy de niggers, sellin' hawgs and cowhides.

"Old massa he sho' a good old man, but de old missy, she a tornado! Her name Miss 'Liza. She could be terrible mean. But sometime she take her old morrel—dat a sack make for to carry things in—and go out and come back with plenty joints of sugar cane. She take a knife and sit on de gallary and peel dat cane and give a joint to every one de li'l chillen.

"Mama, she work up in de big house, doin' cookin' and washin'. Old massa go buy a cullud man name Uncle Charley Fenner. He a good old cullud man. Massa brung him to de quarters and say, 'Renee, here you husband,' and den he turn to Uncle and say, 'Charley, dis you woman.' Den dey consider marry. Dat de way dey marry den, by de massa's word. Uncle Charley, he good step-pa to us.

"De white folks have de good house with a brick chimney. Us quarters de good, snug li'l house with flue and oven. Dey didn't bother to have much furn'chure, 'cause us in dere only to sleep. Us have homemake bench and 'Georgia Hoss' bed with hay mattress. All us cookin' and eatin' done in de kitchen de big house. Us have plenty to eat, too. De smokehouse allus full white 'taters and cracklin's hangin' on de wall. Us git dem mos' any time us want, jes' so long us didn't waste nothin'. Dey have big jar with buttermilk and 'low us drink all us want.

"Old lady 'Liza, she have three women to spin when she git ready make de clothes for everybody. Dey spin and weave and make all us clothes. Us all wear shirt tail till us 'bout twelve or fourteen, boys and gals, too. You couldn't tell us apart.

"Us chillen start to work soon's us could toddle. First us gather firewood. Iffen it freezin' or hot us have to go to toughen us up. When us git li'l bigger us tend de cattle and feed hosses and hawgs. By time us good sprouts us pickin' cotton and pullin' cane. Us ain't never idle. Sometime us git far out in de field and lay down in de corn row and nap. But, Lawdy, iffen dey cotch you, dey sho' wore you out! Sunday de onliest rest day and den de white folks 'low us play.

"Massa never whup Uncle Charley, 'cause he good nigger and work hard. It make missy mad and one time when massa gone she go down in de field. Uncle Charley hoein' corn jes' like massa done told him, jes' singin' and happy. Old missy she say, 'Nigger, I's sho gwineter whup you.' He say, 'What for you whup me. I doin' every bit what old massa done tell me.' But missy think he gittin' it too good, 'cause he ain't never been whupped. She clumb over de fence and start down de row with de cowhide. Uncle Charley, he ain't even raise he voice, but he cut de las' weed outen dat corn and commence to wave he hoe in de air, and he say, 'Missy, I ain't 'vise you come any step closeter.' Dat sho' make her mad, but she 'fraid to do nothin'.

"One time she have 'nother nigger name Charlie. Massa go on de trip and she tell dis Charley iffen he ain't finish grindin' all de cornmeal by Monday she gwineter give him a t'ousand lashes. He try, but he ain't able make dat much meal, so come Monday he runned off in de bayou. Dat night come de big freeze and he down dere with water up to he knees and when massa come home and go git him, he so froze he couldn't walk. Dey brung him in de kitchen and old missy cuss him out. Soon's he thaw out, he done die right dere on de spot.

"My pore mama! Every washday old missy give her de beatin'. She couldn't keep de flies from speckin' de clothes overnight. Old missy git up soon in de mornin', 'fore mama have time git dem specks off. She snort and say, 'Renee, I's gwineter teach you how to wash.' Den she beat mama with de cowhide. Look like she cut my mama in two. Many's de time I edges up and tries take some dem licks off my mama.

"Slavery, one to 'nother, was purty rough. Every plantation have to answer for itself.

"I used to know lots of songs, but I don't know many now. Spiritual songs, dey comes through visions. Dat's why cullud folks can make dem better dan white folks. I knowed one song what start out—

"'De Jews done kill pore Jesus,

And bury him in de sepulchur;

De grave wouldn't hold him,

Dey place guards all 'round him,

But de angels move de stone,

De Jews done kill pore Jesus,

But de grave it wouldn't hold him.'

"Dey 'nother song what say—

"'Run, sinner, run,

Gawd is a-callin' you.

Run, sinner, run,

De fire'll overtake you.'

"When I 'bout ten dey sets me ginnin' cotton. Old massa he done make de cotton with de hand crank. It built on a bench like. I gin de cotton by turnin' dat crank. When I gits a lapful I puts it in de tow sack and dey take it to Miss Susan to make de twine with it. I warm and damp de cotton 'fore de fireplace 'fore I start ginnin' it.

"Dere school for de white chillen in Double Bayou and I used to go meet de chillen comin' home and dey stop longside de way and teach me my ABC. Dey done carry me as far as Baker in de book when old missy find it out and make dem stop. De war comin' on den and us daren't even pick up a piece of paper. De white folks didn't want us to larn to read for fear us find out things.

"Us livin' down by de Welborn's den and I seed dem haul de logs out of Pine Island to make dat Welborn house. Old man Hamshire and old man Remington builded dat Welborn house. It 'cross de bayou, left hand side Smith's ferry. Dat house still standin' in parts.

"One mornin' Eleck and me git up at crack of dawn to milk. All at once come a shock what shake de earth. De big fish jump clean out de bay and turtles and alligators run out dere ponds. Dey plumb ruint Galveston! Us runned in de house and all de dishes and things done jump out de shelf. Dat de first bombardment of Galveston. De sojers put powder under people's houses and blowin' up Galveston.

"Young massa Shake Stevenson he vol'teer and git kilt somewheres in Virginny. Young massa Tucker Stevenson, he ain't 'lieve in war and he say he never gwine fight. He hide in de woods so de conscrip' men can't find him. Old man LaCour come 'round and say he have orders for find Tucker and bring him in dead or 'live. But 'cause he old massa's friend, he say, 'Why don't you buy de boy's services off?' So old massa take de boat, 'Catrig,' us calls it, and loads it with corn and sich and us pole it down to Galveston. De people need dat food so much, dat load supplies done buy off Massa Tucker from fightin'.

"After war starts lots of slaves runned off to git to de Yankees. All dem in dis part heads for de Rio Grande river. De Mexicans rig up flat-boats out in de middle de river, tied to stakes with rope. When de cullud people gits to de rope dey can pull deyself 'cross de rest de way on dem boats. De white folks rid de 'Merican side dat river all de time, but plenty slaves git through, anyway.

"I wait on lots of sojers. I have to get smartweed and bile it in salt water to bath dem in. Dat help de rheumatism. Dem sojers have rheumatism so bad for standin' day and night in de water.

"Us sho' in good health dem days. Iffen a cullud man weak dey move de muscles in he arms, bleed him and give him plenty bacon and cornbread, and he git so strong he could lift a log. Dey didn't go in for cuttin', like dey do now. Dey git herbs out de woods, blue mass and quinine and calomel. I think people jes' die under pills, now. Old lady Field she make medicine with snakeroot and larkspur and marshroot and redroot.

"After war am over Massa Tucker brung de freedom papers and read dem. He say us all am free as Hell. Old man Charley so happy he jes' roll on de floor like a hoss and kick he heels. De nex' mornin' mama start do somethin' and missy cuss her out. I runned to missy and say, 'Us free as de bird.' She sho' whup me for dat, but no more, 'cause she so mean us all leave.

"Dat funny. Old man LaFour, what de head de patterrollers and so mean, he de first to help us niggers after freedom. He loan us he ox team and pay Uncle Charley a dollar de day for work and a dollar every time my mama wash for he wife.

"Old massa and missy split up. She so bad she ain't give him no better show dan she done us. Old massa gittin' some peaches one day and she come after him with de buggy whip. He git on he hoss and say, 'Liz, you's gittin' broad as de beef. You too big for me.' She so mad she spit fire. Lightenin' done kill her, she upstairs and de big streak hits her. It knock her under de bed.

"De first freedom work I done am pullin' up potato hills at two bits a hunnerd. 'Bout two bits de most us could make in one day. I work two days to buy mama de turkey hen for Christmas. Anything mama want I think she got to have. I's growed 'fore I gits much as four bits a day. I's done earn as much as $1.50 in my time, though.

"When I's 25 year old I marries Betty Baker but she dead now. De Rev. Patterson he marry us. Us has four chillen livin'. Turah and Renee, dat my gals, and Enrichs and Milton, dat my boys. Milton work in Houston and Enrich help me farm. I's a Mason 30 year. De lodge split up now, but it answer.

Slave Narratives

WILLIAM BRANCH

WILLIAM BRANCH, born 1850, 322 Utah St., San Antonio, Texas. Eyesight is so poor someone must lead him to the store or to church. William kneels at his bedside each evening at five and says his praye rs. In this ceremony he spends a half hour or more chanting one Negro spiritual after another.

"Yahsur, I was a slave. I was bo'n May 13, 1850, on the place of Lawyer Woodson in Lunenburg County, Virginia. It was 'bout 75 miles southwest of Richmond. They was two big plantations, one on one side the road, yother the yother.

My marster owned 75 slaves. He raised tobacco and cotton. I wukked tobacco sometime, sometime cotton. Dere wasn't no whippin' or switchin'. We had to wuk hard. Marster Woodson was a rich man. He live in a great big house, a lumber house painted white. And it had a great big garden.

"De slaves lives in a long string of log houses. Dey had dirt floors and shingle roofs. Marster Woodson's house was shingle roof too. We had home cured bacon and veg'tables, dried co'n, string beans and dey give us hoe cakes baked in hot ashes. Dere always was lots of fresh milk.

"How'd us slaves git de clothes? We carded de cotton, den de women spin it on a spinnin' wheel. After dat day sew de gahment togeddah on a sewin' machine. Yahsur, we's got sewin' machine, wid a big wheel and a handle. One woman tu'n de handle and de yuther woman do de sewin'.

"Dat's how we git de clothes for de 75 slaves. Marster's clothes? We makes dem for de whole fam'ly. De missis send de pattren and de slaves makes de clothes. Over nigh Richmond a fren' of Marster Woodson has 300 slaves. Dey makes all de clothes for dem.

"I was with Marster twel de Yankees come down to Virginia in 1861. De sergeant of de Yankees takes me up on his hoss and I goes to Washington wid de Yankees. I got to stay dere 'cause I'd run away from my marster.

"I stay at de house of Marse Frank Cayler. He's an ole time hack driver. I was his houseboy. I stay dere twel de year 1870, den I goes to Baltimore and jines de United States Army. We's sent to Texas 'count of de Indians bein' so bad. Dey put us on a boat at Baltimore and we landed at Galveston.

"Den we marches from Galveston to Fort Duncan. It was up, up, de whole time. We ties our bedclothes and rolls dem in a bundle wid a strap. We walks wid our guns and bedclothes on our backs, and de wagons wid de rations follows us. Dey is pulled by mules. We goes 15 miles ev'ry day. We got no tents, night come, we unrolls de blankets and sleeps under de trees, sometime under de brush.

"For rations we got canned beans, milk and hardtack. De hard tacks is 3 or 4 in a box, we wets 'em in water and cooks 'em in a skillet. We gits meat purty often. When we camps for de night de captain say, 'You'all kin go huntin'.' Before we git to de mountains dere's deer and rabbits and dey ain't no fences. Often in de dark we sees a big animal and we shoots. When we bring 'im to camp, de captain say, 'Iffen de cow got iron burns de rancher gwineter shoot hisself a nigger scout.' But de cow ain't got no iron, it's—what de name of de cow what ain't feel de iron? Mavrick, yahsur. We eats lots of dem Mavricks. We's goin' 'long de river bottom, and before we comes to Fort Duncan we sees de cactus and muskeet. Dere ain't much cattle, but one colored scout shoots hisself a bear. Den we eats high. Fort Duncan were made of slab lumber and de roof was gravel and grass.

"Den we's ordered to Fort Davis and we's in de mountains now. Climb, climb all day, and de Indians give us a fit ev'ry day. We kills some Indians, dey kills a few soldiers. We was at Fort Clark a while. At Fort Davis I jines de colored Indian Scouts, I was in Capt. George L. Andrew's Co. K.

"We's told de northern Cheyennes is on a rampus and we's goin' to Fort Sill in Indian Territory. Before we gits to Fort Concho (San Angelo) de Comanches and de Apaches give us a fit. We fitten' 'em all de time and when we gits away from de Comanches and Apaches we fitten de Cheyennes. Dey's seven feet tall. Dey couldn't come through that door.

"When we gits to Fort Sill, Gen. Davidson say de Cheyennes is off de reservation, and he say, 'You boys is got to git dem back. Iffen you kill 'em, dey can't git back to de reservation.' Den we goes scoutin' for de Cheyennes and dey is scoutin' for us. Dey gits us first, on de Wichita River was 500 of 'em, and we got 75 colored Indian Scouts. Den Red Foot, de Chief of de Cheyennes, he come to see Capt. Lawson and say he want rations for his Indians. De captain say he cain't give no rations to Indians off de reservation. Red Foot say he don't care 'bout no reservation and he say he take what we got. Capt. Lawson 'low we gotter git reinforcements. We got a guide in de scout troop, he call hisself Jack Kilmartin. De captain say, 'Jack, I'se in trouble, how kin I git a dispatch to Gen. Davidson?' Jack say, 'I kin git it through.' And Jack, he crawl on his belly and through de brush and he lead a pony, and when he gits clear he rides de pony bareback twel he git to Fort Sill. Den Gen. Davidson, he soun' de gin'ral alarm and he send two companies of cavalry to reinforce us. But de Cheyennes give 'em a fit all de way, dey's gotter cut dere way through de Cheyennes.

"And Col. Shafter comes up, and goes out in de hills in his shirt sleeves jus' like you's sittin' dere. Dey's snow on de groun' and de wind's cole, but de colonel don't care, and he say, 'Whut's dis order Gen. Davidson give? Don' kill de Cheyennes? You kill 'em all from de cradle to de Cross.'

"And den we starts de attack. De Cheyennes got Winchesters and rifles and repeaters from de government. Yahsur, de government give 'em de guns dey used to shoot us. We got de ole fashion muzzle loaders. You puts one ball in de muzzle and shove de powder down wid de ramrod. Den we went in and fit 'em, and 'twas like fightin' a wasp's nest. Dey kills a lot of our boys and we nearly wipes 'em out. Den we disarms de Cheyennes we captures, and turns dere guns in to de regiment.

"I come to San Antonio after I'se mustered out and goes to

work for de Bell Jewelry Company and stays dere twel I cain't work no more. Did I like de army? Yahsur, I'd ruthuh be in de army dan a plantation slave."

United States.Work Project Administration

CLARA BRIM

CLARA BRIM, slave of William Lyons of Branch, Louisiana, now lives in Beaumont, Texas. The town of Branch was known in slave days as Plaquemine Bouley. Clara estimates her age to be 100 or 102, and from various facts known to her and her family, this would seem to be correct.

"Old massa's name was William Lyons. I didn't have no old missus, 'cause he was a bachelor. He had a big plantation. I don't know how big but dey somethin' like twenty fam'lies of slaves and some dem fam'lies had plenty in dem. My ma was Becky Brim and pa, he name Louis Brim. She come from Old Virginny. Dey work in de field. I had two sister name Cass and Donnie and a brudder name Washington. He went off to de war. When it break out dey come and take him off to work in de army. He lost in dat war. He didn't come back. Nobody ever know what happen to him.

"Some de houses log house and some plank, but dey all good. Dey well built and had brick chimneys. Dey houses what de wind didn't blow in. Us had beds, too, not dem built in de wall. Us sho' treat good in slavery times, yes, suh. Old massa give us plenty clothes to keep us good and warm. He sho' did.

"Old massa, he wasn't marry and eat de same things de slaves eat. He didn't work dem in de heat of de day. 'Bout eleven o'clock, when dat sun git hot, he call dem out de field. He give dem till it git kind of cool befo' he make dem go back in de field. He didn't have no overseer. He seed 'bout de plantation hisself. He raise cotton and corn and sweet 'taters and peas and cane, didn't fool with rice. He didn't go in for oats, neither.

"When Sunday come Old Massa ask who want to go to church. Dem what wants could ride hoss-back or walk. Us go to de white folks church. Dey sot in front and us sot in back. Us had prayer meetin', too, reg'lar every week. One old cullud man a sort of preacher. He de leader in 'ligion.

"When de slaves go to work he give dem de task. Dat so much work, so many rows cotton to chop or corn to hoe. When dey git through dey can do what dey want. He task dem on Monday. Some dem git through Thursday night. Den dey can hire out to somebody and git pay for it.

"Old Massa even git de preacher for marryin' de slaves. And when a slave die, he git de preacher and have Bible readin' and prayin'. Mostest de massas didn't do dat-a-way.

"I as big in war time as I is now. I used to do anything in de field what de men done. I plow and pull fodder and pick cotton. But de hardes' work I ever done am since I free. Old Massa, he didn't work us hard, noway.

"He allus give us de pass, so dem patterrollers not cotch us. Dey 'bout six men on hoss-back, ridin' de roads to cotch niggers what out without de pass. Iffen dey cotch him it am de whippin'. But de niggers on us place was good and civ'lized folks. Dey didn't have no fuss. Old Massa allus let dem have de garden and dey can raise things to eat and sell. Sometime dey have some pig and chickens.

"I been marry his' one time and he been dead 'bout forty-one years now. I stay with Old Massa long time after freedom. In 1913 I come live with my youngest girl here in Beaumont. You see, I can't 'member so much. I has lived so long my 'memberance ain't so good now.

SYLVESTER BROOKS

SYLVESTER BROOKS, 87, was born in Green County, Alabama, a slave of Josiah Collier. The old Negro's memory is poor, but he managed to recall a few incidents of slave days. He lives in Mart, Texas.

"I's born 'bout de year 1850, near de Tom Bigbee river in Alabama, on a plantation own by Marse Josiah Collier. My folks was Henderson and Martha Brooks and I's de only child den.

"Marse Collier owned seventy fam'lies of slaves and dey all lived in dey quarters 'bout a mile from de big house. When freedom come Marse Collier sent for all de slaves and lines us up in a row, two deep, and helt up he hands and say, 'Boys, you is free as I is. All of you what wants to can go, and all of you what wants to can work for me on wages dis year. Next year I'll give you a crop or work for wages.' Dey all stays but two, and one of dem two my daddy, and he lef' mammy and six chillen and never come back.

"Us stays on till Marse Collier and Missus both dies, and den stays with he oldes' gal, and didn't go 'way till we's growed and has fam'lies of our own.

"I 'members best de Fourth of July. De white folks have lots to eat for dem and us and we plays games and goes swimmin'.

"Next thing I 'members is de patterrollers, 'cause dey whip me every time dey cotches me without my pass. Dat de way dey make us stay home at night, and it made good niggers out of us, 'cause we couldn't chase round and git in no meanness.

"Old Marse often told me 'bout de stars fallin'. It was 'long 'bout sundown and growed dark all a sudden and de chickens goes to roost. Den some stars with long tails 'gins to shoot, den it look like all de stars had come out of Heaven, and did dey fall! De stars not all what fell. De white folks and de niggers fell on dere knees, prayin' to Gawd to save dem iffen de world comin' to a end, and de women folks all run down in de cellar and stayed till mornin'. Old Marse say it was in 1833, and he say dem stars fall awhile and quit awhile, like de showers when it rains.

"'Bout a year after freedom Old Marse give us a piece of land for a church and dis was de school, too. De preacher's name was Christmas Crawford, and dat de reason I 'members it, it so funny to us. De nigger teacher named Nimron. De niggers has de blueback spellers and larns 'rithmetic, too.

"On Thanksgivin' Day de niggers goes round to de white folks houses and gives a ser'nade, like dis:

"'De old bee make de honeycomb,

De young bee make de honey—

De nigger make de cotton and corn,

And de white folks git de money.

"'De raccoon he a curious man,

He never works till dark;

Nothin' ever 'sturbs he mind,

Till he hear old Towser bark.'

"Den de white folks asks us in and help ourselves to de cake or wine or whatever dey has, and we does dis on Christmas, too.

"We had a song we'd sing when we's thinkin' of comin' to

Texas:

"'We'll put for de South, for seven-up and loo,

Chime in, niggers, won't you come 'long, too?

No use talkin' when de nigger wants to go,

Where de corn top blossoms and canebrakes grow.

Come 'long, Cuba, and dance de polka juba,

Way down South, where de corn tops grow.'

"I'd like to be in old Alabama to die, but Old Marse and Missus gone, and it ain't no use goin' dere no more.

United States.Work Project Administration

DONAVILLE BROUSSARD

DONAVILLE BROUSSARD, a polished gentleman of his race, was the son of a mulatto slave of Emilier Caramouche. He was born in 1850, but appears vigorous. Light skinned, with blue eyes and a genial expression, he gave the story of his life in the French patois spoken by Louisiana French Negroes, which has been translated into English.

"My mama was daughter of one of the Carmouche boys. One of M'sieur Francois' sons. She call herself Armance Carmouche. She was house servant for the family and I worked around the house. I remember my Madame brought me the little basket and it had a strap on it. I put the strap over the shoulder and went round with the sharp stick and picked up the leaves on the ground with the stick.

"It was a great house with trees and flowers. Madame liked all clean and pretty. I never worked hard. The ladies and my mama, too, petted me as if I was the white child.

"M'sieur had a widow sister. She made us learn the prayers. We were glad to go where she was for she always had something good in her bag for us. I never saw the baptizing. In those days all the slaves had the religion of the master and the Catholics didn't have no baptizing. They didn't have to half-drown when they got their religion. The church was 15 or 20 miles off. The priest came and held Mass for the white folks sometimes.

"I remember one wedding. My aunt got married. M'sieur Caramouche killed a big pig. The white folks ate in the house. The slaves sat under the trees and ate in the yard. At four o'clock the justice of the peace came. He was the friend of M'sieur Caramouche. He made my aunt and the man hold hands and jump over the broom handle. When the priest came he made M'sieur sign some papers.

"A slave always had to ask M'sieur to marry. He always let the women slaves marry who they wanted. He didn't loose by that. He was so good the men would come to his plantation.

"We all wore the long chemise. Made out of heavy cloth. They made the cloth on the place and the women sewed it up. We didn't wear the shoes. We didn't like them when we had them.

"Each slave could have the little garden. They raised vegetables and had a couple of beehives for the honey.

"When the Yankees came they told us we could be free, but I don't know of any slaves that left. Old M'sieur died of the fever in the second year of the war. His wife died before he did. No children. They sold us, the house and everything. M'sieur Cyprien Arceneaux of Lafayette bought me and Madame Arvillien Bernard of St. Pierre bought the mama. They used to call it St. Pierre. They call it Carenero now. When war was finished I left M'sieur Arceneaux and lived with mama.

"A year and a half after that the mama married a black man and us three farmed the little farm. My steppapa didn't like me. I was light. He and me couldn't get along. So when I had 20 years I left there and hired myself out. I saved till I bought a little piece of land for myself. Then I married and raised the family. Me and my wife and the children farmed that place up to ten years ago and then she died. My son farms the place now and I came to Beaumont. I live with my girl.

"I remember me in time of war we danced. Round dances. We sang and danced La Boulangere in time of war. De song go:

"'La Boulangere ait ta victoire
Et nous, qui sont en guerre,
Voici le jour que je dois partir.

"'Mon cher ami, tu pars,
Tu me laisses un enfant dans les bras
et prend tes armes.
Et moi, je vais dans le moment
verser des larmes.

"'Quand je serai en le guerre, [*Handwritten Note*: à la guerre?]
Tu serais de garnison,
Et tu m'oublirais moi,
Qui serai en les haillons.

"'J'entends le tombour qui m'appelle
A les points de jour.
Mon cher Armande, si tu m'aimes
Tu penserais à moi, quand tu serais, Dans tes plaisir Moi—
que serai au bout du fusil!

"I got one real scare. I was with M'sieur Arceneaux in Lafayette. There was the battle. Lots of fighting. Lots of killing. The Yankees came right inside the house. I stayed hid.

"I don't know whether it's been better since the war. At all times one has his miseries. We managed to get along on the farm. But now I have nothing. Oh, I don't mean slavery was better than to be free. I mean times were better.

"The reason I'm so light is, my mama was half-white. My papa was Neville Broussard and he was all white.

United States.Work Project Administration

FANNIE BROWN

FANNIE BROWN, aged Negro of Waco, Texas, does not know her age. She was born near Richmond, Virginia, a slave of the Koonce family. They sold her to Mrs. Margaret Taylor, of Belton, Texas, when Fannie was only five years old, and she never saw her mother again.

"I was borned near Richmond, over in Virginy, but Massa Koonce sold me. When I was five year old he brung me to Belton and sold me to Missy Margaret Taylor, and she kep' me till she died. I was growed den and sold to Massa Jim Fletcher and dere I stayed till I was freed.

"Dere no spring near Massa Fletcher's place and us have to git water out de well, what dey call de sweep well. Dey cut down a young saplin' and weight it on one end with rocks and tie de bucket on a rope on de other end and brace de pole over de well.

"While de big house bein' built dey slep' in a big wagon and cook over a fireplace make out of rock what us niggers pick up in de woods. Us cook lots of good eatin' out on dat fireplace, dem wild turkeys and wild meat sho' tasted good.

"Massa trades ten yards of red calico and two hatchets to de Indians for some skins and take de skins to Austin and traded dem fer de spinnin' wheel and loom, and hauls dem to Belton in de ox carts.

"My missy larnt me to spin and weave and did dis child git many a whuppin' 'fore I could do it good. Den she larnt me to cook and start me cookin' two or three days 'fore company come. Dat when us have de good old pound cake. De li'l chillen stand round when I bake, so as to git to lick de spoons and pans, and how dey pop dere lips when dey lickin' dat good dough!

"Massa have garden seed he brung to Texas, but he didn't think it would grow, so he kep' it several months, but den he plants it and up it come, jus' like in de old states. Us used dem tomatoes for flowers, 'cause us thunk dem pretty red things would kill us or put de spell on us. But de white folks et dem and us larn to.

"I was growed and have chillen 'fore de freedom war. I never did have no special husban' 'fore de war. I marries after de war.

"My, how dem niggers could play de fiddle back in de good old days. On de moonlight nights, us dance by de light of de moon under a big oak tree, till most time to go to work next mornin'.

"De fus' barb wire us ever seen, us scairt of it. Us thunk lightnin' be sho' to strike it. It sho' keep de stock in, though.

"I seed men ridin' hosses with dead men tied 'cross dey hoss, endurin' de freedom war. But I can't tell much 'bout dat war, 'cause I couldn't read and I never git any place 'cept home at my work. I love dem days better dan I do dese times now, but I'm too old to 'member much.

FRED BROWN

FRED BROWN, 84, 1414 Jones St., Fort Worth, Texas, was born a slave to Mr. John Brown, who owned a plantation along the Mississippi River, in Baton Rouge Parish, Louisiana. Fred was eight years old when the Civil War started. During the War, he and a number of other slaves were taken to Kaufman Co., Texas, as refugees, by Henry Bidder, an overseer. He worked five years as a laborer after he was freed, then worked as a cook until 1933.

"Sho', I has time to talk to you 'bout my life, 'cause I can't work any more and I has nothin' but time. It am de rhumatis' in de leg, it ketch me dat way, from de hip to de knee,—zip—dat pain goes!

"I's bo'n in ole Louisiana, in Baton Rouge Parish, on de 16th of November, in 1853. I knows, 'cause massa give dis nigger a statement. You see, dey don' larn de niggers to read in dem days, nor figger, but I can read figgers. See dem on dat car? Dat am 713. Dat am bad figgers, I never has any truck with sich numbers as de 7 or de 13.

"Massa have quite pert a plantation in Louisiana, dis side de Mississippi River. De slaves him own am from 40 to 50 sometimes. In our family am pappy, mammy and three brudders and one sister, Julia, and six cousins. Dat am 13 and dat's why massa had so much trouble with niggers runnin' 'way!

"Everyone have dere certain wo'k and duties for to do. Mammy am de family cook and she he'p at de loom, makin' de cloth. My daddy am de blacksmith and shoemaker and de tanner. I 'spains how he do tannin.' He puts de hides in de water with black-oak bark and purty soon de hair come off and den he rolls and poun's de hides for to make dem soft.

"When I's 'bout 8 years old, or sich, dey starts me to he'pin' in de yard and as I grows older I he'ps in de fields. Massa, him raises cane and co'n mostly, no cotton.

"De buildings on de place am de resident of de massa and de quarters for de niggers. Dey am built from logs and de quarters has no floors and no windows, jus' square holes whar de windows ought to be. Dey have bunks for sleepin' and a table and benches, and cooks in de fireplace.

"We allus have plenty for to eat, plenty co'nmeal, 'lasses and heavy, brown sugar. We gits flour bread once de week, but lots of butter and milk. For de coffee, we roasts meal bran and for de tea, de sassafras. Den we has veg'tables and fruit dat am raised on de place. De meat mostly am de wil' game, deer and de turkey, but sometimes hawg meat.

"Massa have overseer and overlooker. De overseer am in charge of wo'k and de overlooker am in charge of de cullud women. De overseer give all de whippin's. Sometimes when de nigger gits late, 'stead of comin' home and takin' de whippin' him goes to de caves of de river and stays and jus' comes in night time for food. When dey do dat, de dawgs is put after dem and den it am de fight 'tween de nigger and de dawg. Jus' once a nigger kills de dawg with de knife, dat was close to freedom and it come 'fore dey ketches him. When dey whips for runnin' off, de nigger am tied down over a barrel and whipped ha'd, till dey draws blood, sometimes.

"Dem fool niggers what sneak off without de pass, have two things for to watch, one is not to be ketched by de overseer and de other am de patter-rollers. De nigger sho' am skeert of de patters. One time my pappy and my mammy goes out without de pass and de patters takes after dem. I'se home, 'cause I's too young to be pesterin' roun'. I sees dem comin,' and you couldn' catched dem with a jackrabbit. One time anoudder nigger am runnin' from de patters and hides under de house. Dey fin' him and make him come out. You's seen de dawg quaver when him's col'? Well, dat nigger have de quaverment jus' like dat. De patters hits him five or six licks and lets him go. Dat nigger have lots of power—him gits to de quarters ahead of his shadow.

"Now, I tell 'bout some good times. We is 'lowed to have parties and de dance and we has for music, sich as de banjo and de jew's harp and a 'cordian. Dey dance de promenade and de jeg. Sometimes day have de jiggin' contest and two niggers puts a glass of water on dere heads and den see who can dance de longes' without spillin' any water. Den we has log-rollin'. Dere was two teams, 'bout three to de team, and dey see which can roll de log de fastes'. Den sometimes a couple am 'lowed to git married and dere am extry fixed for supper. De couple steps over de broom laid en de floor, dey's married den.

"Sometimes de overlooker don' let dem git married. I 'splains it dis way. He am used for to father de chillun. Him picks de portly, and de healthy women dat am to rear de portly chillen. De overlooker, he am portly man. Dem dat him picks he overlooks, and not 'low dem to marry or to go round with other nigger men. If dey do, its whippin' sho.' De massa raises some fine, portly chillen, and dey sel' some, after dey's half-grown, for $500 and sometimes more.

"De war didn' make no diff'runce, dat I notices, 'cept massa and one overseer jines de army. Massa come back, but de overseer am captured by de Yankees, so massa says, and we never hears 'bout him after dat. De soldiers passes by lots of times, both de 'federates and de 'blue bellies', but we's never bothered with dem. De fightin' was not close enough to make trouble. Jus' 'fore freedom come, de new overseer am 'structed to take us to Texas and takes us to Kaufman County and we is refugees dere. De Yankee mans tells us we am free and can do sich as we pleases. Dat lef' us in charge of no one and we'uns, jus' like cattle, wen' wanderin'.

"Pappy, him goes back to Lousiana to massa's place. Dat am de las' we hears from him. Mammy and I goes to Henderson and I works at dis and dat and cares for my mammy ten years, till she dies. Den I gits jobs as cook in Dallas and Houston and lots of other places.

"I gits married in 1901 to Ellen Tilles and I cooks till 'bout four years ago, till I gits de rhumatis'. Dat's all I can tell you 'bout de ole days.

JAMES BROWN

JAMES BROWN, 84, blind for the last 12 years and now living alone in a shack at 408 W. Belknap, Fort Worth, Texas, was born a slave of Mr. Berney in Bell Co., Texas, in 1853. While still an infant, he and his mother were sold to Mr. John Blair, who farmed four miles south of Waco, Texas. JAMES has no known living relatives and a pension of $14.00 a month is his sole support.

"My fust Marster was named Marster Berney. I'se don' 'member hims fust name nor nothin' 'bout him. I'se don' know nothin' 'bout my pappy, but Marster Blair told me hims name was John Brown.

"Marster Blair have hims farm four miles south of Waco. We'uns lived in de cabins and have de fiddle and de banjoes. We'uns sing and have music on Sundays. Marster never whups we'uns and him was allus good to us. Him gives us plenty to eat, and meat, too. Hims keeps 'bout 20 hawgs dere all de time. De women makes de clothes and we'uns have all we need.

"De fust work I does is drivin' de Marster to town. Marster have fine hosses. Marster have hims office in Waco and we drive dere every day. I'se stays all day ready to drive him home. Mos' every day hims give me five cents or maybe de dime. Hims was a big law man and went to de legislature down in Austin. His picture am in Austin, 'cause I'se down dere years ago and seen his picture in a case wid Gov'ner Ross' picture.

"Anudder thing dat Marster does powe'ful good am trade de niggers. He buys and sells 'em all de time. You see, dere was traders dat traveled from place to place dem days and dey takes sometimes as much as 100 niggers for to trade. Dere was sheds outside of town, whar dey keeps de niggers when dey comes to town.

"De Marster and de trader talks dis away: 'How you trade?' 'I'se gives you even trade.' 'No, I'se wants $25.00 for de diff'runce.' 'I'se gives you $5.00.' Dat's de way dey talks on and on. Maybe dey makes de trade and maybe dey don'.

"Dey have auction sometime and Marster allus tend 'em. At de auction I'se seen dem sell a family. Maybe one man buy de mammy, anudder buy de pappy and anudder buy all de chillens or maybe jus' one, like dat. I'se see dem cry like dey at de funeral when dey am parted. Dey has to drag 'em away.

"When de auction begin, he says: 'Dis nigger is so and so ole, he never 'bused, he soun' as a dollar. Jus' look at de muscle and de big shoulders. He's worth a thousan' of any man's money. How much am I offered?' Den de biddin' starts. It goes like dis: '$200 I'se hear, does I'se hear $250, does I hear $300.' Den de nigger takes hims clothes—dey have one extry suit—and goes wid de man dat buys him.

"De day befo' Marster gives we'uns freedom, he says to we'uns, 'I'se wants all you niggers to come to de front of de house Sunday mornin'!' We'uns was dere and he was standin' on de gallery, holdin' a paper in hims han' and readin'. Dere was tears in hims eyes and some drap on de paper. I'se have tears in my eyes, too; mos' of 'em have. When hims done readin', hims says: 'You darkies is as free as I'se is. You can go or you can stay. Those dat stay till de crops laid by, I'se will give $5.00 a month.'

"Den he takes de little niggers and says, 'De little fellows who I'se have sold dere mammies will stay wid me till dey am 21 years ole. You little fellows, I'se know you's age and I'se give yous de statement.'

"Mos' of de niggers stays wid him, but dey lef' fust one and den tudder. I'se stays on wid him for many years and works as coachman. When I lef' de Marster, 'twas to work for a farmer for one year, den I'se comes to Fort Worth. I'se works in lumberya'd for long time.

"For de las' 12 years I'se been blin'. I'se had hard time after dat till de las' year but I'se gits de pension each month, dat am a heap of help. Dis nigger am thankful for what de Lawd have blessed me wid.

United States.Work Project Administration

JOSIE BROWN

JOSIE BROWN was born about 1859, in Victoria, Texas. She belonged to George Heard. Her mother was born free, a member of the Choctaw Nation, but she was stolen and sold as a slave. Josie now lives in Woodville, Texas.

"I's bo'n on Christmas day, in Victoria. Got here jus' in time for de eggnog! Dat 'bout 1859, 'cause I's six year ole de Christmas 'fore freedom. My mudder was a free bo'n Injun woman. Jus' like any ole, demmed Choctaw down in de woods. She was stole and sol' by a spec'lator's gang. Us move to Tyler when I one mont' ole.

"We lib on a big farm and my mudder suckle her thirteen chillun and ole mistus seven. Bob, my brudder, he go to Mansfiel' and we never hear of him no more. He wen' with young marster, Wesley Heard. I 'member de mornin' dey lef', dey had to wait for him, 'cause he'd been out seein' his gal.

"De marstar hab a big log house close to de road. De quarters was 'cordin' to de family what live dere. De stage line through Woodville pass close by. I 'member sittin' on de rail fence to see de stage go by. Dat was a fine sight! De stage was big, rough carriage and dey was four or five hosses on de line. De bugle blow when dey go by, with de dus' behin' dem. Dey was comin' from Jasper, in Louisian', and everywhere.

"When us little dey hab to keep us in de house 'cause de bald eagle pick up chillen jus' like de hawk pick up chicken. Dey was lots of catamoun' and bears and deer in de woods. Us never 'llowed play 'lone in de woods.

"I didn' do nothin' 'cep' eat and sleep and foller ole mistus 'round. She giv me good clothes 'cause my mudder was de weaver. De clothes jus' cut out straight down and dyed with all kinds of bark. I hab to keep de head comb and grease with lard. De lil' white chillun play with me but not de udder nigger chilluns much. Us pull de long, leaf grass and plait it and us make rag doll and playhouse and grapevine swing. Dere's plenty grapes, scudlong, sour blue grape and sweet, white grape. Dey make jelly and wine outta dem. Dey squeeze de grapes and put de juice in a jimmijohn(demijohn) to fo'men'.

"My mudder name was Keyia. Dat Injun. Daddy's name was Reuben. I 'member when I's lil' us goes visit my uncle, Major Scott. He lib in Polk County and he wore earring in he ears and beads and everyt'ing. He's a Injun. He dead now, many year.

"My daddy work in de fiel'. He sow de rice and raise t'baccy. Dey have fiel's of it. Dey put it in de crack of de fence to press, den dey dry it on de barn roof. Dat was smokin' t'baccy! For de chewin' t'baccy, dey soak it in sugar and honey. Us never see snuff den.

"On Sunday us didn' work. We has chu'ch meetin'. But dey has to have it in de ya'd, so de white folks could see de kin' of religion 'spounded.

"I seed some bad sight in slavery, but ain' never been 'bused myself. I seed chillun too lil' to walk from dey mammies sol' right off de block in Woodville. Dey was sol' jus' like calfs. I seed niggers in han' locks.

"After freedom dey wuk a whole year and den Major Sangers, he finally come and make de white folks tu'n us loose. I stay on for years, 'till ole mistus die. She larn me to knit and spin and sich like.

"In de early day, us hab to be keerful. Dey say witches ride dey hosses on de da'k nights. Us allus put hossshoes over de door to keep de witch out. Iffen us go out at night, us go roun' de house three time so de witch not come in while us gone.

"I's fifteen year ole when I marry. Giles Paul was from de Wes'. He was de fus' husban'. Us hab a real weddin' with a bride veil. My weddin' dress hang 'way back on de flo', and shine like silver. Dey hab big dance and eat supper.

"My second husban' name' Robert Brown and I's mudder of ten chillun. 'Sides dat, I raises six or seven day I pick up on de street 'cause dey orfums and hab nobody to care for dem. Some dem chillun drif' 'bout now and I wouldn' know 'em if I seed 'em!

United States.Work Project Administration

ZEK BROWN

ZEK BROWN, 80, was born a slave of Green Brown, owner of six slave families, in Warren County, Tennessee. Zek came to Texas in 1868, with Sam Bragg. Zek now lives at 407 W. Bluff St., in Fort Worth, Texas.

"My name am Zek Brown and Massa Green Brown owned me. He have a plantation in Tennessee and own all my folks, what was my pappy and mammy and two sisters. I never seed any of dem since I ran 'way from there, when I's ten years old.

"I sometimes wishes I's back on de plantation. I's took good care of dere and massa am awful good. Each fam'ly have dere own cabin and it warn't so much for niceness but we lives comfor'ble and has plenty to eat and wear. My mammy work de loom, makin' cloth, and us chillen wears linsey cloth shirts till dey gives us pants. Massa buy he fam'ly nice clothes but dey wears linsey clothes everyday. Same with shoes, dey am made on de plantation and de first store shoes I has am after surrender. My mammy buys me a pair with brass tips on de toe, and am I dress up den!

"De food am bester dan what I's had since dem days. Dey raises it all but de salt and sich. You wouldn't 'lieve how us et den. It am ham and bacon, 'cause dey raises all de hawgs. It am cornmeal and some white flour and fruit and honey and 'lasses and brown sugar. De 'lasses am black as I is and dat am some black. I wishes I was dere and mammy call me, and I can smell dat ham fryin' right now.

"Not once does I know of de massa whippin' and him don't talk rough even. Jus' so de work am done we does as we pleases, long as us reas'ble. Us have parties and dancin' and singin'. De music am de banjo and de fiddle.

"I don't 'member when de war start but I 'member when it stop and massa call all us together and tell us we's no more slaves. Him talk lots 'bout what it mean and how it am diff'rent and we'uns have to make our own way and can't 'pend on him like. He say if us stay dere'll be wages or we can share crop and everybody stay. My folks stays one year and den moves to 'nother he farms. Pappy keep de farm and mammy teach school. Her missie done larnt her to read and sich from time she a young'un, so she have eddication so good dey puts her to teachin'.

"De way I leaves home am dis. One day mammy teachin' school and me and my sister am home, and I 'cides she need de haircut. She want it, too. So I gits de shears and goes to work and after I works a while de job don't look so good, so I cuts some more and den it look worse and I tries to fix it and first thing I knows dere ain't no hair left to cut. When mammy come home she pays me for de work with de rawhide whip and dat hurts my feelin's so bad I 'cides to git even by runnin' 'way a few days. It am 'bout sundown and I starts to go and comes to Massa Sam Bragg's place. I's tired den and not so strong 'bout de idea and 'cides to rest. I walks into he yard and dere am a covered wagon standin' and loaded with lots of stuff and de front end open. I finds de soft place in de back and goes to sleep, and when I wakes up it am jus' gittin' daylight and dat wagon am a-movin'."

"I don't say nothin'. I's skeert and waits for dat wagon to stop, so's I can crawl out. I jus' sits and sits and when it stop I crawls out and Massa Bragg say, 'Good gosh, look what am crawlin' out de wagon! He look at me a while and den he say, 'You's too far from home for me to take you back and you'll git lost if you tries to walk home. I guesses I'll have to take you with me.' I thinks him am goin' some place and comin' back, but it am to Texas him come and stop at Birdville. Dat am how dis nigger come to Texas.

"I's often wish my mammy done whip me so hard I couldn't walk off de place, 'cause from den on I has mighty hard times. I stays with Massa Bragg four years and then I hunts for a job where I can git some wages. I gits it with Massa Joe Henderson, workin' on he farm and I's been round these parts ever since and farmed most my life.

"I gits into a picklement once years ago. I's 'rested on de street. I's not done a thing, jus' walkin' 'long de street with 'nother fellow and dey claim he stole somethin'. I didn't know nothin' 'bout since. Did dey turn me a-loose? Dey turn me loose after six months on de chain gang. I works on de road three months with a ball and chain on de legs. After dat trouble, I sho' picks my comp'ny.

"I marries onct, 'bout forty years ago, and after four years she drops dead with de heart mis'ry. Us have no chillen so I's alone in de world. It am all right long as I could work, but five years ago dis right arm gits to shakin' so bad I can' work no more. For a year now dey pays me $9.00 pension. It am hard to live on dat for a whole month, but I's glad to git it.

United States.Work Project Administration

MADISON BRUIN

MADISON BRUIN, 92, spent his early days as a slave on the Curtis farm in the blue grass region of Kentucky, where he had some experience with some of the fine horses for which the state is famous. Here, too, he had certain contacts with soldiers of John Morgan, of Confederate fame. His eyes are keen and his voice mellow and low. His years have not taken a heavy toll of his vitality.

"I's a old Kentucky man. I's born in Fayette County, 'bout five miles from Lexington, right where dere lots of fine hosses. My old massa was name Jack Curtis and de old missus was Miss Addie. My mother name Mary and she die in 1863 and never did see freedom. I don't 'member my daddy a-tall.

"De place was jis' a farm, 'cause dey didn't know nothin' 'bout plantations up dere in Kentucky. Dey raise corn and wheat and garlic and fast hosses. Dey used to have big hoss races and dey had big tracks and I's stood in de middle of dat big track in Lexington and watch dem ex'cise de hosses. Sometimes I got to help dem groom some dem grand hosses and dat was de big day for me. I don't 'member dem hosses names, no, suh, but I knowed one big bay hoss what won de race nearly every time.

"I had two sisters name Jeanette and Fanny and a brother, Henry, and after my daddy die, my mother marries a man name Paris and I had one half-brother call Alfred Paris.

"Old massa was good to us and give us plenty food. He never beat us hard. He had a son what jis' one month older'n me and we run 'round and play lots. Old massa, he whip me and he own son jis' de same when we bad. He didn't whip us no more'n he ought to, though. Dey was good massas and some mean ones, and some worthless cullud folks, too.

"Durin' de war de cholera broke out 'mongst de people and everybody scairt dey gwine cotch it. Dey say it start with de hurtin' in de stomach and every time us hurt in de stomach, missus make us come quick to de big house. Dat suit us jis' right and when dey sends Will and me to hoe or do somethin' us didn't want to do, pretty soon I say, 'Willie, I think my stomach 'ginnin to hurt. I think dis mis'ry a sign I gittin' de cholera.' Den him say, 'Us better go to de big house like ma say,' and with dat, us quit workin'. Us git out lots of work dat way, but us ain't ever took de cholera yit.

"Durin' de war John Morgan's men come and took all de hosses. Dey left two and Willie and me took dem to hide in de plum thicket, but us jis' git out de gate when de sojers come 'gain and dey head us off and take de last two hosses.

"My mother she wore de Yankee flag under her dress like a petticoat when de 'federates come raidin'. Other times she wore it top de dress. When dey hears de 'federates comin' de white folks makes us bury all de gold and de silver spoons out in de garden. Old massa, he in de Yankee army, 'cause dey 'script him, but he sons, John and Joe, dey volunteers.

"Old massa he never sold none of he slaves. I used to hear him and missus fussin' 'bout de niggers, 'cause some 'long to her and some to him and dey have de time keepin' dem straighten' out.

Us boys have good time playin'. Us draw de line and some git on one side and some de other. Den one sing out

"'Chickama, Chickama, craney crow,
Went to de well to wash my toe;
When I git back my chicken was gone,

What time, old witch?'

"Den somebody holler out, 'One o'clock' or 'Two o'clock' or any time, and dem on one side try to cotch dem on de other side.

"When I's young I didn't mind plowin', but I didn't like to ride at fust, but dey make me larn anyhow. Course, dat white boy and me, us like most anything what not too much work. Us go down to de watermelon patch and plug dem melons, den us run hide in de woods and eat watermelon. Course, dey lots of time dey 'low us to play jis' by ourselves. Us play one game where us choose sides and den sing:

"'Can, can, candio,
Old man Dandio,
How many men you got?
More'n you're able to cotch.'

"Endurin' de war us git whip many a time for playin' with shells what us find in de woods. Us heered de cannons shootin' in Lexington and lots of dem shells drap in de woods.

"What did I think when I seed all dem sojers? I wants to be one, too. I didn't care what side, I jis' wants a gun and a hoss and be a sojer. John Morgan, he used to own de hemp factory in Lexington. When young massa jine Woolford's 11th Kentucky Cavalry, dey come to de place and halt befo' de big house in de turnpike. Dey have shotguns and blind bridles on dere hosses, not open bridle like on de race hosses. Dey jis' in reg'lar clothes but next time dey come through dey in blue uniforms. All my white folks come back from de war and didn't git kilt. Nobody ever telt me I's free. I's happy dere and never left dem till 1872. All de others gone befo' dat, but I gits all I wants and I didn't need no money. I didn't know what paper money was and one time massa's son give me a paper dime to git some squab and I didn't know what money was and I burned it up.

"Dey's jis' one thing I like to do most and dat's eat. Dey allus had plenty of everything and dey had a big, wooden tray, or trough and dey put potlicker and cornbread in dat trough and set it under de big locust tree and all us li'l niggers jis' set 'round and eat and eat. Jis' eat all us wants. Den when us git full us fall over and go to sleep. Us jis' git fat and lazy. When us see dat bowl comin', dat bowl call us jis' like hawgs runnin' to de trough.

"Dey was great on gingerbread and us go for dat. Dey couldn't leave it in de kitchen or de pantry so old missus git a big tin box and hide de gingerbread under her bed and kept de switch on us to keep us 'way from it. But sometime us sneak up in de bedroom and git some, even den.

"When I 'bout 17 I left Kentucky and goes to Indiana and white folks sends me to school to larn readin' and writin', but I got tired of dat and run off and jine de army. Dat in 1876 and dey sends me to Arizona. After dat I's at Fort Sill in what used to be Indian Territory and den at Fort Clark and Fort Davis, dat in Garfield's 'ministration, den in Fort Quitman on de Rio Grande. I's in skirmishes with de Indians on Devil's River and in de Brazos Canyon, and in de Rattlesnake Range and in de Guadalupe Mountains. De troops was de Eighth Cavalry and de Tenth Infantry. De white and de cullud folks was altogether and I have three hosses in de cavalry. De fust one plays out, de next one shot down on campaign and one was condemn. On dat campaign us have de White Mountain 'paches with us for scouts.

"When I git discharge' from de Army I come to Texas and work on de S.P. Railroad and I been in Texas ever since, and when I's in Dallas I got 'flicted and got de pension 'cause I been in de army. I ain't done much work in ten year.

"I gits married in San Antonio on December 14, 1882 and I marries Dolly Gross and dat her right dere. Us have de nice weddin', plenty to eat and drink. Us have only one chile, a gal, and she dead, but us 'dopt sev'ral chillen.

"Us come to Beaumont in 1903 and I works 'round Spindletop and I works for de gas people and de waterworks people. I's been a carpenter and done lots of common work wherever I could find it.

"It's been long time since slavery and I's old, but me and my old lady's in good health and us manage to git 'long fairly well. Dat's 'bout all I can 'member 'bout de old times."

United States.Work Project Administration

MARTHA SPENCE BUNTON

MARTHA SPENCE BUNTON, 81, was born a slave, Jan. 1, 1856, on the John Bell plantation, in Murphfreesboro, Tennessee. Mr. Bell sold Martha, her mother and four sisters to Joseph Spence, who brought them to Texas. Martha married Andy Bunton in 1880, and they had nine children. Martha now lives with her sister, Susan, on twelve acres of land which their father bought for $25.00 an acre. The farm is picturesquely located on a thickly wooded hill about six miles east of Austin, Texas.

"I was born on New Year's Day. Yes, suh, in 1856, on Massa Bell's plantation over in Tennessee. De name of de town was Murphreesboro, and my mammy and my four sisters and me all 'longed to Massa John Bell, but he done sold us to Massa Joseph Spence, and dat how I come by my name.

"I 'members how Massa Spence brung us to Texas in wagons, and the way we knowed when we hit Texas am 'cause massa 'gin to talk 'bout a norther. When dat norther done strike, all de weeds and leaves jus' starts rollin'. Us poor, ig'rant niggers thunk at first dey was rabbits, 'cause we'd never seed a rabbit den. Massa Spence rid his hoss and Missie Spence come 'long in de richer way, in a coach. De chillen walked mornin's and de older folks walked afternoons.

"Massa Spence come to Montopolis, right nigh to Austin, and settled down. I helped carry dinner pails to de field workers, and dey was full of meat and cabbage and biscuit.

Pappy wasn't dere then, 'cause he was own by Massa Burrows, over in Tennessee. But when his massa died, my massa bought pappy and he come out to Texas. Befo' I's a sizeable child, mammy took sick with diphtheria and died and pappy had to be mammy and pappy to us. Pappy was a big-bodied man and on Sunday mornin' he'd git out of bed and make a big fire and say, 'Jiminy cripes! You chillen stay in you beds and I'll make de biscuits.' He would, too. I laughs when I thinks 'bout dem big, rye biscuits, what was so big we called dem 'Nigger heels.' Dey sho' was big biscuits, but dey was good. We never did git no butter, though, and sometimes we'd ask the white chillen to give us a piece of biscuit with butter on it. We got plenty other eats—sliced meat and roastin' ears and sweet milk.

"After freedom pappy sent us to school to de white teacher, and dat's why I can read and write. I went to de sixth grade and quit. Pappy was drinkin' a lot then. He'd take alcohol and mix it with 'lasses and water. But he was good to us. Sometimes a Texas norther come up and we'd be on the way home and we'd see something comin' what look like a elephant and it was pappy, with a bundle of coats.

"I was twenty-four years old when I married Andy Bunton and he jes' rented farms here and yonder. We had a big weddin' and pork and turkey and cake. Aunt Lucy Hubbard, what weighed three hundred pounds, done de cookin' dat day. We had such a good time nobody knowed when one de guests stole a whole turkey.

"I was mother of nine chillen and three of dem is livin' now. Andy made a purty good livin till he had a paral'sis stroke. Poor old feller! In de end, I took care of him and had to work like I was young again. I cut wood and carried water and washed and cooked. I had to feed him.

"I owns my place here. It am twelve acres and pappy bought it long ago for $25.00 de acre. My sister lives here too, and my son, Howard, comes home sometimes, but he's got eight houn' dogs he can't feed. I sho' can't feed dem on dat $11.00 pension what I gits.

United States.Work Project Administration

ELLEN BUTLER

E LLEN BUTLER was born a slave to Richmond Butler, near Whiska Chitto, in the northern part of Calcasieu Parish (now a part of Beauregard Parish), in Louisiana. Ellen is about 78 years old. She now lives in Beaumont, Texas.

"My old massa was name Richmond Butler and he used to have a big plantation over on Whiska Chitto, in Louisiana, and that's where I was born. They used to call the place Bagdad. I was his slave till I six year old and then freedom come.

"I don't 'member my daddy, but my mammy was name Dicey Ann Butler. I have seven sister and three brudder, and they was Anderson and Charlie and Willie, and the girls was Laura and Rosa and Rachel and Fannie and Adeline and Sottie and Nora.

"Us used to live in a li'l log house with one room. The floor was dirt and the house was make jus' like they used to make 'tater house. They was a little window in the back. When I was a baby they wrop me up in cotton and put me in a coffee pot—that how li'l I was. But I grows to be more sizable.

"The plantation were a good, big place and they have 'bout 200 head of niggers. When I gets big enough they start me to totin' water to the field. I gits the water out the spring and totes it in gourds. They cut the gourds so that a strip was left round and cross the top and that the handle. They was about a foot 'cross and a foot deep. Us used to have one good gourd us kep' lard in and li'l gourds to drink out of.

"Massa never 'lowed us slaves go to church but they have big holes in the fields they gits down in and prays. They done that way 'cause the white folks didn't want them to pray. They used to pray for freedom.

"When the white folks go off they writes on the meal and flour with they fingers. That the way they know if us steal meal. Sometime they take a stick and write in front of the door so if anybody go out they step on that writin' and the massa know. That the way us larn how to write.

"Old massa didn't give 'em much to eat. When they comes in out of the field they goes work for other folks for something to eat.

"They jus' have a old frame with planks to sleep on and no mattress or nothin'. In winter they have to keep the fire goin' all night to keep from freezin'. They put a old quilt down on the floor for the li'l folks. They have a li'l trough us used to eat out of with a li'l wooden paddle. Us didn't know nothin' 'bout knives and forks.

"I never did git nothin' much to eat. My sister she de cook and sometime when the white folks gone us go up to the big house and she give us somethin'. But she make us wash the mouth after us finish eatin', so they won't be no crumbs in our mouth.

"Massa used to beat 'em all the time. My brudder tell old massa sometime he git hongry and gwine have to come ask de niggers for somethin' to eat. He say he never do that, but he did, 'cause after freedom he go to West Texas and some niggers with him and he los' everything and, sho' 'nough, old massa have to go to my brudder and ask him for food and a shelter to sleep under. Then he say if he had it to do over, he wouldn't treat the hands so bad.

"One time my brudder slip off de plantation and they almost beat him to death. He told 'em he had to do somethin' to git somethin' to eat. They used to put 'em 'cross a log or barrel to beat 'em. My mammy had a strop 'bout eight inch wide they used to beat 'em with.

"Most clothes what we git is from the Iles, what was rich folks and lives close by. They folks lives in DeRidder, in Louisiana, I hears. They treated the slaves like white folks.

"On Christmas time they give us a meal. I 'member that. I don't 'member no other holidays.

"When us git sick us go to the woods and git herbs and roots and make tea and medicine. We used to git Blackhaw root and cherry bark and dogwood and chinquapin bark, what make good tonic. Black snakeroot and swamproot make good medicine, too.

"My mammy told us we was free and we starts right off and walks to Sugartown, 'bout 8 mile away. I 'member my brudder wades 'cross a pool totin' me.

"I used to nuss Dr. Frasier. He used to be the high sheriff in DeRidder.

United States.Work Project Administration

HENRY H. BUTTLER

HENRY H. BUTTLER, 87, venerable graduate of Washburn College, Topeka, Kansas, and ex-school teacher, was born a slave to Mr. George Sullivan on his 300 acre plantation in Farquier Co., Virginia. Henry and a number of other slaves were transported to Arkansas in 1863, and Henry escaped and joined the Union Army. He now lives at 1308 E. Bessie St., Fort Worth, Texas.

"My name is Henry H. Buttler and I am past 87 years of age. That figure may not be accurate, but you must realize that there were no authentic records made of slave births. I estimate my age on the work I was doing at the commencement of the Civil War and the fact that I was large enough to be accepted as a soldier in the Union Army, in the year of 1864.

"I was born on the plantation of George Sullivan, in Farquier Co., Virginia. The plantation was situated in the valley at the base of Bull Mountain, and presented a beautiful picture. The plantation consisted of about 30 acres, with about 30 slaves, though this number varied and sometimes reached 50. Mr. Sullivan owned my mother and her children, but my father was owned by Mr. John Rector, whose place was adjacent to ours.

"The slave quarters consisted of a group of one-room log cabins, with no flooring, and very crude furnishings. There were bunks and benches and a table and the fireplace provided the means for cooking and heating.

"The food was wholesome and of sufficient quantity. In that period about all the food was produced and processed on the plantation, which eliminated any reason for failure to provide ample food. The meat was home cured and the ham and bacon had a superior flavor.

"On the Sullivan place there existed consideration for human feelings but on the Rector place neither the master nor the overseer seemed to understand that slaves were human beings. One old slave called Jim, on the Rector place, disobeyed some rule and early one morning they ordered him to strip. They tied him to the whipping post and from morning until noon, at intervals, the lash was applied to his back. I, myself, saw and heard many of the lashes and his cries for mercy.

"One morning a number of slaves were ordered to lay a fence row on the Rector place. The overseer said, 'This row must be laid to the Branch and left in time to roll those logs out in the back woods.' It was sundown when we laid the last rail but the overseer put us to rolling logs without any supper and it was eleven when we completed the task. Old Pete, the ox driver, became so exhausted that he fell asleep without unyoking the oxen. For that, he was given 100 lashes.

"The slaves were allowed to marry but were compelled to first obtain permission from the master. The main factor involved in securing the master's consent was his desire to rear negroes with perfect physiques. On neither plantation was there any thought or compassion when a sale or trade was in question. I have seen the separation of husband and wife, child and mother, and the extreme grief of those involved, and the lash administered to a grieving slave for neglecting their work. All this made the marriages a farce.

"In 1863 Mr. Sullivan transported about 40 of us slaves to Arkansas, locating us on a farm near Pine Bluff, so we would not be taken by the Federal soldiers. The general faithfulness of the slave was noticeable then, as they had a chance to desert and go to free states. But I think I was the only one who deserted Mr. Sullivan. I went to Federal Headquarters at Fort Smith, Arkansas, and was received into the army. We campaigned in Arkansas and nearby territory. The major battle I fought in was that of Pine Bluff, which lasted one day and part of one night.

"After I was mustered out of the army, I set out to get an education and entered a grade school at Pine Bluff. I worked after school at any job I could secure and managed to enter Washburn College, in Topeka, Kansas. After I graduated I followed steam engineering for four years, but later I went to Fort Worth and spent 22 years in educational work among my people. I exerted my best efforts to advance my race.

"I married Lucia Brown in 1880 and we had three children, all of whom are dead. There is just my wife and me left of the family, and we have a $75.00 per month Union soldier's pension.

United States.Work Project Administration

WILLIAM BYRD

WILLIAM BYRD, 97, was born a slave of Sam Byrd, near Madisonville, Texas. William was with his master during the Civil War. The old Negro is very feeble, but enjoyed talking about old times. He lives in Madisonville.

"I has a bill of sale what say I's born in 1840, so I knows I's ninety-seven years old, and I's owned by Marse Sam Byrd. My mother's name was Fannie and I dunno pappy's name, 'cause my mother allus say she found me a stray in the woods. I allus 'lieves my master was my pappy, but I never did know for sho'.

"Our quarters was log and the bed built with poles stuck in the cracks and cowhide stretched over, and we'd gather moss 'bout once a month and make it soft. When it was real cold we'd git close together and I don't care how cold it got, we'd sleep jes' as warm as these here feather beds.

"I split rails and chopped cotton and plowed with a wooden plow and druv Marse Byrd lots, 'cause he was a trader, slave trade most the time. He was good to us and give us lots to eat. He had a big garden and plenty sugar cane, and brown sugar. We'd press the juice out the cane 'tween two logs and cook it in the big washpot.

"We had sheepskin clothes in cold weather, with the fur part inside, no shoes less'n we wropped our feet in fur hides. But them clothes was warmer than these here cotton overalls. They're plumb cold!

"Marse Sam was full of life and Missus Josie was real good. They had a nice home of that day, made out split logs and four rooms and a hall two ways through it.

"That great iron piece hung jes' outside the door and Marse Sam hit it at 3:30 every mornin'. If we didn't muster out he come round with that cat-o-nine-tails and let us have it, and we knowed what that bell was for nex' mornin'. Sometimes when Marse Sam was gone, we'd have a overseer. He'd let us go swimmin' in the creek when the work was done.

"If a nigger was mean Marse Sam give him fifty licks over a log the first time and seventy-five licks the second time and 'bout that time he most gen'rally had a good nigger. If they was real mean and he couldn't do nothin' with 'em, he put them in the jail with a chain on the feets for three days, and fed 'em through a crack in the wall.

"On Christmas Marse Sam had a great big eggnog and kilt a big beef and had fireworks, and the nigger, he know Christmas was come. We had plenty to eat and eggnog and did 'bout what we pleased that day and New Year's. The white folks allus said what we'd do on them days we'd do all year. That's all foolishment, but some still believes in it.

"They give a big dance and all night supper when war started. Then Marse Sam, he carries me for waterboy and cook and to tend his hosses. He had two, and rid one this day and the other nex' day. He was 'fraid one git kilt and then he wouldn't be slam a-foot.

"When them big guns went to poppin', I jes' couldn't stand it without gittin' in a brush top. Then marse goes and gits shot and I has to be his nuss. But, Lawd-a-me, one them Yankee gals, she falls in love with marse whilst he lays nearly dead, and she say, 'William, he's mine, so you got to take good care of him.' And him with a plumb good wife back home!

"When Marse Sam git well, he say he's goin' to 'nother place to fight. He was with General Lee when that old war was over and that there Yankee General Grant takes General

Lee prisoner, and Marse Sam won't leave his general, and he say to me, 'William, you got to go home alone.'

"I lights out a-foot to Texas and it's most a year befo' I gits home. I travels day and night at first. I buys some things to eat but every time I goes by a farmhouse I steals a chicken. Sometimes I sho' gits hongry. When I git to the house, Missus Josie faints, 'cause she thunk Marse Sam ain't with me and he mus' be dead. I tells her he's in prison and she say she'll give me $2.00 a month to stay till he gits back. I's plumb crazy 'bout a little gal called 'Cricket,' 'cause she so pert and full of live, so I stays. We gits us a cabin and that's all to our weddin'. We stays a year befo' Marse Sam comes back.

"He was the plumb awfulest sight you ever done seed! His clothes is tore offen his body and he ain't shaved in three months and he's mos' starved to death. Missus Josie she don't even rec'nize him and wouldn't 'low him in till I tells her dat am Marse Sam, all right. He stays sick a whole year.

"I thinks if them Yankees didn't 'tend to fix some way for us pore niggers, dey oughtn't turn us a-loose. Iffen de white folks in de South hadn't been jes' what they is, us niggers been lots worser off than we was. In slavery time when the nigger am sick, his master pay de bills, but when nigger sick now, that's his own lookout.

"I never done nothin' but farm and odd jobs. I been married five times, but only my las' wife am livin' now. My four boys and two gals is all farmin' right here in the county and they helps us out. We gits by somehow.

United States.Work Project Administration

Slave Narratives

LOUIS CAIN

LOUIS CAIN, 88, was born in North Carolina, a slave of Samuel Cain. After Louis was freed, he came to Texas, and has farmed near Madisonville over sixty years.

"I knows I's birthed in 1849, 'cause I had a bill of sale. It say that. My master traded me to Massa Joe Cutt for a hundred acres of land. That's in 1861, and I 'members it well. My daddy was Sam Cain, name after old Massa Cain, and mammy was Josie Jones, 'cause she owned by 'nother master. Mammy was birthed in North Carolina, but daddy allus say he come from Africy. He say they didn't work hard over there, 'cause all they et come out the jungle, and they had all the wives they wanted. That was the 'ligion over there.

"Our quarters was made of logs, in a long shed six rooms long, like cowsheds or chicken houses, and one door to each room. The bed was a hole dug in a corner and poles around and shucks and straw. We'd sleep warm all night long, but it wouldn't do in this country in summertime.

"Massa give us plenty to eat. Our cornbread was what you calls water pone bread and cooked in the ashes. We didn't have no stove. Massa was a great hunter and allus had venison and game. They was plenty fish, too.

"Massa Cain was purty good to his slaves and mean to them if they didn't behave. Missy was a good woman. They lived in a two-story rock house with plenty trees all 'round.

"We worked long as we could see, from four o'clock in the mornin', and them milked twenty cows and fed the work stock. They was fifty acres and not 'nough niggers to work it easy.

"If some niggers was mean they'd git it. Massa tied they hands to they feet and tied them to a tree and hit 'bout twenty-five or fifty licks with a rawhide belt. Hide and blood flew then. Next mornin' he'd turn them loose and they'd have to work all day without nothin' to eat. He had a cabin called jail for the nigger women, and chain them in with cornbread and one glass of water.

"One nigger run to the woods to be a jungle nigger, but massa cotched him with the dogs and took a hot iron and brands him. Then he put a bell on him, in a wooden frame what slip over the shoulders and under the arms. He made that nigger wear the bell a year and took it off on Christmas for a present to him. It sho' did make a good nigger out of him.

"In the summer time they had camp meetin' and baptized in the creek, white folks first while the old nigger mammies shouts, and then the niggers.

"On Saturday mornin' us men grated corn for bread the next week and the women washed massa's clothes and our'n. On Saturday night we'd have a dance all night long, and Sunday the men went to see they wives or sweethearts and us young'uns went swimmin' in the creek. Every night but Saturday we had to go to bed at nine o'clock. Massa hit the big steel piece and we knowed it was time to put out the torches and pile in.

"On Christmas I'd stand by the gate, to open it for the company, and they'd throw nuts and candy to me. That night all the slaves what could brung they banjoes and fiddles and played for the white folks to dance all night. Them great old days are done gone. Most the men be full that good, old eggnog.

"After war come they ain't no more dances and fun, and not

much to eat or nothin'. Massa git kilt in a big battle and missy took four slaves and brung him home and buried him under a big shade tree in the yard. That the saddes' time I ever seen, nobody there to do anythin' but missy and neighbor women and some real young niggers like me. She was cryin' and all us slaves takin' on. It's a wonder we ever did git massa buried. We carried him on our backs to the grave.

"After that we had to carry missy to the mountains and hide her, 'cause everything, house and sheds and all, was burnt, and all her stock kilt by sojers and outlaws. When she come out of hidin' she didn't have a thing, not even a bed.

"But she was a brave woman, and said, 'Louis, we'll fix some kind of quarters for you.' She went to work to rebuild the place. She said, 'You niggers is free, but I need you and I'll pay you $2.00 a month.' She did, too. She cut some logs and builded her one room and then we all build us a room and that was the best we could do. I 'lieve the Lawd blessed that woman. After freedom, that's how I lived the first year, and she paid me every cent she promised. I stayed with her three years.

"Then I heared of a railroad job in Texas, and married Josie Sewel in a big weddin' and we had a great time. I gits a job on that railroad for fifty cents a day and it never lasted more'n a year, so I goes to farmin'.

"We had fourteen chillun, four dead now, and the rest farmin' all over Texas. I has more'n a hundred grandchillun. Josie, she done die twenty years ago.

"I don't know as I 'spected massa's land to be 'vided and give us, but they was plenty of land for everybody, and missy allus treated us right. Wages was terrible small for a long time after I married and sometimes they wouldn't pay us, and we had to beg or steal. I's went a whole two days without nothin' to eat. If it hadn't been for them there Klu Klux, sometimes the niggers would have went on the warpath for starvin'. But the Klu Kluxers wouldn't let 'em roam none, if they tried they stretch them out over a log and hit them with rawhide, but never say a word. That was got the niggers—they was so silent, not a sound out of them, and the nigger he can't stand that.

"I gits a pension and works when I can and gits by. Some the young niggers is purty sorry, they's had so much and don't 'preciate none of it. I's glad for what I can git, 'cause I 'members them old times after the war when it was worse'n now.

JEFF CALHOUN

JEFF CALHOUN, about 98, was born a slave of the Calhoun family, in Alton, Alabama. After his master died, a son-in-law, Jim Robinson, brought Jeff and 200 other slaves to Austin, Texas. Jeff was 22 when the Civil War began. He stayed with his old master, who had moved to Stewart Mills Texas, after he was freed, and raised 23 children. He says, "I 'spect I has near a thous- children, grandchildren and great grandchildren." He makes his home among them, drifting over five states when and as he wishes.

"My name am Jeff Calhoun and I was born in Alton, in Alabama, about 1838, 'cause I's told by my massa. Dat makes me 'bout 98 year old now. My father was Henry Robinson and my mammy, she Mary Robinson. She was born in Maryland, in Virginia, but didn't know much 'bout her folks, 'cause she was sold off young. Dere was four of us brothers and ten sisters, but dey all dead now but me.

"We makes our beds out of forked saplings drove in the ground, 'cause de floors was dirt. We sets de pole in dat ground and it run to de top of de cabin and we makes one bed down low and one bed above. De big folks sleeps in de low beds and de chillun above, 'cause dey can climb.

"My massa had 15 chillun and my mamma suckled every one of dem, 'cause his wife was no good to give milk.

"We allus had lots to eat, but for meat we has to go to de woods and git deer and turkey and buffalo and some bear. I have eat hoss and skunk and crow and hawk.

"We has a big fire to cook on, and to make de corn cakes

we put one leaf down and put batter on dat and put another leaf over it and cover with hot ashes and by noon it was done. Same thing for supper. We never have biscuits 'cept on Sunday or Christmas.

"My mama was de spinner so I has plenty shirts and some britches, and we raises indigo on de place and makes dye of it. We never wore no shoes in de summer and some winters neither. We has a good pair of pants and shirt we wears Sundays and holidays and was married in.

"De way dey done at weddings dem days, you picks out a girl and tell your boss. If she was from another plantation you had to git her bosses 'mission and den dey tells you to come up dat night and git hitched up. They says to de girl, 'You's love dis man?' Dey says to de man, 'You loves dis girl?' If you say you don't know, it's all off, but if you say yes, dey brings in de broom and holds it 'bout a foot off de floor and say to you to jump over. Den he says you's married. If either of you stumps you toe on de broom, dat mean you got trouble comin' 'tween you, so you sho' jumps high.

"My massa was good to us. He lived in a log house with a floor and was all fixed up with pretty furniture and mirrors and silver on de table. De missus was little and frail, but she was good to us and so was de massa. He wasn't no hand to whip like some of he neighbors. Dey would tied de slaves' hands to a pole and whip de blood out of them. Dey was whipped for runnin' away.

"I knowed a slave call Ben Bradley and he was sold on de auction block and his massa chained him hand and foot and started for Texas. Dey got to de Red River and was crossin' and de chains helt him down and he never came up. And I have a uncle what run off and dey took a pack of hounds—a pack were twelve—and dey got on his trail and I heared dem runnin' him. Dey run him three days and nights and took a gun loaded with buck shot but was sposed not to shoot above de legs. Dey come back and said he got away, but some boys was out huntin' and finds him and he been shot four times with buck shot.

"De only time we got to rest was Sunday and de fourth of July and Christmas, and one day Thanksgiving. We got de big dinners on holidays. After supper was have corn shuckings, or on rainy days, and sometimes we shucks 500 bushels. We allus picked de cotton in big baskets, and when we gits it all picked we spreads on big and has a celebration.

"I was in Texas when de war broke out and I hauls corn lots of times to de gin where was de soldier camp, and I helped cook awhile and would have been in de battle of Vicksburg only dey takes another man 'stead of me and he gits kilt. I's glad I's a sorry cook, or I'd got kilt 'stead of him.

United States.Work Project Administration

SIMP CAMPBELL

SIMP CAMPBELL was born January 1860, in Harrison County, Texas, He belonged to W.L. Sloan and stayed with him until 1883, when Simp married and moved to Marshall. He and his wife live in Gregg Addition, Marshall, Texas, and Simp works as porter for a loan company.

"My name is Simpson Campbell, but everybody, white and black, calls me Simp. I's born right here in Harrison County, on Bill Sloan's place, nine miles northwest of Marshall. I got in on the last five years of slavery.

"Pappy was Lewis Campbell, and he was sold by the Florida Campbells to Marse Sloan and fotched to Texas, but he allus kep' the Campbell name. Mammy was Mariah and the Sloans brung her out of South Carolina. She raised a passel of chillen. Besides me there was Flint, Albert and Clinton of the boys, and—let me count—Dinah, Clandy, Mary, Lula, Liza, Hannah, Matilda and Millie of the girls.

"The Sloans lived in a big house, but it wasn't no shanty. They was fixed 'bout as good as anybody in the county and driv as good hosses and rigs as anybody. They wasn't a mean streak in the whole Sloan family.

"The slave quarters sot in rows right down in the field from the big house. They had beds made to the wall, and all the cookin' was on the fireplace. We raised all our meat and corn and garden truck right there on the place and Marse Sloan brung wheat and other rations from Shreveport. The nigger women spinned all the cloth and pappy made shoes by hand, when they kilt a beef. The beef was dried and jetted and hung in the smokehouse.

"Marse's place civered a thousand acres and he had over a hunderd slaves, with a overseer, Johnson, and a nigger driver. Us niggers was treated well but the overseer had order to whip us for fightin'. If the nigger driver hit too many licks, the overseer sold him off the place.

"We worked from four till six and done a task after that, and sot round and talked till nine and then had to go to bed. On Saturday night you'd hear them fiddles and banjoes playin' and the niggers singin'. All them music gadgets was homemade. The banjoes was made of round pieces of wood, civered with sheepskin and strung with catgut strings.

"They wasn't no school but Marse Bill larnt some his niggers readin' and writin' so we could use them bookin' cotton in the field and sich like. They was a church on the Sloan place and white preachers done most the 'xhorting. Mammy allus say the cullud preachers had to preach what they's told—obey you master and missus.

"I seed Yankee sojers and wagons comin' home from Mansfield. Marse Tom sot us free right after surrender, but my folks stayed on with him till he died, in 1906. I lef when I's twenty-three and marries and made a livin' from public work in Marshall all my life. I worked as day laborer and raised two boys and two girls and the boys is farmin' right here in the county and doin' well.

"When I's eighteen they got up a 'mendment to the Constitution and got out a "People's Party Ticket." It was a Democratic ticket and control by Southerners. They told us niggers if we'd vote that ticket we'd be rec'nized as white folks, but I didn't 'lieve a word of it. Old Man Sloan told all his niggers that and they all voted that ticket but two—that was Charley Tang and Simp Campbell.

"I 'lieve the young race of our people is progressin' fine. If they had priv'lege to use they educations, they'd make more progress, but the color line holds them back.

United States.Work Project Administration

JAMES CAPE

JAMES CAPE, centenarian, now living in a dilapidated little shack in the rear of the stockyards in Fort Worth, Texas, was born a slave to Mr. Bob Houston, who owned a large ranch in southeast Texas. James' parents came direct from Africa into slavery. James spent his youth as a cowboy, fought in the Confederate army, was wounded and has an ugly shoulder scar. After the war, James unknowingly took a job with the outlaw, Jesse James, for whom he worked three years, in Missouri. He then came back to Texas, and worked in the stockyards until 1928. Documentary proof of James' age is lacking, but various facts told him by his parents and others lead him to think he must be over 100 years old.

"I's bo'n in yonder southeast Texas and I don' know what month or de year for sho', but 'twas more dan 100 years ago. My mammy and pappy was bo'n in Africa, dats what dey's tol' me. Dey was owned by Marster Bob Houston and him had de ranch down dere, whar dey have cattle and hosses.

"When I's old 'nough to set on de hoss, dey larned me to ride, tendin' hosses. 'Cause I's good hoss rider, dey uses me all de time gwine after hosses. I goes with dem to Mexico. We crosses de river lots of times. I 'members once when we was a drivin' 'bout 200 hosses north'ards. Dey was a bad hail storm comes into de face of de herd and dat herd turns and starts de other way. Dere was five of us riders and we had to keep dem hosses from scatterment. I was de leader and do you know what happens to dis nigger if my hoss stumbles? Right dere's whar I'd still be! Marster give me a new saddle for savin' de hosses.

"One day Marster Bob comes to me and says, 'Jim, how you like to jine de army?' You see, de war had started. I says to him, 'What does I have to do?' And he says, 'Tend hosses and ride 'em.' I was young den and thought it would be lots of fun, so I says I'd go. So de first thing I knows, I's in de army away off east from here, somewhar dis side of St. Louis and in Tennessee and Arkansas and other places. I goes in de army 'stead of Dr. Carroll.

"After I gits in de army, it wasn' so much fun, 'cause tendin' hosses and ridin' wasn' all I does. No, sar, I has to do shootin' and git shooted at! One time we stops de train, takes Yankee money and lots of other things off dat train. Dat was way up de other side of Tennessee.

"You's heard of de battle of Independence? Dat's whar we fights for three days and nights. I's not tendin' hosses dat time. Dey gives me a rifle and sends me up front fightin', when we wasn' running'. We does a heap of runnin' and dat suits dis nigger. I could do dat better'n advance. When de order comes to 'treat, I's all ready.

"I gits shot in de shoulder in dat fight and lots of our soldiers gits killed and we loses our supply, jus' leaves it and runs. 'Nother time we fights two days and nights and de Yankees was bad dat time, too, and we had to run through de river. I sho' thought I's gwine git drowned den. Dat's de time we tries to git in St. Louis, but de Yankee mans stop us.

"I's free after de war and goes back to Texas, to Gonzales County, and gits a job doin' cowboy work for Marster Ross herdin' cattle. And right dere's whar I's lucky for not gittin' in jail or hanged. It was dis way: I's in town and dat man, Ross, says to me, 'I unnerstan' you's a good cowhand,' and he hires me and takes me way out. No house for miles 'fore we comes to de ranch with cattle and I goes to work. After I's workin' a while, I wonders how come dey brings in sich fine steers so often and I says to myself, 'Marster Ross mus' have heaps of money for to buy all dem steers.' Dey pays no 'tention to de raisin' of cattle, jus' brings 'em in and drives dem 'way.

"One time Marster Ross and six mens was gone a week and when dey comes back, one of 'em was missin'. Dey had no steers dat time and dey talks 'bout gittin' frusterated and how one man gits shot. I says to myself, 'What for was dey chased and shot at?' Den I 'members Marster Bob Houston done tol' me 'bout rustlers and how dey's hanged when dey's caught, and I knows den dat's how come all dem fine steers is driv in and out all de time. But how to git 'way, dere's de puzzlement. I not know which way to go and dere's no houses anywhere near. I keeps gittin' scarter, and ever' time somebody comes, I thinks its de law. But Marster Ross drives de cattle north and I says to him, 'I's good hand at de drive. Kin I go with you nex' time you goes north?' And not long after dat we starts and we gits to Kansas City. After Marster Ross gets shut of de critters, he says, 'We'll res' for couple days, den starts back.' I says to me, 'Not dis nigger.'

"I sneaks 'way and was settin' on a bench when 'long comes a white man and he's tall, had dark hair and was fine lookin'. He says to me, 'Is you a cowhand?' So I tells him I is, and he says he wants a hand on his farm in Missouri and he says, 'Come with me.' He tells me his name was James and takes me to his farm whar I tends cattle and hosses for three years and he pays me well. He gives me more'n I earns. After three years I leaves, but not 'cause I larned he was outlaw, 'cause I larned dat long time afterwa'ds. I's lonesome for Texas and dat's how I comes to Fort Worth and here's whar I's stayed ever' since.

"I's married 'bout 40 years ago to a woman dat had eight chillens. We sep'rated 'cause dem chillens cause arg'ments. I can fight one, but not de army.

RICHARD CARRUTHERS

RICHARD CARRUTHERS, 100 year old ex-slave, was born in Memphis, Tennessee. Mr. Billy Coats bought him and his mother and brought them to Bastrop Co., Texas. He came to Houston 20 years ago and lives in a negro settlement known as Acres Home, about 8 miles northeast of Houston. It is a wooded section, with a clearing here and there for a Negro shack and plots of ground for growing "victuals and co'n."

"I wants to tell the Gospel truf. My mammy's name was Melia Carruthers and my papa's name was Max. My papa's papa's name was Carruthers, too. My brothers names was Charlie and Frank and Willie and John and Tom and Adam.

"When I was still little Mr. Billy Coats bought my mama and us and with about 500 of his slaves we set out to come to Texas. We goes to Bastrop County and starts to work. My old missy—her name was Missy Myra—was 99 year old and her head was bald as a egg and had wens on it as big as eggs, too.

"In them days the boss men had good houses but the niggers had log cabins and they burned down oftentimes. The chimney would cotch fire, 'cause it was made out of sticks and clay and moss. Many the time we have to git up at midnight and push the chimney 'way from the house to keep the house from burnin' up.

"The chairs was mostly chunks of cordwood put on end, or slabs, just rough, and the beds was built like scaffoldin'. We made a sort of mattress out of corn shucks or moss.

"My missy, she was good, but the overseer, he rough. His temper born of the debbil, himse'f. His name was Tom Hill, but us called him 'Debbil Hill.'

Old Debbil Hill, he used to whup me and the other niggers if we don't jump quick enough when he holler and he stake us out like you stake out a hide and whup till we bleed. Many the time I set down and made a eight-plait whup, so he could whup from the heels to the back of the head 'til he figger he get the proper ret'ibution. Sometime he take salt and rub on the nigger so he smart and burn proper and suffer mis'ry. They was a caliboose right on the plantation, what look like a ice-house, and it was sho' bad to git locked up in it.

"Us got provisions 'lowanced to us every Saturday night. If you had two in the family, they 'lowanced you one-half gallon 'lasses and 12 to 15 pounds bacon and a peck of meal. We have to take the meal and parch it and make coffee out of it. We had our flours. One of them we called biscuit flour and we called it 'shorts.' We had rye and wheat and buck grain.

"If they didn't provision you 'nough, you jus' had to slip 'round and git a chicken. That easy 'nough, but grabbin' a pig a sho' 'nough problem. You have to cotch him by the snoot so he won't squeal, and clomp him tight while you knife him. That ain't stealin', is it? You has to keep right on workin' in the field, if you ain't 'lowanced 'nough, and no nigger like to work with his belly groanin'.

"When the white preacher come he preach and pick up his Bible and claim he gittin the text right out from the good Book and he preach: 'The Lord say, don't you niggers steal chickens from your missus. Don't you steal YOUR MARSTER'S hawgs.' That would be all he preach.

"Us niggers used to have a prayin' ground down in the hollow and sometime we come out of the field, between 11 and 12 at night, scorchin' and burnin' up with nothin' to eat, and we wants to ask the good Lawd to have mercy. We puts grease in a snuff pan or bottle and make a lamp. We takes a pine torch, too, and goes down in the hollow to pray. Some gits so joyous they starts to holler loud and we has to stop up they mouth. I see niggers git so full of the Lawd and so happy they draps unconscious.

"I kep' a eye on the niggers down in the cotton patch. Sometime they lazy 'round and if I see the overseer comin' from the big house I sings a song to warn 'em, so they not git whupped, and it go like this:

"'Hold up, hold up, American Spirit!
Hold up, hold up, H-O-O-O-O-O-O-O!'
"We used to go huntin' and they was lots of game, bears and panthers and coons. We have bear dawgs, fox dawg and rabbit dawg that mostly jus' go by the name of houn' dawg. Then they have a dawg to run niggers.

"I never tried the conjure, but they would take hair and brass nails and thimbles and needles and mix them up in a conjure bag. But I knows one thing. They was a old gin between Wilbarger and Colorado and it was hanted with spirits of kilt niggers. Us used to hear that old mill hummin' when dark come and we slip up easy, but it stop, then when you slip away it start up.

"I 'member when the stars fell. We runs and prays, 'cause we thinks it jedgment day. It sure dumb old Debbil Hill, them stars was over his power.

"On Sundays we put shoes on our feet and they was brass toed. They was so hard and stiff they go 'tump, tump, tump,' when we walk. That's the only day we got 'cept Christmas and we jus' got somethin' extry to eat. All them women sho' knowed how to cook! I often tell my wife how glad I was one mornin' when my missy give me a hot, butter biscuit. I goes down and shows it to all the other boys. We didn't git them hot, butter biscuits in them days.

"I used to dance the pigeon wing and swing my partners 'round. Was them womenfolks knock-kneed? You sho' couldn't tell, even when you swung 'em 'round, 'cause they dresses was so long.

"I's been all 'round the mountain and up on top of it in my day. Durin' slave time I been so cold I mos' turn white and they sot me 'fore the fire and poultice me with sliced turnips. Come a norther and it blow with snow and sleet and I didn't have 'nough clothes to keep me warm.

"When a nigger marry, he slick up his lowers and put on his brass-toed shoes, then the preacher marry him out of the Bible. My pappy have a pass to visit my mammy and if he don't have one, the paddle roller conk him on the head. My grandma and grandpa come here in a steamboat. The man come to Africa and say, 'Man and woman, does you want a job?' So they gits on the boat and then he has the 'vantage.

"When I was 21 and some more, I don't know jus' how old, I was a free man. That the day I shouted. We niggers scattered like partridges. I had a fiddle and I'd play for the white folks wherever I went, when they has the balls. I marries after 'while, but I don't know what year, 'cause we never done paid no 'tention to years. My first wife died after a long time, I think 'bout 34 year and I married another and she died this very year. Jus' three months later I marries my housekeeper, named Luvena Dixon, cause I allus lived a upright life and I knowed the Lawd wouldn't like it if I went on livin' in the same house with Luvena without we was married. She is 52 year old, and we is happy.

CATO CARTER

CATO CARTER was born in 1836 or 1837, near Pineapple, Wilcox County, Alabama, a slave of the Carter family. He and his wife live at 3429 Booth St., Dallas, Texas.

"I'm home today 'cause my li'l, old dog is lost and I has to stay 'round to hunt for him. I been goin' every day on the truck to the cotton patches. I don't pick no more, 'count my hands git too tired and begin to cramp on me. But I go and set in the field and watch the lunches for the other hands.

"I am a hunerd one years old, 'cause I's twenty-eight, goin' on twenty-nine, a man growned, when the breakin' up come. I'm purty old, but my folks live that way. My old, black mammy, Zenie Carter, lived to be a hunerd twenty-five, and Oll Carter, my white massa—which was the brother of my daddy—lived to be a hunerd four. He ain't been so long died. Al Carter, my own daddy, lived to be very ageable, but I don't know when he died.

"Back in Alabama, Missie Adeline Carter took me when I was past my creepin' days to live in the big house with the white folks. I had a room built on the big house, where I stayed, and they was allus good to me, 'cause I's one of their blood. They never hit me a lick or slapped me once, and told me they'd never sell me away from them. They was the bes' quality white folks and lived in a big, two-story house with a big hall what run all the way through the house. They wasn't rough as some white folks on their niggers.

"My mammy lived in a hewn-oak log cabin in the quarters. There was a long row of cabins, some bigger than t'others, 'count of fam'ly size. My massa had over eighty head of slaves. Them li'l, old cabins was cozy, 'cause we chinked 'em with mud and they had stick chimneys daubed with mud, mixed with hawg-hair.

"The fixin's was jus' plain things. The beds was draw-beds—wooden bedsteads helt together with ropes drawed tight, to hold them. We scalded moss and buried it awhile and stuffed it into tickin' to make mattresses. Them beds slep' good, better'n the ones nowadays.

"There was a good fireplace for cookin' and Sundays the Missie give us niggers a pint of flour and a chicken, for to cook a mess of victuals. Then there was plenty game to find. Many a time I've kilt seventy-five or eighty squirrels out of one big beech. There was lots of deer and bears and quails and every other kind of game, but when they ran the Indians out of the country, the game jus' followed the Indians. I've seed the bigges' herds of deer followin' the way the Indians drifted.

Whenever the Indians lef', the game all lef' with them, for some reason I dunno.

"Talkin' 'bout victuals, our eatin' was good. Can't say the same for all places. Some of the plantations half starved their niggers and 'lowanced out their eatin' till they wasn't fittin' for work. They had to slip about to niggers on other places to piece out their meals. They had field calls and other kinds of whoops and hollers, what had a meanin' to 'em.

"Our place was fifteen hunerd acres in one block, and 'sides the crops of cotton and corn and rice and ribbon cane we raised in the bottoms, we had veg'tables and sheep and beef. We dried the beef on scaffolds we built and I used to tend it. But bes' of anythin' to eat, I liked a big, fat coon, and I allus liked honey. Some the niggers had li'l garden patches they tended for themselves.

"Everythin' I tell you am the truth, but they's plenty I can't tell you. I heard plenty things from my mammy and grand-pappy. He was a fine diver and used to dive in the Alabama river for things what was wrecked out of boats, and the white folks would git him to go down for things they wanted. They'd let him down by a rope to find things on the bottom of the riverbed. He used to git a piece of money for doin' it.

"My grandmammy was a juksie, 'cause her mammy was a nigger and her daddy a Choctaw Indian. That's what makes me so mixed up with Indian and African and white blood. Sometimes it mattered to me, sometimes it didn't. It don't no more, 'cause I'm not too far from the end of my days.

"I had one brother and one sister I helped raise. They was mostly nigger. The Carters told me never to worry 'bout them, though, 'cause my mammy was of their blood and all of us in our fam'ly would never be sold, and sometime they'd make free man and women of us. My brother and sister lived with the niggers, though.

"I was trained for a houseboy and to tend the cows. The bears was so bad then, a 'sponsible pusson who could carry a gun had to look after them.

"My massa used to give me a li'l money 'long, to buy what I wanted. I allus bought fine clothes. In the summer when I was a li'l one, I wore lowerin's, like the rest of the niggers. That was things made from cotton sackin'. Most the boys wore shirttails till they was big yearlin's. When they bought me red russets from the town, I cried and cried. I didn't want to wear no rawhide shoes. So they took 'em back. They had a weakness for my cryin'. I did have plenty fine clothes, good woolen suits they spinned on the place, and doeskins and fine linens. I druv in the car'age with the white folks and was 'bout the mos' dudish nigger in them parts.

"I used to tend the nurslin' thread. The reason they called it that was when the mammies was confined with babies havin' to suck, they had to spin. I'd take them the thread and bring it back to the house when it was spinned. If they didn't spin seven or eight cuts a day, they'd git a whuppin'. It was consid'ble hard on a woman when she had a frettin' baby. But every mornin' them babies had to be took to the big house, so the white folks could see if they's dressed right. They was money tied up in li'l nigger young'uns.

"They whupped the women and they whupped the mens. I used to work some in the tan'ry and we made the whips. They'd tie them down to a stob, and give 'em the whuppin'. Some niggers, it taken four men to whup 'em, but they got it. The nigger driver was meaner than the white folks. They'd better not leave a blade of grass in the rows. I seed 'em beat a nigger half a day to make him 'fess up to stealin' a sheep or a shoat. Or they'd whup 'em for runnin' away, but not so hard if they come back of their own 'cordance when they got hungry and sick in the swamps. But when they had to run 'em down with the nigger dogs, they'd git in bad trouble.

"The Carters never did have any real 'corrigible niggers, but I heard of 'em plenty on other places. When they was real 'corrigible, the white folks said they was like mad dogs and didn't mind to kill them so much as killin' a sheep. They'd take 'em to the graveyard and shoot 'em down and bury 'em face downward, with their shoes on. I never seed it done, but they made some the niggers go for a lesson to them that they could git the same.

"But I didn't even have to carry a pass to leave my own place, like the other niggers. I had a cap with a sign on it: 'Don't bother this nigger, or there will be Hell to pay.' I went after the mail, in the town. It come in coaches and they put on fresh hosses at Pineapple. The coachman run the hosses into Pineapple with a big to-do and blowin' the bugle to git the fresh hosses ready. I got the mail. I was a trusty all my days and never been 'rested by the law to this day.

"I never had no complaints for my treatment, but some the niggers hated syrup makin' time, 'cause when they had to work till midnight makin' syrup, its four o'clock up, jus' the same. Sun-up to sundown was for fiel' niggers.

"Corn shuckin' was fun. Them days no corn was put in the cribs with shucks on it. They shucked it in the fiel' and shocked the fodder. They did it by sides and all hands out. A beef was kilt and they'd have a reg'lar picnic feastin'. They was plenty whiskey for the niggers, jus' like Christmas.

"Christmas was the big day at the Carter's. Presents for every body, and the bakin' and preparin' went on for days. The li'l ones and the big ones were glad, 'specially the nigger mens, 'count of plenty good whiskey. Mr. Oll Carter got the bes' whiskey for his niggers.

"We used to have frolics, too. Some niggers had fiddles and played the reels, and niggers love to dance and sing and eat.

"Course niggers had their ser'ous side, too. They loved to go to church and had a li'l log chapel for worship. But I went to the white folks church. In the chapel some nigger mens preached from the Bible, but couldn't read a line no more than a sheep could. The Carters didn't mind their niggers prayin' and singin' hymns, but some places wouldn't 'low them to worship a-tall, and they had to put their heads in pots to sing or pray.

"Mos' the niggers I know, who had their mar'age put in the book, did it after the breakin' up, plenty after they had growned chillen. When they got married on the places, mostly they jus' jumped over a broom and that made 'em married. Sometimes one the white folks read a li'l out of the Scriptures to 'em and they felt more married.

"Take me, I was never one for sickness. But the slaves used to git sick. There was jaundice in them bottoms. First off they'd give some castor oil, and if that didn't cure they'd give blue mass. Then if he was still sick they'd git a doctor.

"They used to cry the niggers off jus' like so much cattle, and we didn't think no diff'rent of it. I seed them put them on the block and brag on them somethin' big. Everybody liked to hear them cry off niggers. The cryer was a clown and made funny talk and kep' everybody laughin'.

"When massa and the other mens on the place went off to war, he called me and said, 'Cato, you's allus been a 'sponsible man, and I leave you to look after the women and the place. If I don't come back, I want you to allus stay by Missie Adeline!' I said, 'Fore Gawd, I will, Massa Oll.' He said, 'Then I can go away peaceable.'

"We thought for a long time the sojers had the Fed'rals whupped to pieces, but there was plenty bad times to go through. I carried a gun and guarded the place at nighttime. The paddyrollers was bad. I cotched one and took him to the house more'n once. They wore black caps and put black rags over their faces and was allus skullduggerying 'round at night. We didn't use torches any more when we went 'round at night, 'cause we was afeared. We put out all the fires 'round the house at nighttime.

"The young mens in grey uniforms used to pass so gay and singin', in the big road. Their clothes was good and we used to feed them the best we had on the place. Missie Adeline would say, 'Cato, they is our boys and give them the best this place 'fords.' We taken out the hams and the wine and kilt chickens for them. That was at first.

"Then the boys and mens in blue got to comin' that way, and they was fine lookin' men, too. Missie Adeline would cry and say, 'Cato, they is just mens and boys and we got to feed them, too.' We had a pavilion built in the yard, like they had at picnics, and we fed the Fed'rals in that. Missie Adeline set in to cryin' and says to the Yankees, 'Don't take Cato. He is the only nigger man I got by me now. If you take Cato, I just don't know what I'll do.' I tells them sojers I got to stay by Missie Adeline so long as I live. The Yankee mens say to her, 'Don't 'sturb youself, we ain't gwine to take Cato or harm nothin' of yours.' The reason they's all right by us, was 'cause we prepared for them, but with some folks they was rough somethin' ter'ble. They taken off their hosses and corn.

"I seed the trees bend low and shake all over and heard the roar and poppin' of cannon balls. There was springs not too far from our place and the sojers used to camp there and build a fire and cook a mule, 'cause they'd got down to starvation. When some of the guerillas seed the fire they'd aim to it, and many a time they spoiled that dinner for them sojers. The Yankees did it and our boys did it, too. There was killin' goin' on so ter'ble, like people was dogs.

"Massa Oll come back and he was all wore out and ragged. He soon called all the niggers to the front yard and says, 'Mens and womens, you are today as free as I am. You are free to do as you like, 'cause the damned Yankees done 'creed you are. They ain't a nigger on my place what was born here or ever lived here who can't stay here and work and eat to the end of his days, as long as this old place will raise peas and goobers. Go if you wants, and stay if you wants.' Some of the niggers stayed and some went, and some what had run away to the North come back. They allus called, real humble like, at the back gate to Missie Adeline, and she allus fixed it up with Massa Oll they could have a place.

"Near the close of the war I seed some folks leavin' for Texas. They said if the Fed'rals won the war they'd have to live in Texas to keep slaves. So plenty started driftin' their slaves to the west. They'd pass with the womens ridin' in the wagons and the mens on foot. Some took slaves to Texas after the Fed'rals done 'creed the breakin' up.

"Long as I lived I minded what my white folks told me, 'cept one time. They was a nigger workin' in the fiel' and he kept jerkin' the mules and Massa Oll got mad, and he give me a gun and said, 'Go out there and kill that man.' I said, 'Massa Oll, please don't tell me that. I ain't never kilt nobody and I don't want to.' He said, 'Cato, you do what I tell you.' He meant it. I went out to the nigger and said, 'You has got to leave this minute, and I is, too, 'cause I is 'spose to kill you, only I ain't and Massa Oll will kill me.' He drops the hanes and we run and crawled through the fence and ran away.

"I hated to go, 'cause things was so bad, and flour sold for $25.00 a barrel, and pickled pork for $15.00 a barrel. You couldn't buy nothin' lessen with gold. I had plenty of 'federate money, only it wouldn't buy nothin'.

"But today I is a old man and my hands ain't stained with no blood. I is allus been glad I didn't kill that man.

"Mules run to a ter'ble price then. A right puny pair of mules sold for $500.00. But the Yankees give me a mule and I farmed a year for a white man and watched a herd of mules, too. I stayed with them mules till four o'clock even Sundays. So many scoundrels was goin' 'bout, stealin' mules.

"That year I was boun' out by 'greement with the white man, and I made $360.00. The bureau come by that year lookin' at nigger's contracts, to see they didn't git skunt out their rightful wages. Missie Adeline and Massa Oll didn't stay mad at me and every Sunday they come by to see me, and brung me li'l del'cate things to eat.

"The Carters said a hunerd times they regretted they never larned me to read or write, and they said my daddy done put up $500.00 for me to go to the New Allison school for cullud folks. Miss Benson, a Yankee, was the teacher. I was twenty-nine years old and jus' startin' in the blueback speller. I went to school a while, but one mornin' at ten o'clock my poor old mammy come by and called me out. She told me she got put out, 'cause she too old to work in the fiel'. I told her not to worry, that I'm the family man now, and she didn't never need to git any more three-quarter hand wages no more.

"So I left school and turnt my hand to anything I could find for years. I never had no trouble findin' work, 'cause all the white folks knowed Cato was a good nigger. I lef' my mammy with some fine white folks and she raised a whole family of chillen for them. Their name was Bryan and they lived on a li'l bayou. Them young'uns was crazy 'bout mammy and they'd send me word not to worry about her, 'cause she'd have the bes' of care and when she died they'd tend to her buryin'.

"Finally I come to Texas, 'cause I thought there was money for the takin' out here. I got a job splittin' rails for two years and from then on I farmed, mostly. I married a woman and lived with her forty-seven years, rain or shine. We had thirteen chillen and eight of them is livin' today.

"Endurin' the big war I got worried 'bout my li'l black mammy and I wanted to go back home and see her and the old places. I went, and she was shriveled up to not much of anything. That's the last time I saw her. But for forty-four years I didn't forget to send her things I thought she'd want. I saw Massa Oll and he done married after I left and raised a family of chillen. I saw Missie Adeline and she was a old woman. We went out and looked at the tombstones and the rock markers in the graveyard on the old place, and some of them done near melted away. I looked good at lots of things, 'cause I knowed I wouldn't be that way 'gain. So many had gone on since I'd been there befo'.

"After my first wife died I married 'gain and my wife is a good woman but she's old and done lost her voice, and has to be in Terrell most the time. But I git 'long all right, 'cept my hands cramps some.

"You goin' take my picture? I lived through plenty and I lived a long time, but this is the first time I ever had my picture took. If I'd knowed you wanted to do that, I'd have tidied up and put on my best.

JACK CAUTHERN

JACK CAUTHERN, 85, was born near Austin, Texas. Dick Townes owned Jack and his parents. After they were freed, the family stayed on the plantation, but Jack went to San Angelo, because "times was too dull in Travis County."

"My master was Dick Townes and my folks come with him from Alabama. He owned a big plantation fifteen miles from Austin and worked lots of slaves. We had the best master in the whole county, and everybody called us "Townes' free niggers," he was so good to us, and we worked hard for him, raisin' cotton and corn and wheat and oats.

"Most the slaves lived in two-room log cabins with dirt floors, over in the quarters, but I lived in master's yard. That's where I was born. There was a tall fence 'tween the yard and the quarters and the other nigger boys was so jealous of me they wouldn't let me cross that fence into the quarters. They told me I thinked I was white, jes' for livin' in master's yard.

"Me and young master had the good times. He was nigh my age and we'd steal chickens from Old Miss and go down in the orchard and barbecue 'em. One time she cotched us and sho' wore us out! She'd send us to pick peas, but few peas we picked!

"Old Miss was good to her cullud folks. When she'd hear a baby cryin' in the night she'd put on boots and take her lantern and go see about it. If we needed a doctor she'd send for old Dr. Rector and when I had the measles he give me some pills big as the end of my finger.

"We went to church all the time. Young Miss come over

Sunday mornin' and fotched all us chillen to the house and read the Bible to us. She was kind of a old maid and that was her pleasure. We had baptisin's, too. One old cullud man was a preacher. Lawd, Lawd, we had shoutin' at them camp meetin's!

"I guess we was glad to be free. Old master done die and Old Miss was managin' the plantation. She had the whole bunch in the yard and read the freedom paper. The old slaves knowed what it meant, but us young ones didn't. She told everybody they could stay and work on shares and most of 'em did, but some went back to they old homes in Alabama.

"I stayed a while and married, and came to San Angelo. The reason I come, times was dull in Travis County and I done hear so much talk 'bout this town I said I was comin' and see for myself. That was in 1900 and it was jes' a forest here then. I worked eighteen years in McCloskey's saloon, and he gave me ten dollars every Christmas 'sides my pay and a suit every year. I wish he was livin' now. My wife and I was together fifty-two years and then she died. After a long time I married again, and my wife is out pickin' cotton now.

"It seem mighty hard to me now by side of old times, but I don't know if it was any better in slavery days. It seems mighty hard though, since I'm old and can't work.

SALLY BANKS CHAMBERS

SALLY BANKS CHAMBERS, wife of Ben Chambers of Liberty, does not know her age. She was born a slave of Jim Moore, in Oakland, Louisiana. Sally has been married three times and has had seven children, about 54 grandchildren and 13 great-grandchildren. Heavy gold earrings hang from her ears and she dresses, even in midsummer, in a long-sleeved calico shirt, heavy socks and shoes, and a sweeping skirt many yards wide.

"Befo' I marry de first time my name am Sally Banks, and I's borned in de old states, over in Louisiana, round Oakland. I ain't 'member nothin' 'bout dat place, 'cause I's so small when dey brung me to Texas.

"Old massa name Jim Moore. He a fair old gen'man, with a big bald place on he head, and he am good to de slaves. Not even as stric' as old missus, what was de big, stout woman. She am terrible stric', but she whip de li'l white chillen too, so dey be good.

"My daddy name John Moore and mama name Car'line, and dey borned in Louisiana. My grandpa was Lewis Moore and grandma name Polly, but dey wasn't reg'lar Africy people. My grandma, she have right smart good blood in her.

"When old massa come to Texas he brung us over first by wagon, a mule wagon with a cover over de top, and he rent de house clost to Liberty. But de nex' year he find a place on de river bottom near Grand Cane and it jes' suit him for de slaves he have, so he brung all de rest over from Louisiana.

"My mama have four chillen when us come to Texas, but she have eleven more after freedom. When war broke out she have six, but she multiply after dat. She de milker and washwoman and spinner, and make de good, strong clothes.

"Dey have li'l separate houses make outten logs for us slaves. De white folks house was one dese big, old double-pen house, with de hall down de middle. Dey have right nice things in it.

"De white folks 'lowance out de food every Saturday night and dat spose last de week. All de cullud folks cook for deyself 'cept'n de single mens, and dey eats up in de big kitchen. Us have syrup and cornbread and lots of sweet 'taters and homecure' meat what dey salt down and hang in de smokehouse.

"De old missus, she ain't 'low no dancin' or huzzawin' round dat place, 'cause she Christian. Dey 'low us Saturday and Sunday off, and de women do dey own washin den'. De menfolks tend to de gardens round dey own house. Dey raise some cotton and sell it to massa and git li'l money dat way. Us don't never have no presents, but dey give eatments mostly.

"De young massas both go to war. Dey John Calhoun Moore and William. De oldes' goes crazy, kind of shellshock like. As far as I knowed, he ain't never git no more better. Young William and de old man comes back without no scratch, but dey ain't serve long. All dey three 'lists by deyselfs, 'cause dey didn't have no truck with dem conscrip'ers. One my uncles, Levy Moore, he go to war to wait on de massas, and he struck with de fever at Sabine Pass and die right dere.

"After freedom riz up, old massa come home. Den he call all de growed folks and tell dem dey's free. A heap left, dey jes' broke ranks and left. My daddy and mama both stay. Dey de fav'rites. Old missus make present to my mama of a heap of things she need. But de white folks was jus' rentin' and when dey have no slaves no more dey give it up and move to Tarkington Prairie. Us lost track of dem and ain't never seed dem no more.

"My daddy come back to Liberty den and work in de woodyard. Mama, she larn me to work and cook and sich and hire me out to nuss a white baby. I ain't knowed how much dey pay, 'cause mama she collec' de money.

"I's 19 year old when I marry de first time. You know I got two dead men, dat Dick Owens and Nero Williams, both of Liberty. I has two gals, Alice and Airy, for Dick, and five chillen for Nero. Dey all dead but Adlowyer and Mamie, and dey lives right here. I been marry some thirty odd year to Ben Chambers but us ain't never have no chillen.

"Goodness, I dunno how many grandchillen I has. I jedge 'bout 54 in all and 13 great ones.

"I loves to work and I ain't gwineter beg, though I's got too old to do much. I can't take it but a li'l at a time, but I gits by somehow.

United States.Work Project Administration

JEPTHA CHOICE

JEPTHA CHOICE, 1117 Brashear St., Houston, Texas, was born in slavery, on the plantation of Jezro Choice, about 6 miles south of Henderson, Texas. Jeptha was sent to school with the white children, and after he was freed, he was sent to school for several years, and became a teacher. He moved to Houston in 1888 and opened a barber shop. Jeptha claims to have been born on Oct. 17, 1835, which would make him 101 years old. He has the appearance of extreme age, but has a retentive memory, and his manner of speaking varies from fairly good English to typical Negro dialect and idiom.

"I'll be 102 years old, come fall, 'cause my mother told me I was born on Oct. 17, 1835, and besides, I was about 30 years old at the end of the Civil War. We belonged to the Choices and I was born on their plantation. My mother's name was Martha and she had been brought here from Serbia. My father's name was John and he was from the East Indies. They was brought to this country in a slave boat owned by Captain Adair and sold to someone at New Orleans before Master Jezro Choice bought them. I had five sisters and one brother but they are all dead, 'cepting one brother who lives near Henderson.

"Master Jezro was right kind. He had 50 or 60 slaves and a grist mill and tannery besides the plantation. My white folks sort of picked me out and I went to school with the white children. I went to the fields when I was about 20, but I didn't do much field works, 'cause they was keepin' me good and they didn't want to strain me.

"On Sunday we just put an old Prince Albert coat on some good nigger and made a preacher out of him. We niggers had our band, too, and I was one of the players.

"The master was mighty careful about raisin' healthy nigger families and used us strong, healthy young bucks to stand the healthy nigger gals. When I was young they took care not to strain me and I was as handsome as a speckled pup and was in demand for breedin'. Later on we niggers was 'lowed to marry and the master and missus would fix the nigger and gal up and have the doin's in the big house. The white folks would gather round in a circle with the nigger and gal in the center and then master laid a broom on the floor and they held hands and jumped over it. That married 'em for good.

"When babies was born old nigger grannies handled them cases, but until they was about three years old they wasn't 'lowed round the quarters, but was wet nursed by women who didn't work in the field and kept in separate quarters and in the evenin' their mammies were let to see 'em.

"We was fed good and had lots of beef and hawg meat and wild game. Possum and sweet yams is mighty good. You parboil the possum about half done and put him in a skewer pan and put him in a hot oven and just 'fore he is done you puts the yams in the pan and sugar on 'em. That's a feast.

"Sometimes when they's short of bread the old missus would say, 'How 'bout some ash cakes?' Then they'd mix cornmeal and water and sweep ashes out of the open hearth and bake the ash cakes.

"The master and his boys was all kilt in the war and after freedom I stayed all summer. It was pretty tough on us niggers for a while, 'cause the womenfolks what was left after the war didn't have money. But Colonel Jones, the master's son-in-law, took me to live in Henderson and paid twenty-five cents a week for more schoolin' for me and I learned through fractions. Then I got me a job teachin' school about six months a year and in off times I'd farm. I did lots of different kinds of work, on the narrow gauge railroad out of Longview and I learned to be a barber, too. But I had to give it up a few years back 'cause I can't stand up so long any more and now I'm tryin' to help my people by divine healing.

United States.Work Project Administration

AMOS CLARK

A MOS CLARK, 96, was born a slave of Robert Clark, in Washington County, Texas. After Amos was freed, he farmed near Belton, Texas. Amos now lives in Waco.

"I was borned on the second of April, in 1841. Mammy say dat de year, 'cause Marse Bob's brother, Tom, done go tradin' and has a lot of trouble with de Indians, and come back with scars all over he arms. It warn't all dey fault, 'cause Marse Tom allus gittin' in trouble with somebody.

"When I was still half-growed, Marse Bob traded me to Marse Ed Roseborough, and we come to Belton to live. Us piled ox wagons high with beddin' and clothes and sich, and Old Marse had he books in a special horsehair trunk, what de hide still had hair on. It had brass tacks all trimmin' it up, and it was sho' a fine trunk, and he say, 'Amos, you black rascal, keep you eye on dat trunk, and don't git it wet crossin' de water and don't let no Indian git it.' Us had a sizeable drove of cattle and some sheep and pigs and chickens and ducks.

"Marse and Missis finds where dey wants de house and us gits dem axes out and in a few days dere am a nice log house with two big rooms and a hall 'tween dem, mos' as big as de rooms. Us been on de road 'bout six weeks and Missis sho' proud of her new house. Den us makes logs into houses for us and a big kitchen close to de big house. Den us builds a office for Old Marse and makes chairs and beds and tables for everybody. Old Miss brung her bed and a spindly, li'l table, and us make all de rest.

"For eatin' de good shooters and scouters gits birds and rabbits and wild turkeys and sometimes a lot of wild eggs or honey, when dey chops a bee tree down. A old Indian come to holp us hunt. He'd work a week if Marse Ed give him some red calico or a hatchet. Old Miss done bring a dozen hens and a bag of seeds, and folks come ridin' twenty miles to swap things.

"Dere warn't no mill to grind corn, so de boss carpenter, he hollows out a log and gits some smooth, hard rocks and us grind de corn like it was a morter. Old Man Stubblefield builded a watermill on de creek 'bout eight miles from us, and den us tooken de corn dere.

"Dere was three hundred acres and more'n fifty slaves, and lots of work, clearin' and buildin' and plantin'. Some de cabins didn't git no floor for two years. Jes' quick as dey could, de men gits out clapboards for de walls and split puncheon slabs for floors and palin's for fences.

"Missis, she takes two de likelies' young slaves and makes

a garden, come spring. Somehow she git herself roses and posies and vegetables.

"Dere warn't no overseer. Marse Ed, he jes' ride round on he big hoss and see to things. Us didn't know nothin 'bout de war much, 'cause none us could read or write.

"Dere was two fiddlers 'mongst us, Jim Roseborough and Tom. Dey'd have de big barbecue for folks come from miles round, and coffee and chicken and turkey and dancin' and fiddlin' all night. Come daybreak, dey jes' goin' good. Us niggers dance back de quarters, and call

"'All eight balance and all eight swing,
All left allemond and right hand grand,
Meet your partner and prom'nade, eight,
Den march till you come straight.

"'First lady out to couple on de right,
Swing Mr. Adam and swing Miss Eve,
Swing Old Adam befo' you leave,
Don't forgit your own—now you're home.'
"Two, three years after dat I marries Liza Smith. Us has four chillen and all dead 'cept John, and he lives out west.

"After freedom Old Marse say kill a yearlin' and have de big dinner and dance. De young ones he told to scatter out and hunt work, not to steal and work hard. Some de oldes' ones he give a cabin and a patch of land. He say de niggers what want to stay on and work for him can, iffen he make enough to feed dem. I stays with Marse Ed, but he give me a patch of twenty acres and a sorghum mill to make a livin' on. Dat how I gits on my way after freedom.

"I gits dat sorghum mill to workin' good and works de Roseborough land and my patch, and raises corn and cotton and wheat. I was plumb good at farmin'. I allus had a piece or two of money in my pocket since I can 'member, but now de old man's too old. De gov'ment gives me seven or eight dollars a month and I has a few chickens and gits by, and de good white folks nigh by sees dat dis old boy don't git cold.

ANNE CLARK

MOTHER ANNE CLARK, 112 years old, lives at 3602 Alameda Ave., El Paso, Texas. She is too crippled to walk, but a smile lights up the tired old eyes that still see to sew without glasses. One tooth of a third set is in her upper gum. She is deaf, but can hear if you speak close to her ear. She says, "Lemma git my ears open, bofe of 'em," wets her finger, then pulls so hard on the ear lobes it seems they would be injured.

"I'll be 112 years old, come first day of June (1937). Bo'n in Mississippi. I had two marsters, but I've been free nearly 80 years. I was freed in Memphis.

"My marster was a Yankee. He took me to Louisiana and

made a slave outta me. But he had to go to war. He got in a quarrel one day and grabbed two six-shooters, but a old white man got him down and nearly kilt him. Our men got him and gave him to the Yankees.

"Capt. Clark, my second marster, took a shot at him and he couldn' come south no more. You don' know what a time I seen! I don' wanna see no more war. Why, we made the United States rich but the Yankees come and tuk it. They buried money and when you bury money it goes fu'ther down, down, down, and then you cain't fin' it.

"You know, the white folks hated to give us up worse thing in the world. I ploughed, hoed, split rails. I done the hardest work ever a man ever did. I was so strong, iffen he needed me I'd pull the men down so the marster could handcuff 'em. They'd whop us with a bullwhip. We got up at 3 o'clock, at 4 we done et and hitched up the mules and went to the fiel's. We worked all day pullin' fodder and choppin' cotton. Marster'd say, 'I wan' you to lead dat fiel' today, and if you don' do it I'll put you in de stocks.' Then he'd whop me iffen I didn' know he was talkin' to me.

"My poppa was strong. He never had a lick in his life. He helped the marster, but one day the marster says, 'Si, you got to have a whoppin', and my poppa says, 'I never had a whoppin' and you cain't whop me.' An' the marster says, 'But I kin kill you,' an' he shot my poppa down. My mama tuk him in the cabin and put him on a pallet. He died.

"My mama did the washin' for the big house. She tuk a big tub on her head and a bucket of water in her hand. My mama had two white chillen by marster and they were sold as slaves. I had two chillen, too. I never married. They allus said we'd steal, but I didn' take a thing. Why, they'd put me on a hoss with money to take into town and I'd take it to the store in town, and when I'd git back, marster'd say, 'Anne, you didn' take a thing.'

"When women was with child they'd dig a hole in the groun' and put their stomach in the hole, and then beat 'em. They'd allus whop us."

"Don' gring me anything fine to wear for my birthday. I jus' wan' some candy. I'm lookin' for Him to take me away from here."

United States.Work Project Administration

THOMAS COLE

THOMAS COLE was born in Jackson Co., Alabama, on the 8th of August, 1845, a slave of Robert Cole. He ran away in 1861 to join the Union Army. He fought at Chickamauga, under Gen. Rosecran and at Chattanooga, Look Out Mt. and Orchard Knob, under Gen. Thomas. After the war he worked as switchman in Chattanooga until his health failed due to old age. He then came to Texas and lives with his daughter, in Corsicana. Thomas is blind.

"I might as well begin far back as I remember and tell you all about myself. I was born over in Jackson County, in Alabama, on August 8, 1845. My mother was Elizabeth Cole, her bein' a slave of Robert Cole, and my father was Alex Gerrand, 'cause he was John Gerrand's slave. I was sposed to take my father's name, but he was sech a bad, ornery, no-count sech a human, I jes' taken my old massa's name. My mother was brung from Virginny by Massa Dr. Cole, and she nussed all his six chillen. My sister's name was Sarah and my brother's name was Ben and we lived in one room of the big house, and allus had a good bed to sleep in and good things to eat at the same table, after de white folks gits through.

"I played with Massa Cole's chillen all de time, and when I got older he started me workin' by totin' wood and sech odd jobs, and feedin' de hawgs. Us chillen had to pick cotton every fall. De big baskets weigh about seventy-five to a hundred pounds, but us chillen put our pickin's in some growed slave's basket. De growed slaves was jes' like a mule. He work for grub and clothes, and some of dem didn't have as easier a time as a mule, for mules was fed good and slaves was sometimes half starved. But Massa Cole was a smart man and a good man with it. He had 'spect for the slaves' feelin's and didn't treat dem like dumb brutes, and 'lowed dem more privileges dan any other slaveholder round dere. He was one of de best men I ever knows in my whole life and his wife was jes' like him. Dey had a big, four-room log house with a big hall down the center up and down. De logs was all peeled and de chinkin' a diff'rent color from de logs and covered with beads. De kitchen am a one-room house behin' de big house with de big chimney to cook on. Dat where all de meals cooked and carry to de house.

"In winter massa allus kill from three to four hundred hawgs, de two killin's he done in November and January. Some kill and stick, some scald and scrape, and some dress dem and cut dem up and render de lard. Dey haul plenty hick'ry wood to de smokehouse and de men works in shifts to keep de smoke fire goin' sev'ral days, den hangs de meat in de meathouse. First us eat all de chitlin's, den massa begin issuin' cut-back bones to each fam'ly, and den 'long come de spareribs, den de middlin' or a shoulder, and by dat time he kill de second time and dis was to go all over 'gain. Each fam'ly git de same kind of meat each week. Iffen one git a ham, dey all git a ham. All de ears and feet was pickle and we eats dem, too. If de meat run out 'fore killin' time, us git wild turkeys or kill a beef or a goat, or git a deer.

"Massa let us plant pumpkins and have a acre or two for watermelons, iffen us work dem on Saturday evenin's. Dere a orchard of 'bout five or six acres peaches and apples and he 'low us to have biscuits once a week. Yes, we had good eatin' and plenty of it den.

"Massa had one big, stout, healthy lookin' slave 'bout six foot, four inches tall, what he pay $3,000 for. He bought six slaves I knows of and give from $400 up for dem. He never sold a slave 'less he git onruly.

"Massa allus give us cotton clothes for summer and wool for winter, 'cause he raised cotton and sheep. Den each fam'ly have some chickens and sell dem and de eggs and maybe go huntin' and sell de hides and git some money. Den us buy what am Sunday clothes with dat money, sech as hats and pants and shoes and dresses.

"We'd git up early every day in de year, rain or shine, hot or cold. A slave blowed de horn and dere no danger of you not wakin' up when dat blowed long and loud. He climb up on a platform 'bout ten feet tall to blow dat bugle. We'd work till noon and eat in de shade and rest 'bout a hour or a little more iffen it hot, but only a hour if it cold. You is allus tired when you makes de day like dat on de plantation and you can't play all night like de young folks does now. But us lucky, 'cause Massa Cole don't whip us. De man what have a place next ours, he sho' whip he slaves. He have de cat-o-nine tails of rawhide leather platted round a piece of wood for a handle. De wood 'bout ten inches long and de leather braided on past de stock quite a piece, and 'bout a foot from dat all de strips tied in a knot and sprangle out, and makes de tassle. Dis am call de cracker and it am what split de hide. Some folks call dem bullwhips, 'stead of cat-o-nine tails. De first thing dat man do when he buy a slave, am give him de whippin'. He call it puttin' de fear of Gawd in him.

"Massa Cola 'low us read de Bible. He awful good 'bout dat. Most de slaveowners wouldn't 'low no sech. Uncle Dan he read to us and on Sunday we could go to church. De preacher baptize de slaves in de river. Dat de good, old-time 'ligion, and us all go to shoutin' and has a good time. Dis gen'ration too dig'fied to have de old-time 'ligion.

"When baptizin' comes off, it almost like goin' to de circus.

People come from all over and dey all singin' songs and everybody take dere lunch and have de good time. Massa Cole went one time and den he git sick, and next summer he die. Missy Cole, she moves to Huntsville, in Alabama. But she leave me on de plantation, 'cause I'm big and stout den. She takes my mother to cook and dat de last time I ever seed my mother. Missy Cole buys de fine house in Huntsville my mother tells me to be good and do all de overseer tells me. I told her goodbye and she never did git to come back to see me, and I never seed her and my brother and sister 'gain. I don't know whether dey am sold or not.

"I thinks to myself, dat Mr. Anderson, de overseer, he'll give me dat cat-o-nine tails de first chance he gits, but makes up my mind he won't git de chance, 'cause I's gwine run off de first chance I gits. I didn't know how to git out of dere, but I's gwine north where dere ain't no slaveowners. In a year or so dere am 'nother overseer, Mr. Sandson, and he give me de log house and de gal to do my cookin' and sich. Dere am war talk and we 'gins gwine to de field earlier and stayin' later. Corn am haul off, cotton am haul off, hawgs and cattle am rounded up and haul off and things 'gins lookin' bad. De war am on, but us don't see none of it. But 'stead of eatin' cornbread, us eats bread out of kaffir corn and maize. ""We raises lots of okra and dey say it gwine be parch and grind to make coffee for white folks. Dat didn't look good either. Dat winter, 'stead of killin' three or four hundred hawgs like we allus done befo', we only done one killin' of a hundred seventy-five, and dey not all big ones, neither. When de meat supply runs low, Mr. Sandson sends some slaves to kill a deer or wild hawgs or jes' any kind of game. He never sends me in any dem bunches but I hoped he would and one day he calls me to go and says not to go off de plantation too far, but be sho' bring home some meat. Dis de chance I been wantin', so when we gits to de huntin' ground de leader says to scatter out, and I tells him me and 'nother man goes north and make de circle round de river and meet 'bout sundown. I crosses de river and goes north. I's gwine to de free country, where dey ain't no slaves. I travels all dat day and night up de river and follows de north star. Sev'ral times I thunk de blood houn's am trailin' me and I gits in de big hurry. I's so tired I couldn't hardly move, but I gits in a trot.

"I's hopin' and prayin' all de time I meets up with dat Harriet Tubman woman. She de cullud women what takes slaves to Canada. She allus travels de underground railroad, dey calls it, travels at night and hides out in de day. She sho' sneaks dem out de South and I thinks she's de brave woman.

"I eats all de nuts and kills a few swamp rabbits and cotches a few fish. I builds de fire and goes off 'bout half a mile and hides in de thicket till it burns down to de coals, den bakes me some fish and rabbit. I's shakin' all de time, 'fraid I'd git cotched, but I's nearly starve to death. I puts de rest de fish in my cap and travels on dat night by de north star and hides in a big thicket de nex' day and along evenin' I hears guns shootin'. I sho' am scart dis time, sho' 'nough. I's scart to come in and scart to go out, and while I's standin' dere, I hears two men say, 'Stick you hands up, boy. What you doin?' I says, 'Uh-uh-uh, I dunno. You ain't gwine take me back to de plantation, is you?' Dey says, 'No. Does you want to fight for de North?' I says I will, 'cause dey talks like northern men. Us walk night and day and gits in Gen. Rosecran's camp and dey thunk I's de spy from de South. Dey asks me all sorts of questions and says dey'll whip me if I didn't tell dem what I's spyin' 'bout. Fin'ly dey 'lieves me and puts me to work helpin' with de cannons. I feels 'portant den, but I didn't know what was in front of me, or I 'spects I'd run off 'gain.

"I helps sot dem cannons on dis Chickamauga Mountain,

in hidin' places. I has to go with a man and wait on him and dat cannon. First thing I knows, bang, bang, boom, things has started, and guns am shootin' faster dan you can think, and I looks round for de way to run. But dem guns am shootin' down de hill in front of me and shootin' at me, and over me and on both sides of me. I tries to dig me a hole and git in it. All dis happen right now, and first thing I knows, de man am kickin' me and wantin' me to holp him keep dat cannon loaded. Man, I didn't want no cannon, but I has to help anyway. We fit till dark and de Rebels got more men dan us, so Gen. Rosecran sends de message to Gen. Woods to come help us out. When de messenger slips off, I sho' wish it am me slippin' off, but I didn't want to see no Gen. Woods. I jes' wants to git back to dat old plantation and pick more cotton. I'd been willin' to do mos' anything to git out that mess, but I done told Gen. Rosecran I wants to fight de Rebels and he sho' was lettin' me do it. He wasn't jes' lettin' me do it, he was makin' me do it. I done got in dere and he wouldn't let me out.

"White folks, dere was men layin' wantin' help, wantin' water, with blood runnin' out dem and de top or sides dere heads gone, great big holes in dem. I jes' promises de good Lawd if he jes' let me git out dat mess, I wouldn't run off no more, but I didn't know den he wasn't gwine let me out with jes' dat battle. He gwine give me plenty more, but dat battle ain't over yet, for nex' mornin' de Rebels 'gins shootin' and killin' lots of our men, and Gen. Woods ain't come, so Gen. Rosecran orders us to 'treat, and didn't have to tell me what he said, neither. De Rebels comes after us, shootin', and we runs off and leaves dat cannon what I was with settin' on de hill, and I didn't want dat thing nohow.

"We kep' hotfootin' till we gits to Chattanooga and dere is where we stops. Here comes one dem Rebel generals with de big bunch of men and gits right on top of Look Out

Mountain, right clost to Chattanooga, and wouldn't let us out. I don't know jes' how long, but a long time. Lots our hosses and mules starves to death and we eats some de hosses. We all like to starve to death ourselves. Chattanooga is in de bend de Tennessee River and on Look Out Mountain, on de east, am dem Rebels and could keep up with everything we done. After a long time a Gen. Thomas gits in some way. He finds de rough trail or wagon road round de mountain 'long de river and supplies and men comes by boat up de river to dis place and comes on into Chattanooga. More Union men kep' comin' and I guess maybe six or eight generals and dey gits ready to fight. It am long late in Fall or early winter.

"Dey starts climbin' dis steep mountain and when us gits three-fourths de way up it am foggy and you couldn't see no place. Everything wet and de rocks am slick and dey 'gins fightin'. I 'spect some shoots dere own men, 'cause you couldn't see nothin', jes' men runnin' and de guns roarin'. Fin'ly dem Rebels fled and we gits on Look Out Mountain and takes it.

"Dere a long range of hills leadin' 'way from Look Out Mountain, nearly to Missionary Ridge. Dis ridge 'longside de Chickamauga River, what am de Indian name, meanin' River of Death. Dey fights de Rebels on Orchard Knob hill and I wasn't in dat, but I's in de Missionary Ridge battle. We has to come out de timber and run 'cross a strip or openin' up de hill. Dey sho' kilt lots our men when we runs 'cross dat openin'. We runs for all we's worth and uses guns or anything we could. De Rebels turns and runs off and our soldiers turns de cannons round what we's capture, and kilt some de Rebels with dere own guns.

"I never did git to where I wasn't scart when we goes into de battle. Dis de last one I's in and I's sho' glad, for I never seed de like of dead and wounded men. We picks dem up, de Rebels like de Unions, and doctors dem de bes' we could. When I seed all dat sufferin', I hopes I never lives to see 'nother war. Dey say de World War am worse but I's too old to go.

"I sho' wishes lots of times I never run off from de plantation. I begs de General not to send me on any more battles, and he says I's de coward and sympathizes with de South. But I tells him I jes' couldn't stand to see all dem men layin' dere dyin' and hollerin' and beggin' for help and a drink of water, and blood everywhere you looks. Killin' hawgs back on de plantation didn't bother me none, but dis am diff'rent.

"Fin'ly de General tells me I can go back to Chattanooga and guard de supplies in camp dere and take care de wounded soldiers and prisoners. A bunch of men is with me and we has all we can do. We gits de orders to send supplies to some general and it my job to help load de wagons or box cars or boats. A train of wagons leaves sometimes. We gits all dem supplies by boat, and Chattanooga am de 'stributing center. When winter comes, everybody rests awhile and waits for Spring to open. De Union general sends in some more cullud soldiers. Dere ain't been many cullud men but de las' year of war dere am lots. De North and de South am takin' anything dey can git to win de war.

"When Spring breaks and all de snow am gone, and de trees 'gins puttin' out and everything 'gins to look purty and peaceable-like, makin' you think you ought to be plowin' and plantin' a crop, dat when de fightin' starts all over 'gain, killin' men and burnin' homes and stealin' stock and food. Den dey sends me out to help clear roads and build temp'rary bridges. We walks miles on muddy ground, 'cross rivers, wadin' water up to our chins. We builds rafts and pole bridges to git de mules and hosses and cannons 'cross, and up and down hills, and cuts roads through timber.

"But when dey wants to battle Gen. Thomas allus leaves me in camp to tend de supplies. He calls me a coward, and I sho' glad he thunk I was. I wasn't no coward, I jes' couldn't stand to see all dem people tore to pieces. I hears 'bout de battle in a thick forest and de trees big as my body jes' shot down. I seed dat in de Missionary Ridge battle, too.

"I shifts from one camp to 'nother and fin'ly gits back to Chattanooga. I bet durin' my time I handles 'nough ammunition to kill everybody in de whole United States. I seed mos' de mainest generals in de Union Army and some in de Rebel Army.

"After de war am over we's turned loose, nowhere to go and nobody to help us. I couldn't go South, for dey calls me de traitor and sho' kill me iffen dey knows I fit for de North. I does any little job I can git for 'bout a year and fin'ly gits work on de railroad, in Stevenson, in Alabama. I gits transfer to Chattanooga and works layin' new tracks and turn tables and sich.

"In 'bout two weeks I had saw a gal next door, but I's bashful. But after payday I dresses up and takes her to a dance. We sparks 'bout two months and den we's married at her uncles. Her name am Nancy. We buys a piece of land and I has a two-room house built on it. We has two chillen and I's livin' with de baby gal now.

"I 'lieve de slaves I knowed as a whole was happier and better off after 'mancipation dan befo'. Of course, de first few years it was awful hard to git 'justed to de new life. All de slaves knowed how to do hard work, and dat de old slaves life, but dey didn't know nothin' 'bout how to 'pend on demselves for de livin'. My first year was hard, but dere was plenty wild game in dem days. De south was broke and I didn't hear of no slaves gittin' anything but to crop on de halves. Dey too glad to be free and didn't want nothin'.

"Things 'gin to git bad for me in Chattanooga as de white men finds out I run off from de South and jined de North. Some de brakemen try to git my job. I fin'ly quits when one of dem opens a switch I jus' closed. I seed him and goes back and fixes de switch, but I quits de job. I goes up north but dey ain't int'rested, so I comes back and sells my home and buys me a team and wagon. I loads it with my wife and chillen and a few things and starts for Texas. We's on de road 'bout six weeks or two months. We fishes and hunts every day and de trip didn't cost much. I buys ninety acres in timber in Cass County and cuts logs for a house and builds a two-room house and log crib. My wife built a stomp lot for de team and cow and a rail fence.

"We got 'nough land cleared for de small crop, 'bout thirty acres, and builds de barn and sheds outselves. We lived there till de chillen am growed. My wife died of chills and fever and den my boy and I built a four-room house of planks from our timber. Den I gits lonesome, 'cause de chillen gone, and sells de place. I bought it for fifty cents de acre and sold it for $12.00 de acre.

"I buys sixty acres in Henderson County for $15.00 a acre and marries de second time. I didn't care for her like Nancy. All she think 'bout am raisin' de devil and never wants to work or save anything. She like to have broke me down befo' I gits rid of her. I stayed and farmed sev'ral years.

"My son-in-law rents land in Chambers Creek bottom, and he usually gits he crop 'fore de flood gits it. We has some hawgs to kill ev'ry winter and we has our cornmeal and milk and eggs and chickens, so de 'pression ain't starved us yit. We all got might' nigh naked durin' de 'pression. I feeds de hawgs and chickens night and mornin'. I can't see dem, but I likes to listen to dem eatin' and cackle. People don't know how dey's blessed with good eyes, till dey loses dem. Everybody ought to be more thankful dan they is.

"I ain't never voted in my life. I leans to de 'publicans. I don't know much 'bout politics, though.

"Today I is broke, 'cause I spent all my money for med'cine and doctors, but I gits a small pension and I spends it mos' careful.

United States.Work Project Administration

ELI COLEMAN

ELI COLEMAN, 91, was born a slave of George Brady, in Kentucky. Eli's memory is poor and his story is somewhat sketchy. He now lives in Madisonville, Texas.

"I has a old bill of sale, and it shows I's born in 1846 and my massa am George Brady. I know my pappy's name was same as mine, and mammy was Ella, and I had one brother named Sam, and my sisters was Sadie and Rosa and Viola. They's all dead now.

"Pappy was owned by Massa Coleman, what was brother to Massa Brady. Pappy could only see mammy once a week when he's courtin' for her. I heard pappy tell 'bout his pappy, over in Africy, and he had near a hundred wives and over three hundred chillen.

"Pappy never did work. All he ever did was trade. He'd make one thing and 'nother and trade it for something to eat. He could get lots of fruit and game out of the woods them days, and there was lots of fish.

"Our log house was built of logs, trimmed, and had six rooms. It was long, like a cowbarn or chicken house, and my room was third. We had one door to each room, covered over with hides. We dug out one corner for the bed and fenced it up and gathered straw and moss and tore-up corn shucks, and put in the corner to sleep on. What I mean, it was a warm bed.

"We did all kinds of work, choppin' cotton and split rails and cut rock, and work in the tobacco field. We'd cut that tobacco and hang it in the shed to dry. It had to be hanged by the stubble end.

"We had plenty to eat, sech as corn pones. The corn was grated by hand and cooked in ashes, and no salt or soda or fancy things like they put in bread now.

"There was possum and rabbit and we cooked them different to now. A great big, old pot hung over the old rock fireplace. Food cooked that way still eats good. Massa Brady allus give us lots out of the garden. He fed us reg'lar on good, 'stantial food, jus' like you'd tend to you hoss, if you had a real good one.

"Massa Brady, he was one these jolly fellows and a real good man, allus good to his black folks. Missy, she was plumb angel. They lived in a old stone house with four big rooms. It was the best house in the whole county and lots of shade trees by it.

"We had 'bout a hundred acres in our plantation and started to the field 'fore daylight and worked long as we could see, and fed ane stock and got to bed 'bout nine o'clock. Massa whopped a slave if he got stubborn or lazy. He whopped one so hard that slave said he'd kill him. So Massa done put a chain round his legs, so he jus' hardly walk, and he has to work in the field that way. At night he put 'nother chain round his neck and fastened it to a tree. After three weeks massa turnt him loose and that the proudes' nigger in the world, and the hardes' workin' nigger massa had after that.

"On Saturday night we could git a pass or have a party on our own place. Through the week we'd fall into our quarters and them patterrollers come walk all over us, and we'd be plumb still, but after they done gone some niggers gits up and out.

"On Christmas Day massa make a great big eggnog and let us have all we wants with a big dinner. He kilt a yearlin' and made plenty barbecue for us.

"Massa was a colonel in the war and took me along to care for his hoss and gun. Them guns, you couldn't hear nothin' for them poppin'. Us niggers had to go all over and pick up them what got kilt. Them what was hurt we carried back. Them what was too bad hurt we had to carry to the burying place and the white man'd finish killin' them, so we could roll them in the hole.

"When massa say we're free, we all 'gun to take on. We didn't have no place to go and asked massa could we stay, but he say no. But he did let some stay and furnished teams and something to eat and work on the halves. I stayed and was sharecropper, and that was when slavery start, for when we got our cop made it done take every bit of it to pay our debts and we had nothing left to buy winter clothes or pay doctor bills.

"'Bout a year after the war I marries Nora Brady, jus' a home weddin'. I asks her to come live with me as my wife and she 'greed and she jus' moved her clothes to my room and we lived together a long time. One mornin' Nora jus' died, and there warn't no chillen, so I sets out for Texas. I done hear the railroad is buildin' in Texas and they hires lots of niggers. I gits a hoss from massa and rolls up a few clothes and gits my gun.

"I never got very far 'fore the Indians takes my hoss away from me. It was 'bout fifty mile to a train and I didn't have no money, but I found a white man what wants wood cut and I works near a month for him and gits $2.00. I gits on a train and comes a hundred mile from where that railroad was goin' 'cross the country, and I has to walk near all that hundred miles. Once and now a white man comin' or goin' lets me ride. But I got there and the job pays me sixty cents a day. That was lots of money them days. Near as I 'member, it was 1867 or 1868 when I comes to Texas.

"Then I marries Agnes Frazer, and we has a big weddin' and a preacher and a big supper for two or three weeks. Her pappy kilt game and we et barbecue all the time. We had eleven chillen, one a year for a long time, five boys and six gals. One made a school teacher and I ain't seen her nearly forty-five years, 'cause she done took a notion to go north and they won't let her back in Texas 'cause she married a white man in New York. I don't like that. She don't have no sense or she wouldn't done that, no, sir.

"Since the nigger been free it been Hell on the poor old nigger. He has advance some ways, but he's still a servant and will be, long as Gawd's curse still stay on the Negro race. We was turnt loose without nothin' and done been under the white man rule so long we couldn't hold no job but labor. I worked most two years on that railroad and the rest my life I farms. Now I gits a little pension from the gov'ment and them white folks am sho' good to give it to me, 'cause I ain't good for work no more.

PREELY COLEMAN

PREELY COLEMAN was born in 1852 on the Souba farm, near New Berry, South Carolina, but he and his mother were sold and brought to Texas when Preely was a month old. They settled near Alto, Texas. Preely now lives in Tyler.

"I'm Preely Coleman and I never gits tired of talking. Yes, ma'am, it am Juneteenth, but I'm home, 'cause I'm too old now to go on them celerabrations. Where was I born? I knows that 'zactly, 'cause my mammy tells me that a thousand times. I was born down on the old Souba place, in South Carolina, 'bout ten mile from New Berry. My mammy belonged to the Souba family, but its a fact one of the Souba boys was my pappy and so the Soubas sells my mammy to Bob and Dan Lewis and they brung us to Texas 'long with a big bunch of other slaves. Mammy tells me it was a full month 'fore they gits to Alto, their new home.

"When I was a chile I has a purty good time, 'cause there was plenty chillen on the plantation. We had the big races. Durin' the war the sojers stops by on the way to Mansfield, in Louisiana, to git somethin' to eat and stay all night, and then's when we had the races. There was a mulberry tree we'd run to and we'd line up and the sojers would say, 'Now the first one to slap that tree gits a quarter,' and I nearly allus gits there first. I made plenty quarters slappin' that old mulberry tree!

"So the chillen gits into their heads to fix me, 'cause I wins all the quarters. They throws a rope over my head and started draggin down the road, and down the hill, and I was nigh 'bout choked to death. My only friend was Billy and he was a-fightin', tryin' to git me loose. They was goin' to throw me in the big spring at the foot of that hill, but we meets Capt. Berryman, a white man, and he took his knife and cut the rope from my neck and took me by the heels and soused me up and down in the spring till I come to. They never tries to kill me any more.

"My mammy done married John Selman on the way to Texas, no cere'mony, you knows, but with her massa's consent. Now our masters, the Lewises, they loses their place and then the Selman's buy me and mammy. They pays $1,500 for my mammy and I was throwed in.

"Massa Selman has five cabins in he backyard and they's built like half circle. I grows big 'nough to hoe and den to plow. We has to be ready for the field by daylight and the conk was blowed, and massa call out, 'All hands ready for the field.' At 11:30 he blows the conk, what am the mussel shell, you knows, 'gain and we eats dinner, and at 12:30 we has to be back at work. But massa wouldn't 'low no kind of work on Sunday.

"Massa Tom made us wear the shoes, 'cause they's so many snags and stumps our feets gits sore, and they was red russet shoes. I'll never forgit 'em, they was so stiff at first we could hardly stand 'em. But Massa Tom was a good man, though he did love he dram. He kep' the bottle in the center of the dining table all the time and every meal he'd have the toddy. Us slaves et out under the trees in summer and in the kitchen in winter and most gen'rally we has bread in pot liquor or milk, but sometimes honey.

"I well 'members when freedom come. We was in the field and massa comes up and say, 'You all is free as I is.' There was shoutin' and singin' and 'fore night us was all 'way to freedom.

HARRIET COLLINS

HARRIET COLLINS was born in Houston, Texas, in 1870. Her family had been slaves of Richard Coke, and remained with him many years after they were freed. Harriet recalls some incidents of Reconstruction days, and believes in the superstitions handed down to her from slave days.

"My birthday done come in January, on de tenth. I's birthed in Houston, in 1870, and Gov. Richard Coke allus had owned my daddy and mammy, and dey stayed with him after freedom. Mammy, what was Julia Collins, didn't die till 1910, and she was most a hundred year old.

"She done told me many a time 'bout how folkses git all worked up over Marse Coke's 'lection. Mammy took lunch to de Capitol House to Marse Richard, and dere he am on de top floor with all he congressmen and dat Davis man and he men on de bottom floor, tryin' to say Marse Richard ain't got no right to be governor dis here State. Old Miss and de folkses didn't sleep a wink dat night, 'cause dey thunk it sho' be a fight. Dat in 1873, Mammy allus say.

"De old place at Houston was like most all old places. Dere was little, small dormer windows, dey call 'em, in upstairs, and big porches everywhere. Dere was 'hogany furniture and rosewood bedsteads, and big, black walnut dressers with big mirrors and little ones down de side. Old Miss allus have us keep de drapes white as drifted snow, and polish de furniture till it shine. Dere was sofies with dem claw foots, and lots of purty chiny and silver.

"On de farm out from town dere was de log house, with quarters and de smokehouse and washhouse and big barns and carriage house. De quarters was little, whitewashed, log houses, one for de family, and a fence of de split palin's round most of dem.

"De white and cullud chillen played together, all over de place. Dey went fishin' and rode de plough hosses and run de calves and colts and sech devilment. De little white gals all had to wear sunbonnets, and Old Miss, she sew dem bonnets on every day, so dey not git sunburnt. Us niggers weared de long, duckin' shirts till us git 'bout growed, and den us weared long, dark blue dresses. Dey had spinnin' and weavin' rooms, where de cullud women makes de clothes.

"Old Miss, she sho' a powerful manager. She knowed jes' how much meal and meat and sorghum it gwine take to run de plantation a year. She know jes' how much thread it take for spinnin', and she bossed de settin' hens and turkeys and fixin' of 'serves and soap. She was sho' good to you iffen you work and do like she tell you. Many a night she go round to see dat all was right. She a powerful good nuss, too, and so was mammy.

"De white folks had good times. Dey'd go hossback ridin' and on picnics, and fishin' and have big dinners and balls. Come Christmas, dey have us slaves cut a big lot of wood and keep fires all night for a week or two. De house be lit with candles from top to toe, and lots of company come. For dinner us have turkey and beef roast and a big 'ginny ham and big bowls of eggnog and a pitcher of apple cider and apple toddy. All us git somethin' on Christmas and plenty eggnog, but no gittin' drunk.

"I can jes' see Marse Dick, tall and kinder stooped like, with de big flop hat and longtail coat and allus carryin' a big, old walkin' stick. He was sho' a brave man and de big men say dey likes dat flop hat, 'cause dey done follow it on de battlefield. He had a big voice and dey do tell how, in de war, he'd holler, 'Come on, boys,' and de bullets be like hail and men fallin' all round, but dat don't stop Marse Dick. He'd take off dat flop hat and plunge right on and dey'd foller he bald head where de fight was hottes'. He was sho' a man!

"When I gits married it was eight folkses dere, I jus' walks off and goes to housekeepin'. I had a calico dress and a Baptist preacher marries us.

"Dere been some queer things white folks can't understand. Dere am folkses can see de spirits, but I can't. My mammy larned me a lots of doctorin', what she larnt from old folkses from Africy, and some de Indians larnt her. If you has rheumatism, jes' take white sassafras root and bile it and drink de tea. You makes lin'ment by bilin' mullein flowers and poke roots and alum and salt. Put red pepper in you shoes and keep de chills off, or string briars round de neck. Make red or black snakeroot tea to cure fever and malaria, but git de roots in de spring when de sap am high.

"When chillen teethin' put rattlesnake rattles round de neck, and alligator teeth am good, too. Show de new moon money and you'll have money all month. Throw her five kisses and show her money and make five wishes and you'll git dem. Eat black-eyed peas on New Year and have luck all dat year:

"'Dose black-eyed peas is lucky,
When et on New Year's Day;
You'll allus have sweet 'taters
And possum come you way.'

"When anybody git cut I allus burns woolen rags and smokes de wound or burns a piece fat pine and drops tar from it on scorched wool and bind it on de wound. For headache put a horseradish poultice on de head, or wear a nutmeg on a string round you neck.

If you kills de first snake you sees in spring, you enemies ain't gwine git de best of you dat year. For a sprain, git a dirt dauber's nest and put de clay with vinegar and bind round de sprain. De dime on de string round my ankle keeps cramps out my leg, and tea from red coon-root good, too. All dese doctorin' things come clear from Africy, and dey allus worked for mammy and for me, too.

ANDREW COLUMBUS (SMOKY)

ANDREW (Smoky) COLUMBUS was born in 1859 on the John J. Ellington plantation, one mile south of Linden, Texas. He continued in the service of the Ellingtons until about 1878, when he moved to Jefferson, Texas. He carried meals to Abe Rothchild, who was in jail, charged with the murder of Diamond Bessie Moore. Andrew was 37 years a servant of Hon. Tom Armistead, and was a porter in the Capital at Austin when Armistead was a senator. Andrew now lives in Marshall, Texas.

"I was bo'n a slave of Master John Ellington, who lived in Davis County (now Cass Co.), Texas. Master John had a big house and close by was a long, double row of slave quarters. It looked like a town. There was four boys and two girls in Master's fam'ly and one daughter, Miss Lula, married Lon Morris, that run the Lon Morris School.

"Master John was one white man that sho' took care of his niggers. He give us plenty warm clothes and good shoes, and come see us and had Dr. Hume doctor us when we was sick. The niggers et ham and middlin' and good eats as anybody. Master John's place joined the Haggard place, where they was lots of wild turkey and the slaves could go huntin' and fishin' when they wanted.

"We had a church and a school for the slaves and the white folks helped us git book learnin'. Mos' of the niggers allus went to preachin' on Sunday.

"The hands didn't work Saturday afternoons. That's when we'd wash our clothes and clean up for Sunday. There was parties and dances on Saturday night for them as wanted them. But there wasn't no whiskey drinkin' and fightin' at the parties. Mammy didn't go to them. She was religious and didn't believe in dancin' and sech like. On Christmas Master John allus give the slaves a big dinner and it didn't seem like slavery time. The niggers had a sight better time than they do now.

"Master John did all the bossin' hisself. None of his niggers ever run off 'cause he was too good for them to do that. I only got one whippin' from him and it was for stealin' eggs from a hen's nest. My pappy was carriage driver for Master. I didn't do much of the work when I was a boy, jes' stayed round the house.

"Master John raised lots of cotton and after it was baled he hauled it to Jefferson on ox wagons. I'd allus go with him, ridin' on top of the bales. I'll never forgit how scared I was when we'd cross Black Cypress on Roger's Ferryboat and it'd begin to rock.

"I don't remember much about the War. When it was over Master John calls all his slaves together and says, 'You'se free now and you can go or stay.' He told the men who wanted to leave they could have a wagon and team, but most of them stayed. Pappy took a wagon and team and left but mammy and us children stayed and lived with Master Ellington 'bout 15 years after the war was over.

"When I left Master John I moved to Jefferson and married Cora Benton and we had three boys and two girls. While I was in Jefferson Sheriff Vine goes to Cincinnati after Abe Rothchild, for killin' 'Diamond Bessie.' Abe shot hisself in the forehead when he heared Sheriff Vine was after him, but it didn't kill him. There was sho' some stirrin' about when the sheriff fotch Abe back to Jefferson.

"Mr. Sam Brown was the jailer. Abe wouldn't eat the jail food and hired me to bring his meals to him from the hotel. His cell was fixed up like a hotel room, with a fine brussels rug and nice tables and chairs. He kep' plenty of whiskey and beer to drink. He'd allus give me a drink when I took his meals.

"I worked 37 years for Mr. Tom Armistead, who helped W.T. Crawford and his brother defend Rothchild. Mr. Eppenstadt, he was mayor of Jefferson then and acted as a go-between man in the case.

"Master Tom Armistead never married and I kep' house and cooked for him. He give me lots of fine clothes. I bet I owned more fine shirts than any nigger in Texas. He got me a job as porter in the Capitol at Austin while he was senator. I was workin' there when they moved in the new Capitol in 1888. They was gonna put on a big party and say all the porters had to wear cutaway suits. I didn't have one, so the day 'fore the party I goes over to Mr. Tom's room at the Bristol Hotel and git one of his. I didn't know then it was a right new one he had made for the party. When I goes back to the Capitol all dressed up in that cutaway suit, I meets Mr. Templeton Houston and he recognises the suit and says, 'You sho' look fine in Mr. Tom's new suit,' 'bout that time Mr. Tom walks up and, you know, he give me that suit and had him another one made for the party! I wouldn't live where there wasn't no good white folks.

United States.Work Project Administration

STEVE CONALLY'S HOUSE

STEVE CONNALLY, 90, was born a slave of Tom Connally, grandfather of United States Senator Tom Connally, from Texas. The family then lived in Georgia, and Steve's master was a member of the Georgia Legislature.

"I was born in Murray County, Georgia, and was a slave of Massa Tom Connally, but they called him Massa "Cushi" Connally. He was a member of de Georgia Legislature. I stayed with Missy Mary Connally till I was sixty-seven and Massa Cushi died when I was sixty-nine.

"My mother, Mandy, weighed two hundred pounds and she was de Connally cook. When I was born, she took de fever and couldn't raise me, so Missy Mary took and kep' me in a li'l cot by her bed. After dat, I'm with her nearly all de time and follows her. When she go to de garden I catches her dresstail and when she go to de doctor, 'bout eighty miles away, I goes with her.

"I mus' tell you why everybody call Massa Connally Cushi. Dere am allus so many Tom Connallys in de fam'ly, dey have to have de nickname to tell one from de other.

"Back dere in Georgia, us have lots and lots of fruit. Come time, de women folks preserves and cans till it ain't no use. My mammy take de prize any day with her jelly and sech, and her cakes jes' nachelly walk off and leave de whole county. Missy Mary sho' de master hand hersef at de fine bakin' and I'd slip round and be handy to lick out de pans.

"Dey didn't have no 'frigerators den, but dey built log houses without a floor over de good, cold spring, and put flat rocks dere to keep de milk and cream and butter cold. Or dey dig out de place so de crock be down in de wet dirt. Dey sho' have to make de latch up high, so de bad chillen couldn't open dat door!

"De plantation in Georgia was de whopper. I don't know 'zactly how many acres, but it a big one. Us make everything and tan hides and make shoes, jes' like all de big places did. De big house and de weavin' house and de tannin' yard and de sugar mill and slave quarters made a li'l town. Dere used to be some mighty big doin's dere. De Connally men and women am allus good lookers and mighty pop'lar, and folkses come from far and near to visit dem. All de 'portant men come and all de sassiety belles jes' drift to our place. Dere sho' lots of big balls and dinners and de house fix mighty fine dem times. De women wore de hoop skirts and de ribbons and laces. My missy was de bes' lookin' from far and near, and all de gem'mans want to dance with her. She sho' look like de queen you see in de picture books and she have mighty high ways with folks, but she's mighty good to dis here li'l black boy.

"I goes in de buggy with Massa Cushi, up to Tennessee, to git his sons what been kilt or wounded. Massa Ned, he dead, and Massa Charles, he shot in de hip, and die after he git brung home. Massa Dick hurt, too, but he didn't die.

"Right after de Civil War, when I'm 'bout nineteen, I comes to Texas with de Connallys, all what didn't git kilt in de war. I stays with Missy Mary till she die in Georgia. Her son, Jones Connally, come to Brazos County, near Bryan, and after dat removes to Eddy. I works for him two years and has lived round Eddy ever since. De Connallys give me a house and lot in Eddy. Some de fool niggers 'spected a lot, but I wasn't worryin' none. All I wanted was to stay near de Connallys. Mos' gen'ly all de slaves what I knowed was found places for and holp git a start at jobs and places to live. All de Connally slaves loved dem. Some de timber land give to Mrs. Rose Staten and when she go up dere a old nigger woman name Lucy sees her. She so happy to see one dem Connally chillen she laugh and cry.

"Massa Jones Connally have de twin gals, name Ola and Ella. Olla born with de lef' arm off at de elbow and she allus follow me round. When I go to milk I puts her in de trough. I saved her life lots of times. One time she's on de cone of de two-story house, when she's 'bout two years old. I eases up and knocks de window out and coaxes her to come to me. 'Nother time, I's diggin' de well and some clods falls down and I looks up and dere am dat Missy Ola leanin' over, mos' tumblin' in de well on her head. I gives de loud yell and her brother-in-law come runnin' and grabs her legs.

"Senator Tom Connally, what am a son of Jones Connally,

often says he'd like to visit his grandpa's old home in Georgia. I'd like mighty well to go with him and take him all over de old home place and out to de old cemetary."

VALMAR CORMIER

VALMAR CORMIER was born a slave to Duplissent Dugat, a small slave-holder of Lafayette, Louisiana. He tells his story in a mixture of English and French. As far as he knows, he is nearly 90 years old. He now lives with his sister, Mary Moses, in the Pear Orchard Settlement, in Beaumont, Texas.

"I 'member de day my old marster go to de war. I kin 'member dat jes' like yesterday. He used to like to play de fiddle and make me dance when I was li'l, but he went to de war and got kilt. He name Duplissent Dugat. Mary, my sister, she don't 'member de old marster.

"De slaves did de work on dat farm. Dey was two growed-ups, my mama, Colaste, and my uncle, and dere was us two chillen. My father was a white man, a white Creole man. I never carry he name till after freedom.

"Marster was jes' a poor man and he have jes' a ordinary house. De slave house was jes' a old plank house 'bout twelve feet by twenty feet and have dirt floor. Us cook in de big fireplace and take a log 'bout four foot long and have a big iron pot with a iron lid. Dey put red hot coals under de pot and on top de lid and dey have a big iron poker with a hook on it what dey took de lid off with.

"Befo' dey have coal oil lamp dey used to use homemake candles. Dey'd kill de brutes and keep and save all de tallow and one day was set off to make de candles. All de neighbors come and dey have kind of party and eat and things. Sometime dey make three, four hunnerd candles in one day and lay dem in a big box, so dey won't git break.

"Us make soap on de plantation, too. Dey melt de tallow and cracklin's and git lye out de fireplace ash. We have cotton and corn and potatoes growin', so we has plenty to eat. Us have coosh-coosh, dat cornbread and meat, and some fish to eat. Snails us jes' go through de woods and pick dem up and eat dem jes' like dat. Us eat plenty crawfish. De chillen git string and old piece fat meat and tie on de end, and us go to de bog and drap de string down dat crawfish hole. When de old man grab de meat with he pincher, den us jerk us up a crawfish, and bile him in hot water, or make de gumbo.

"Us drink French coffee befo' de war, but endurin' de war us couldn't git de good kind. Den us make coffee out of coffee weed. Dey parch dat weed in de iron oven, grind it and put it in de iron pot.

"I seed de sojers and I run under de house, I was so scared. Mary, she hide under de bed in de house. De Yankees come take de cattle and went 'way with dem. I kin sho' rec'lect when dose sojers come and de road was full goin' day and night. De Yankees find a lot of Confed'rate sojers close to Duson, de other side of Rayne and dey captures lots and brung dem back by dere.

"After while it all over and dey told us we free, but my mama kep' working for old missus after freedom, 'cause old marster, he kilt in dat war. Den old missus die and left three li'l chillen, but I don't know what happen to them, 'cause us go to another place and I plow and Mary she he'p pick cotton.

"I git marry at 20 and my first wife de French gal. We marry by de priest in de church. Us have so many chillen us have to keep a map to account for all dem, dere was 19 in all. We stays in Louisiana long time, den come to Texas.

LAURA CORNISH

LAURA CORNISH was born on the plantation of Isaiah Day, near Dayton, Texas. She "reckons I's 'bout twelve or maybe thirteen years old when all de cullud folks was made free." Laura's memory is poor, but she made an effort to recall slave days. She lives at 2915 Nance St., Houston, Texas.

"Lawd have mercy 'pon me, when you calls me Aunt Laura it seems jes' like you must be some of my white folks, 'cause dat what dey calls me. I mean Papa Day's chillen and dere younguns, when dey comes to see me. But it been de long time since any of dem come to see old Aunt Laura, and I reckon dey most all gone now.

"You know where Dayton is at? Well, dat's where Papa Day's plantation was at and where I's borned. I don't know when dat am, 'zactly, but when all de cullud folks was made free, I reckons I's 'bout twelve or thirteen years old.

"Mama's name was Maria Dunlap and daddy's name was Saul. Mamma was de seamstress and don't do nothin' but weave cloth on de spinnin' wheel and make clothes. Daddy from Lake Providence, I heared him say, but I don't know where at dat is. He do all de carpenter work. I has five sisters and two brothers, but dey heaps older dan me and I don't know much 'bout dem.

"We 'longs to Papa Day, his name Isaiah, but us all call him Papa Day, 'cause he won't 'low none he cullud folks to call him master. He say us is born free as he is, only de other white folks won't tell us so, and our souls is jes' as white, and de reason us am darker on de outside is 'cause us is sunburnt. I don't reckon dere am anybody as good to dere cullud folks as he was.

"Miss Martha, he wife, was mighty good, too. Does any us chillen git hurt or scratched, she fix us up and give us a hug. I knows dey has two boys and a gal, and dey comes to see me long time after I's free and brings dere own chillen. But my mem'ry am sort of foggy-like and I can't 'member dere names now.

"De only work Papa Day 'lows us chillen do am pick de boles close to de ground, and dat mostly fun, and us ride to de house on de wagon what takes de pickin' at night. Papa Day don't make he cullud folks work Saturdays and Sundays and dey can visit round on other plantations, and he say nobody better bother us none, either.

"One time us chillen playin' out in de woods and seed two old men what look like wild men, sho' 'nough. Dey has long hair all over de face and dere shirts all bloody. Us run and tell Papa Day and he makes us take him dere and he goes in de briar patch where dem men hidin'. Dey takes him round de knees and begs him do he not tell dere massa where dey at, 'cause dey maybe git kilt. Dey say dey am old Lodge and Baldo and dey run 'way 'cause dere massa whips dem, 'cause dey so old dey can't work good no more. Papa Day has tears comin' in he eyes. Dey can't hardly walk, so he sends dem to de house and has Aunt Mandy, de cook, fix up somethin' to eat quick. I never seed sech eatin', dey so hongry. He puts dem in a house and tells us not to say nothin'. Den he rides off on he hoss and goes to dere massa and tells him 'bout it, and jes' dares him to come git dem. He pays de man some money and Lodge and Baldo stays with Papa Day and I guess day thunk dey in Heaven.

"One mornin' Papa Day calls all us to de house and reads

de freedom papers and say, 'De gov'ment don't need to tell you you is free, 'cause you been free all you days. If you wants to stay you can and if you wants to go, you can. But if you go, lots of white folks ain't gwine treat you like I does.'

"For de longest time, maybe two years, dey wasn't none of Papa Day's cullud folks what left, but den first one fam'ly den 'nother gits some land to make a crop on, and den daddy gits some land and us leaves, too. Maybe he gits de land from Papa Day, 'cause it an't far from his plantation. Us sho' work hard on dat place, but I heared mama say lots of times she wishes we stay on Papa Day's place.

"I 'member one year us don't make no crop hardly and daddy say he gwine git out 'fore us starves to death, and he moves to Houston. He gits a job doin' carpenter work and hires me out for de housegirl. But mama dies and daddy takes sick and dies, too. Lawd have mercy, dat sho' de hard time for me when I loses my mama and daddy, and I has to go to Dayton and stay with my sister, Rachel. Both my husbands what I marries done been dead a long time now, and de only child I ever had died when he jes' a baby. Now I's jes' alone, sittin' and waitin' for de Lawd to call me."

United States.Work Project Administration

JOHN CRAWFORD

JOHN CRAWFORD, 81, was born a slave on Judge Thompson Rector's plantation at Manor, Texas. After emancipation, John was a share-cropper. He has always lived in Travis County and is now cared for by a daughter at Austin.

"John Crawford am me. It am eighty-one years since I's borned and dat's on de old Rector plantation where Manor am now. It wasn't dere den. I knowed the man it was named after.

"Ma's name was Viney Rector and the old judge brung her from Alabama. She milked all the cows two times a day and I had to turn out all de calves. Sometimes dey'd git purty rough and go right to dere mammies.

"Pap's name was Tom Townes, 'cause he 'longed on de Townes place. He was my step-pap and when I's growed I tooken my own pap's name, what was Crawford. I never seed him, though, and didn't know nothin' much 'bout him. He's sold away 'fore I's borned.

"Pap Townes could make most everythin'. He made turnin' plows and hossshoe nails and a good lot of furniture. He was purty good to me, 'siderin' he wasn't my own pap. I didn't have no hard time, noway. I had plenty bacon and side-meat and 'lasses. Every Sunday mornin' the jedge give us our rations for de week. He wasn't short with dem, neither.

"Many was de time Injuns come to Jedge Rector's place. Dem Injuns beg for somethin' and the jedge allus give dem somethin'. They wasn't mean Injuns, jes' allus beggin'.

"I can't read and write to this day. Nobody ever larnt me my A B C's and I didn't git no chance at school.

"On Christmas mornin' Massa Rector come out and give each man and woman a big, red pocket handkerchief and a bottle of liquor. He buyed dat liquor by de barrel and liked it hisself. Dat why he allus had it on de place.

"One mornin' the jedge done send word down by de cook for nobody to go to de fields dat day. We all want up to de big house and de jedge git up to make de speech, but am too choke up to talk. He hated to lose he slaves, I reckon. So his son-in-law has to say, 'You folks am now free and can go where you wants to go. You can stay here and pick cotton and git fifty cents de hunerd.' But only two families stayed. De rest pulled out.

"After freedom we rented land on de halves. Some niggers soon got ahead and rented on de third or fourth. When you rent that-a-way you git three bales and de boss git one. But you has to buy you own teams and seed and all on dat plan.

"Its a fac' we was told we'd git forty acres and a mule. Dat de talk den, but we never did git it.

"De Ku Klux made a lot of devilment round-about dat county. Dey allus chasin' some nigger and beatin' him up. But some dem niggers sho' 'serve it. When dey gits free, dey gits wild. Dey won't work or do nothin' and thinks dey don't have to. We didn't have no trouble, 'cause we stays on de farm and works and don't have no truck with dem wild niggers.

"In 1877 I marries Fannie Black at de town of Sprinkle. It wasn't sech a town, jes' a li'l place. Me and her stayed married fifty-two years and four months. She died and left me eight year ago. We had seven chillen and they is all livin'. Four is here in Austin and two in California and one in Ohio.

"I gits a li'l pension, $9.00 de month, and my gal, Susie, takes care of me. I ain't got long to go now 'fore de Lawd gwine call me.

United States.Work Project Administration

GREEN CUMBY

GREEN CUMBY, 86, was born a slave of the Robert H. Cumby family, in Henderson, Texas. He was about 14 at the close of the Civil War. He stayed with his old master four years after he was freed, then married and settled in Tyler, Texas, where he worked for the compress 30 years. He lives with his daughter at 749 Mesquite St., Abilene, Texas.

"Durin' slavery I had purty rough times. My grandfather, Tater Cumby, was cullud overseer for forty slaves and he called us at four in de mornin' and we worked from sun to sun. Most of de time we worked on Sunday, too.

"De white overseers whupped us with straps when we didn't do right. I seed niggers in chains lots of times, 'cause there wasn't no jails and they jus' chained 'em to trees.

"Spec'lators on hosses drove big bunches of slaves past our place from one place to another, to auction 'em at de market places. De women would be carryin' l'il ones in dere arms and at night dey bed 'em down jus' like cattle right on de ground 'side of de road. Lots of l'il chillun was sold 'way from de mammy when dey seven or eight, or even smaller. Dat's why us cullud folks don't know our kinfolks to dis day.

"De best times was when de corn shuckin' was at hand. Den you didn't have to bother with no pass to leave de plantation, and de patter rolls didn't bother you. If de patter rolls cotch you without de pass any other time, you better wish you dead, 'cause you would have yourself some trouble.

"But de corn shuckin', dat was de gran' times. All de marsters and dere black boys from plantations from miles 'round would be dere. Den when we got de corn pile high as dis house, de table was spread out under de shade. All de boys dat 'long to old marster would take him on de packsaddle 'round de house, den dey bring him to de table and sit by he side; den all de boys dat 'long to Marster Bevan from another plantation take him on de packsaddle 'round and 'round de house, allus singin' and dancin', den dey puts him at de other side de table, and dey all do de same till everybody at de table, den dey have de feast.

"To see de runaway slaves in de woods scared me to death. They'd try to snatch you and hold you, so you couldn't go tell. Sometimes dey cotched dem runaway niggers and dey be like wild animals and have to be tamed over 'gain. Dere was a white man call Henderson had 60 bloodhounds and rents 'em out to run slaves. I well rec'lect de hounds run through our place one night, chasin' de slave what kilt his wife by runnin' de harness needle through her heart. Dey cotch him and de patter rolls took him to Henderson and hangs him.

"De patter rolls dey chases me plenty times, but I's lucky, 'cause dey never cotched me. I slips off to see de gal on de nex' plantation and I has no pass and they chases me and was I scairt! You should have seed me run through dat bresh, 'cause I didn't dare go out on de road or de path. It near tore de clothes off me, but I goes on and gits home and slides under de house. But I'd go to see dat gal every time, patter rolls or no patter rolls, and I gits trained so's I could run 'most as fast as a rabbit.

"De white chillun larned us to read and write at night, but I never paid much 'tention, but I kin read de testament now. Other times at night de slaves gathers round de cabins in little bunches and talks till bedtime. Sometimes we'd dance and someone would knock out time for us by snappin' de fingers and slappin' de knee. We didn't have nothin' to make de music on.

"We mos'ly lived on corn pone and salt bacon de marster give us. We didn't have no gardens ourselves, 'cause we wouldn't have time to work in dem. We worked all day in de fields and den was so tired we couldn't do nothin' more.

"My mammy doctored us when we was feelin' bad and she'd take dog-fenley, a yaller lookin' weed, and brew tea, and it driv de chills and de fever out of us. Sometimes she put horse mint on de pallet with us to make us sweat and driv de fever 'way. For breakfast she'd make us sass' fras tea, to clear our blood.

"My marstar and his two step-sons goes to de war. De marster was a big gen'ral on de southern side. I didn't know what dey fightin' 'bout for a long time, den I heered it 'bout freedom and I felt like it be Heaven here on earth to git freedom, 'spite de fac' I allus had de good marster. He sho' was good to us, but you knows dat ain't de same as bein' free.

United States.Work Project Administration

TEMPIE CUMMINS

TEMPIE CUMMINS was born at Brookeland, Texas, sometime before the Civil War, but does not know her exact age. William Neyland owned Tempie and her parents. She now lives alone in a small, weather-beaten shack in the South Quarters, a section of Jasper, Tex.

"They call me Tempie Cummins and I was born at Brookeland but I don' know jus' the 'xact date. My father's name was Jim Starkins and my mother's name was Charlotte Brooks and both of 'em come from Alabama. I had jus' one brudder, Bill, and four sisters named Margaret and Hannah and Mary and 'Liza. Life was good when I was with them and us play round. Miss Fannie Neyland, she Mis' Phil Scarborough now, she raise me, 'cause I was give to them when I was eight year old.

"I slep' on a pallet on the floor. They give me a homespun dress onct a year at Christmas time. When company come I had to run and slip on that dress. At other time I wore white chillens' cast-off clothes so wore they was ready to throw away. I had to pin them up with red horse thorns to hide my nakedness. My dress was usually split from hem to neck and I had to wear them till they was strings. Went barefoot summer and winter till the feets crack open.

"I never seed my grandparents 'cause my mother she sold in Alabama when she's 17 and they brung her to Texas and treat her rough. At mealtime they hand me a piece of cornbread and tell me 'Run 'long.' Sometime I git little piece of meat and biscuit, 'bout onct a month. I gathered up scraps the white chillens lef'.

"Marster was rough. He take two beech switches and twist them together and whip 'em to a stub. Many's the time I's bled from them whippin's. Our old mistus, she try to be good to us, I reckon, but she was turrible lazy. She had two of us to wait on her and then she didn' treat us good.

"Marster had 30 or 40 acres and he raise cotton, and corn and 'tatoes. He used to raise 12 bales cotton a year and then drink it all up. We work from daylight till dark, and after. Marster punish them what didn' work hard enough.

"The white chillen tries teach me to read and write but I didn' larn much, 'cause I allus workin'. Mother was workin' in the house, and she cooked too. She say she used to hide in the chimney corner and listen to what the white folks say. When freedom was 'clared, marster wouldn' tell 'em, but mother she hear him tellin' mistus that the slaves was free but they didn' know it and he's not gwineter tell 'em till he makes another crop or two. When mother hear that she say she slip out the chimney corner and crack her heels together four times and shouts, 'I's free, I's free.' Then she runs to the field, 'gainst marster's will and tol' all the other slaves and they quit work. Then she run away and in the night she slip into a big ravine near the house and have them bring me to her. Marster, he come out with his gun and shot at mother but she run down the ravine and gits away with me.

"I seed lots of ghosties when I's young. I couldn' sleep for them. I's kind of outgrowed them now. But one time me and my younges' chile was comin' over to church and right near the dippin' vat is two big gates and when we git to them, out come a big old white ox, with long legs and horns and when he git 'bout halfway, he turns into a man with a Panama hat on. He follers us to Sandy Creek bridge. Sometimes at night I sees that same spirit sittin' on that bridge now.

"My old man say, in slavery time, when he's 21, he had to pass a place where patterroles whipped slaves and had kilt some. He was sittin' on a load of fodder and there come a big light wavin' down the road and scarin' the team and the hosses drag him and near kilt him.

United States.Work Project Administration

ADELINE CUNNINGHAM

ADELINE CUNNINGHAM, 1210 Florida St., born 1852, was a slave in Lavaca County, 4-1/2 miles n.e. of Hallettsville. She was a slave of Washington Greenlee Foley and his grandson, John Woods. The Foley plantation consisted of several square leagues, each league containing 4,428.4 acres. Adeline is tall, spare and primly erect, with fiery brown eyes, which snap when she recalls the slave days. The house is somewhat pretentious and well furnished. The day was hot and the granddaughter prepared ice water for her grandmother and the interviewer. House and porch were very clean.

"I was bo'n on ole man Foley's plantation in Lavaca County. He's got more'n 100 slaves. He always buy slaves and he never sell. How many acres of lan' he got? Lawd, dat man ain't got acres, he got leagues. Dey raises cotton and co'n, and cattle and hawgs. Ole man Foley's plantation run over Lavaca and Colorado county, he got 1600 acres in one block and some of it on de Navidad River. Ole man Foley live in a big log house wid two double rooms and a hall, and he build a weavin' house agin his own house and dey's anudder house wid de spinnin' wheels. And ole man Foley run his own cotton gin and his own grindin' mill where dey grinds de co'n and dey got a big potato patch.

"Dey was rough people and dey treat ev'ry body rough. We lives in de quarter; de houses all jine close togedder but you kin walk 'tween 'em. All de cabins has one room and mostly two fam'lies bunks togedder in de one room wid dirt floors. De slaves builds de cabins, de slaves got no money, dey got no land.

"No suh, we never goes to church. Times we sneaks in de woods and prays de Lawd to make us free and times one of de slaves got happy and made a noise dat dey heered at de big house and den de overseer come and whip us 'cause we prayed de Lawd to set us free.

"You know what a stockman is? He is a man dat buys and sells cattle. Ev'ry year de stockman comes to ole man Foley's and he lines us up in de yard and de stockman got a lotta slaves tied togedder and ole man Foley he buys some slaves but he won't sell none. Yassuh, de stockman buys and sells de slaves jes' de same as cattle.

"Dey feeds us well sometimes, if dey warn't mad at us. Dey has a big trough jes' like de trough for de pigs and dey has a big gourd and dey totes de gourd full of milk and dey breaks de bread in de milk. Den my mammy takes a gourd and fills it and gives it to us chillun. How's we eat it? We had oyster shells for spoons and de slaves comes in from de fields and dey hands is all dirty, and dey is hungry. Dey dips de dirty hands right in de trough and we can't eat none of it. De women wuks in de fields until dey has chillun and when de chillun's ole enough to wuk in de fields den de mother goes to ole man Foley's house. Dere she's a house servant and wuks at spinnin' and weavin' de cotton. Dey makes all de clothes for ole man Foley and his fam'ly and for de slaves.

"No suh, we ain't got no holidays. Sundays we grinds co'n and de men split rails and hoes wid de grubbin' hoe. Ole man Foley has a blacksmif shop and a slave does de blacksmiffin. De slaves builds cabins wid split logs and dey makes de roof tight wid co'n shucks and grass. One time a month, times one time in two months, dey takes us to de white folks church.

"Dey's four or five preachers and de slaves. Iffen deys

a marriage de preacher has a book. He's gotter keep it hid, 'cause dey's afraid iffen de slaves learns to read dey learns how to run away. One of de slaves runs away and dey ketches him and puts his eyes out. Dey catches anudder slave dat run away and dey hanged him up by de arm. Yassuh, I see dat wid my own eyes; dey holds de slave up by one arm, dey puts a iron on his knee and a iron on his feet and drag 'im down but his feet cain't reach de groun'.

"Ole man Foley ain't bad, but de overseers is mean. No suh, we never gits no money and we never gits no lan'. Ole man Foley, he wants to give us sumpin for gardens but Mr. John Woods, his gran'son, is agin it.

"Was I glad when dat was over? Wouldn' you be? It's long after we's free dat I gits married. Yassuh, and I live in San Antonio 'bout 20 years."

United States.Work Project Administration

WILL DAILY

WILL DAILY, was born in 1858 in Missouri, near the city of St. Louis. He was a slave of the John Daily family and served as chore boy around the house, carried the breakfast to the field and always drove up the horses on the plantation. The latter duty developed a fondness for horses which led to a career as a race horse rider and trainer. He remained with his white folks several years after freedom and in Missouri many years longer in this work. He came to San Angelo, Texas in 1922 and took up hotel work which he followed until his health broke, only a few years ago. He now lives in his small home, in the colored district of the city and depends on his old age pension for a livelihood.

"Huh! What you say, did you say somethin' 'bout de ole age pension?", questioned Will when approached on the slavery question, but he answered readily, "Sho! sho' I was a slave an' I aint ashamed to admit dat I was. Some of dese here fellers thinks dey sounds ole when dey says dey was slaves and dey denies it but I's proud enough of de good treatment I's got, to allus tell about it. My marster had a driver but he say his niggers was human, wid human feelin's, so he makes dat driver reports to him fer what little thrashin's we gits. Course we had to do de right thing but jes' some how did, mos' of de time 'cause he was good to us. Soon as I was big enough, about four or five years ole, ole miss, she starts trainin' me fer a house boy. I's a doin' all sorts of chores by de time I was six years old. Den ole marster he starts sendin' me out on de plantation to drive up de hosses. I sho' likes dat job 'cause aint nothin' I loves any better den hosses. Den when I was bigger he starts me to carryin' de breakfast to de field whar de grown niggers had been out workin' since way 'fore day. Dey all done dat. Dey say de days wasn't long enough to put in enough time so dey works part of de night.

"We had good grub 'cause we raised all de co'n and de hogs and de cows and chickens and plenty of everything. Mos' times we have biscuits and bacon and syrup for breakfast and butter too if we wants it but mos' niggers dey likes dat fat bacon de bes'.

"Our log cabins was good and comfortable. Dey was all along in a row and built out of de same kind of logs what our marsters house was.

"We had good beds and dey was clean.

"I nev'r had no money when I was a slave 'cause I was jes' a small boy when de slaves was set free.

"We had lots of fish and rabbits, more den we had 'possum

but we sho' likes dat 'possum when we could git it.

"My marster had about three hundred slaves and a big plantation.

"I seen some slaves sold off dat big auction block and de little chillun sho' would be a cryin' when dey takes dere mothers away from dem.

"We didn' have no jail 'cause my marster didn' believe dat way, but I's seen other slaves in dem chains and things.

"We didn' know nothin' 'bout no learnin' nor no church neither and when de slaves die dey was jes' buried without no singin' or nothin'.

"When de war started, my father, he goes and once I remember he comes home on a furlough and we was all so glad, den when he goes back he gits killed and we nev'r see him no mo'.

"We had de doctor and good care when we was sick. I's don't remember much 'bout what kinds of medicine we took but I's know it was mostly home-made.

"We all wears dat asafoetida on a string 'round our necks and sometimes we carry a rabbit's foot in our pockets fer good luck.

"When de war was ended and de slaves was free old Uncle Pete, our oldest slave, comes a-walkin' up from de woods whar he always go to keeps from bein' bothered, to read his Bible, and he had dat Bible under his arm an' he say, 'I's know somethin', me an' de Lawd knows somethin'', and den he tells us. He say, 'You all is free people now, you can go when you please and come when you pleases and you can stay here or go some other place'. Well I had to stay 'cause my mother stayed and I's jes' keeps on ridin' dem race hosses 'til long after my marster was dead, den I's gits me some hosses of my own and train other men's hosses too.

"I's worked at dat racin' business 'til I's come to Texas and when I went to work in hotels dat killed me up. I's done ev'r thing from makin' soap fer de scrubbin', to cookin' de bes' meals fer de bes' hotels. I aint been no good since, though, and I had to quit several years ago.

"De first time I was married was to Phillis Reed in Missouri and we jes' jumps over de broom, and after Phillis die and I comes to Texas I's gits married again to Susie, here in San Angelo; we jes' jumps ov'r de broom too. I's nev'r had no chillun of my own so I's jes' a settin' here a-livin' off de ole age pension."

JULIE FRANCIS DANIELS

JULIA FRANCIS DANIELS, born in 1848, in Georgia, a slave of the Denman family, who moved to Texas before the Civil War. Julia's memory fails her when she tries to recall names and dates. She still tries to take part in church activities and has recently started to learn reading and writing. She lives with a daughter at 2523 Spring St. Dallas, Texas.

"They's lots I disremembers and they's lots I remembers, like the year the war's over and the fightin' all done with, 'cause that the year I larned to plow and that the time I got married. That's the very year they larned me to plow. I larnt all right, 'cause I wasn't one slow to larn anything. Afore to that time, they ain't never had no hoe in the field for me a-tall. I jes' toted water for the ones in the field.

"I had plenty brothers and sisters, 'bout ten of 'em, but I disremembers some they names. There was Tom and George and Marthy and Mandy, and they's all name' Denman, 'cause my mammy and daddy was Lottie and Boyd Denman and they come from Georgia to Cherokee County and then to Houston County, near by to Crockett, with Old Man Denman. He was the one owned all us till he 'vided some with Miss Lizzie when she marries Mr. Cramer.

"My daddy worked in the fields with Uncle Lot and my brothers, and my Uncle Joe, he's driver. But Briscoe am overseer and he a white man. He can't never whup the growed mens like he wants, 'cause they don't let him unless he ask Old Man Denman. I seed him whup 'em, though. He make 'em take off the shirt and whup with the strap.

"Now, my mammy was cook in the Denman house and for our family and Uncle Joe's family. She didn't have much time for anythin' but cookin' all the time. But she's the bestes' cook. Us had fine greens and hawgs and beef. Us et collard greens and pork till us got skittish of it and then they quit the pork and kilt a beef. When they done that, they's jus' pourin' water on our wheels, 'cause us liked best of anythin' the beef, and I do to this day, only I can't never git it.

"Old Man Denman had a boy what kilt squirrels and throwed 'em in the kitchen. The white folks et them. You ain't never seen no white folks then would eat rabbit. I had a brother who hunted. Mostly on Sundays. He'd leave for the swamps 'fore daybreak and we'd know when we'd hear him callin', 'O-o-o-o-o-da-da-ske-e-e-e-t,' he had somethin'. That jus' a make-up of he own, but we knowed they's rabbits for the pot.

"All the mens don't hunt on Sunday, 'cause Uncle Joe helt meetin' in front he house. Us look out the door and seed Uncle Joe settin' the benches straight and settin' he table out under the trees and sweepin' clean the leaves and us know they's gwine be meetin'. They's the loveliest days that ever they was. Night times, too, they'd make it 'tween 'em whether it'd be at our house or Uncle Joe's. We'd ask niggers from other farms and I used to say, 'I likes meetin' jus' as good as I likes a party.'

"When crops is laid by us have the most parties and dence and sing and have play games. The reels is what I used to like but I done quit that foolishness many a year ago. I used to cut a step or two. I remembers one reel call the 'Devil's Dream.' It's a fast song

"'Oh, de Devil drempt a dream,
He drempt it on a Friday—
He drempt he cotch a sinner.'

"Old Man Denman am the great one for 'viding he property and when Miss Lizzie marries with Mr. Creame Cramer, which am her dead sister's husband, Old Man Denman give me and two my sisters to Miss Lizzie and he gives two more my sisters to he son. Us goes with Miss Lizzie to the Cramer place and lives in the back yard in a little room by the back door.

"Everything fine and nice there till one day Miss Lizzie say to me, 'Julia, go down to the well and fetch me some water,' and I goes and I seed in the road a heap of men all in gray and ridin' hosses, comin' our way. I runs back to the house and calls Miss Lizzie. She say, 'What you scairt for?' I tells her 'bout them men and she say they ain't gwine hurt me none, they jus' wants some water. I goes back to the well and heared 'em talk 'bout a fight. I goes back to the house and some of the mens comes to the gate and says to Mr. Cramer, 'How're you, Creame?' He say, 'I's all right in my health but I ain't so good in my mind.' They says, 'What the matter, Creame?' He say, 'I want to be in the fight so bad.'

"When they goes I asks Miss Lizzie what they fightin' 'bout and she say it am 'bout money. That all I knows. Right after that Mr. Cramer goes and we don't never see him no more. Word come back from the fightin' he makes some the big, high mens mad and they puts chains 'round he ankles and make him dig a stump in the hot sun. He ain't used to that and it give him fever to the brain and he dies.

"When Mr. Cramer goes 'way, Miss Lizzie takes us all and goes back to Old Man Denman's. The sojers used to pass and all the whoopin' and hollerin' and carryin' on, you ain't never heered the likes! They hollers, 'Who-o-o-o, Old Man Denman, how's your chickens?' And they chunks and throws at 'em till they cripples 'em up and puts 'em in they bags, for cookin'. Old Man Denman cusses at 'em somethin' powerful.

"My sister Mandy and me am down in the woods a good, fur piece from the house and us keeps heerin' a noise. My brother comes down and finds me and say, 'Come git your dinner.' When I gits there dinner am top the gate post and he say they's sojers in the woods and they has been persecutin' a old woman on a mule. She was a nigger woman. I gits so scairt I can't eat my dinner. I ain't got no heart for victuals. My brother say, 'Wait for pa, he comin' with the mule and he'll hide you out.' I gits on the mule front of pa and us pass through the sojers and they grabs at us and says, 'Gimme the gal, gimme the gal.' Pa say I faints plumb 'way.

"Us heered guns shootin' round and 'bout all the time. Seems like they fit every time they git a chance. Old Man Denman's boy gits kilt and two my sisters he property and they don't know what to do, 'cause they has to be somebody's property and they ain't no one to 'heritance 'em. They has to go to the auction but Old Man Denman say not to fret. At the auction the man say, 'Goin' high, goin' low, goin' mighty slow, a little while to go. Bid 'em in, bid 'em in. The sun am high, the sun am hot, us got to git home tonight.' An old friend of Old Man Denman's hollers out he buys for William Blackstone. Us all come home and my sisters too and Old Man Denman laugh big and say, 'My name allus been William Blackstone Denman.'

"I's a woman growed when the war was to a end. I had my first baby when I's fourteen. One day my sister call me and say, 'They's fit out, and they's been surrenderin' and ain't gwine fight no more.' That dusk Old Man Denman call all us niggers together and stand on he steps and make he speech, 'Mens and womans, you is free as I am. You is free to go where you wants but I is beggin' yous to stay by me till us git the crops laid by.' Then he say, 'Study it over 'fore you gives me you answer. I is always try as my duty to be fair to you.'

"The mens talks it over a-twixt theyselves and includes to stay. They says us might as well stay there as go somewhere else, and us got no money and no place to go.

"Then Miss Lizzie marries with Mr. Joe McMahon and I goes with her to he house near by and he say he larn me to plow. Miss Lizzie say, 'Now, Julia, you knows how to plow and don't make no fool of yourself and act like you ain't never seed no plow afore.' Us make a corn crop and goes on 'bout same as afore.

"I gits married that very year and has a little fixin' for the weddin', bakes some cakes and I have a dress with buttons and a preacher marries me. I ain't used to wearin' nothin' but loring (a simple one piece garment made from sacking). Unnerwear? I ain't never wore no unnerwear then.

"My husband rents a little piece of land and us raise a corn crop and that's the way us do. Us raises our own victuals. I has 17 chillen through the year and they done scatter to the four winds. Some of them is dead. I ain't what I used to be for workin'. I jus' set 'round. I done plenty work in my primer days.

United States.Work Project Administration

KATIE DARLING

KATIE DARLING, about 88, was born a slave on the plantation of William McCarty, on the Elysian Fields Road, nine miles south of Marshall, Texas. Katie was a nurse and housegirl in the McCarty household until five years after the end of the Civil War. She then moved to Marshall and married. Her husband and her three children are dead and she is supported by Griffin Williams, a boy she found homeless and reared. They live in a neat three-room shack in Sunny South addition of Marshall, Texas.

"You is talkin' now to a nigger what nussed seven white chillen in them bullwhip days. Miss Stella, my young missy, got all our ages down in she Bible, and it say I's born in 1849. Massa Bill McCarty my massa and he live east and south of Marshall, clost to the Louisiana line. Me and my three brudders, Peter and Adam and Willie, all lives to be growed and married, but mammy die in slavery and pappy run 'way while he and Massa Bill on they way to the battle of Mansfield. Massa say when he come back from the war, 'That triflin' nigger run 'way and jines up with them damn Yankees.'

"Massa have six chillen when war come on and I nussed all of 'em. I stays in the house with 'em and slep' on a pallet on the floor, and soon I's big 'nough to tote the milk pail they puts me to milkin', too. Massa have more'n 100 cows and most the time me and Violet do all the milkin'. We better be in that cowpen by five o'clock. One mornin' massa cotched me lettin' one the calves do some milkin' and he let me off without whippin' that time, but that don't mean he allus good, 'cause them cows have more feelin' for than massa and missy.

"We et peas and greens and collards and middlin's. Niggers had better let that ham alone! We have meal coffee. They parch meal in the oven and bile it and drink the liquor. Sometime we gits some of the Lincoln coffee what was lef' from the nex' plantation.

"When the niggers done anything massa bullwhip them, but didn't skin them up very often. He'd whip the man for half doin' the plowin' or hoein' but if they done it right he'd find something else to whip them for. At night the men had to shuck corn and the women card and spin. Us got two pieces of clothes for winter and two for summer, but us have no shoes. We had to work Saturday all day and if that grass was in the field we didn't git no Sunday, either.

"They have dances and parties for the white folks' chillen, but missy say, 'Niggers was made to work for white folks,' and on Christmas Miss Irene bakes two cakes for the nigger families but she darsn't let missy know 'bout it.

"When a slave die, massa make the coffin hisself and send a couple niggers to bury the body and say, 'Don't be long,' and no singin' or prayin' 'lowed, jus' put them in the ground and cover 'em up and hurry on back to that field.

"Niggers didn't cou't then like they do now, massa pick out a po'tly man and a po'tly gal and jist put 'em together. What he want am the stock.

"I 'member that fight at Mansfield like it yes'day. Massas's field am all tore up with cannon holes and ever' time a cannon fire, missy go off in a rage. One time when a cannon fire, she say to me, 'You li'l black wench, you niggers ain't gwine be free. You's made to work for white folks.' 'Bout that time she look up and see a Yankee sojer standin' in the door with a pistol. She say, 'Katie, I didn't say anythin', did I?' I say, 'I ain't tellin' no lie, you say niggers ain't gwine git free.'

"That day you couldn't git 'round the place for the Yankees and they stays for weeks at a time.

"When massa come home from the war he wants let us loose, but missy wouldn't do it. I stays on and works for them six years after the war and missy whip me after the war jist like she did 'fore. She has a hun'erd lashes laid up for me now, and this how it am. My brudders done lef' massa after the war and move nex' door to the Ware place, and one Saturday some niggers come and tell me my brudder Peter am comin' to git me 'way from old missy Sunday night. That night the cows and calves got together and missy say it my fault. She say, 'I'm gwine give you one hun'erd lashes in the mornin', now go pen them calves.'

"I don't know whether them calves was ever penned or not, 'cause Peter was waitin' for me at the lot and takes me to live with him on the Ware place. I's so happy to git away from that old devil missy, I don't know what to do, and I stays there sev'ral years and works out here and there for money. Then I marries and moves here and me and my man farms and nothin' 'citin' done happened."

United States.Work Project Administration

CAREY DAVENPORT

CAREY DAVENPORT, retired Methodist minister of Anahuac, Texas, appears sturdy despite his 83 years. He was reared a slave of Capt. John Mann, in Walker Co., Texas. His wife, who has been his devoted companion for 60 years, was born in slavery just before emancipation. Carey is very fond of fishing and spends much time with hook and line. He is fairly well educated and is influential among his fellow Negroes.

"If I live till the 13th of August I'll be 82 years old. I was born in 1855 up in Walker County but since then they split the county and the place I was born is just across the line in San Jacinto County now. Jim and Janey Davenport was my father and mother and they come from Richmond, Virginia. I had two sisters, Betty and Harriet, and a half brother, William.

"Our old master's name was John Mann but they called him Capt. Mann. Old missus' name was Sarah. I'd say old master treated us slaves bad and there was one thing I couldn't understand, 'cause he was 'ligious and every Sunday mornin' everybody had to git ready and go for prayer. I never could understand his 'ligion, 'cause sometimes he git up off his knees and befo' we git out the house he cuss us out.

"All my life I been a Methodist and I been a regular preacher 43 years. Since I quit I been livin' here at Anahuac and seems like I do 'bout as much preachin' now as I ever done.

"I don't member no cullud preachers in slavery times. The white Methodist circuit riders come round on horseback and preach. There was a big box house for a church house and the cullud folks sit off in one corner of the church.

"Sometimes the cullud folks go down in dugouts and hollows and hold they own service and they used to sing songs what come a-gushin' up from the heart.

"They was 'bout 40 slaves on the place, but I never seed no slaves bought or sold and I never was sold, but I seen 'em beat—O, Lawd, yes. I seen 'em make a man put his head through the crack of the rail fence and then they beat him till he was bloody. They give some of 'em 300 or 400 licks.

"Old man Jim, he run away lots and sometimes they git the dogs after him. He run away one time and it was so cold his legs git frozen and they have to cut his legs off. Sometimes they put chains on runaway slaves and chained 'em to the house. I never knowed of 'em puttin' bells on the slaves on our place, but over next to us they did. They had a piece what go round they shoulders and round they necks with pieces up over they heads and hung up the bell on the piece over they head.

"I was a sheep minder them days. The wolves was bad but they never tackled me, 'cause they'd ruther git the sheep. They like sheep meat better'n man meat. Old Captain wanted me to train he boy to herd sheep and one day young master see a sow with nine pigs and want me to catch them and I wouldn't do it. He tried to beat me up and when we git to the lot we have to go round to the big gate and he had a pine knot, and he catch me in the gate and hit me with that knot. Old Captain sittin' on the gallery and he seed it all. When he heered the story he whipped young master and the old lady, she ain't like it.

"One time after that she sittin' in the yard knittin' and she throwed her knittin' needle off and call me to come git it. I done forgot she wanter whip me and when I bring the needle she grab me and I pull away but she hold on my shirt. I run round and round and she call her mother and they catch and whip me. My shirt just had one button on it and I was pullin' and gnawin' on that button and directly it come off and the whole shirt pull off and I didn't have nothin' on but my skin. I run and climb up on the pole at the gate and sot there till master come. He say, 'Carey, why you sittin' up there?' Then I tell him the whole transaction. I say, 'Missus, she whip me 'cause young marse John git whip that time and not me.' He make me git down and git up on his horse behin' him and ride up to the big house. Old missus, she done went to the house and go to bed with her leg, 'cause when she whippin' me she stick my head 'tween her knees and when she do that I bit her.

"Old master's house was two-story with galleries. My mother, she work in the big house and she have a purty good house to live in. It was a plank house, too, but all the other houses was make out of hewed logs. Then my father was a carpenter and old master let him have lumber and he make he own furniture out of dressed lumber and make a box to put clothes in. We never did have more'n two changes of clothes.

"My father used to make them old Carey plows and was good at makin' the mould board out of hardwood. He make the best Carey plows in that part of the country and he make horseshoes and nails and everything out of iron. And he used to make spinning wheels and parts of looms. He was a very valuable man and he make wheels and the hub and put the spokes in.

"Old master had a big farm and he raised cotton and corn and 'taters and peanuts and sorghum cane and some ribbon cane. The bigges' crops was cotton and corn.

"My father told us when freedom come. He'd been a free

man, 'cause he was bodyguard to the old, old master and when he died he give my father he freedom. That was over in Richmond, Virginia. But young master steal him into slavery again. So he was glad when freedom come and he was free again. Old master made arrangement for us to stay with him till after the harvest and then we go to the old Rawls house what 'long to Mr. Chiv Rawls. He and my father and mother run the place and it was a big farm.

"I git marry when I was 'bout 22 years old and that's her right there now. We's been married more'n 60 years and she was 17 years old then. She was raised in Grant's colony and her father was a blacksmith.

"We had it all 'ranged and we stop the preacher one Sunday mornin' when he was on the way to preachin' and he come there to her pa's house and marry us. We's had 11 children and all has deceased but three.

"I was educated since freedom, 'cause they wasn't no schools in slavery days, but after I was freed I went to public schools. Most my learnin' I got from a German man what was principal of a college and he teach me the biggest part of my education.

"When I was 14 a desperado killed my father and then I had my mother and her eight children to take care of. I worked two months and went to school one month and that way I made money to take care of 'em.

CAMPBELL DAVIS

CAMPBELL DAVIS, 85, was born in Harrison Co., Texas, a slave of Henry Hood. He remained on the Hood place about three years after he was freed, then farmed in Louisiana. In 1873 he married and moved back to Harrison Co., where he farmed until old age forced him to stop. He now lives with his nephew, Billie Jenkins, near Karnack. Campbell receives a $12.00 per month old age pension.

"I's big 'nough in slavery time to hear dem tell de darkies to get up and go in the mornin', and to hear the whistlin' of dem whips and howlin' of de dogs. I's birthed up in the northeast part of this county right on the line of Louisiana and Texas, and 'longed to old man Henry Hood. My mammy and daddy was Campbell and Judy Davis and dey both come from Alabama, and was brung here by de traders and sold to Massa Hood. They was nine of us chillen, name Ellis and Hildaman and Henderson and Henrietta and Georgia and Harriet and Patsy.

"Massa Henry didn't have de fine house but it a big one. Us quarters sot off 'cross de field in de edge of a skit of woods. Dey have dirt floors and a fireplace and old pole and plank bunks nail to de walls.

"Dey fed us beef and veg'tables—any kind, jus' name it—and 'low us sop bread in potlicker till de world look level. Dat good eatin' and all my life I ain't have no better.

"Massa didn't 'low no overseer on he place. One my uncles de driver, and massa blow de old conk shell long 'fore day, and if de darkies didn't git goin' you'd hear dem whips crackin'.

"I seed one my sisters whip 'cause she didn't spin 'nough.

Dey pull de clothes down to her waist and laid her down on de stomach and lash her with de rawhide quirt. I's in de field when dey whips my Uncle Lewis for not pickin' 'nough cotton. De driver pull he clothes down and make him lay on de groun'. He wasn't tied down, but he say he scart to move.

"De women am off Friday afternoon to wash clothes and all de hands git Saturday afternoon and mos' de man go huntin' or fishin'. Sometimes dey have parties Saturday night and couples git on de floor and have music of de fiddle and banjo. I only 'members one ring play:

"Hop light, li'l lady,
The cakes all dough,
Don't mind de weather,
Jus' so de wind don't blow.

"De bigges' day to blacks and whites was fourth of July. De hands was off all day and massa give de big dinner out under de trees. He allus barbecue de sheep or beef and have cakes and pies and fancy cookin'. He's one de bes' bosses round dat country. He 'lieve in makin' dem work and when dey need whippin' he done it, but when it come to feedin' he done dat right, too. And on Christmas he give us clothes and shoes and nuts and things and 'nother big dinner, and on Christmas night de darkies sing songs for de white folks.

"Us git some book larnin' 'mongst ourselves, round de quarters, and have our own preacher. Mos' de time us chillen play, makin' frog holes in de sand and mud people and things.

"I done hear lots of talk 'bout ghosts and hants and think I seed one onct. I's comin' home from de neighbors at night, in de moonlight, and 'rectly I seed something white by side de road. De closer I gits de bigger it gits. I's scart but I walks up to it and it nothin' but de big spiderweb on de bush. Den I says to myself, 'Dere ain't nothin' to dis ghost business.'

"Massa have one son go to war and he taken a old cullud man with him. I seed soldiers on hosses comin' and goin' de big road, and lots of dem come to Port Caddo in boats. De pretties' sight I ever seed am a soldier band all dress in de uniforms with brass buttons. When de soldiers come back from de war dey throwed cannon balls 'long de road and us chillen play with dem.

"When de war am over, massa call us all and say we's free, but can stay on and work for de victuals and clothes. A bunch leaves and go to de Progoe Marshal at Shreveport and ask him what to do. He tell dem to go back and wait till dey find work some place. My mammy and me stays at de Hood place 'bout three years. When I's twenty-one I marries and come back to Harrison County. Mammy and me done farm in Louisiana up to dat. My wife and me marries under de big oak tree front of de Leigh Church. Us jus' common folks and doesn't have no infair or big to-do when us marry.

"I's voted but our people won't pull together. I votes de 'publican ticket de long time, but last time I pulls over and votes de Democrat ticket. I 'cides I jus' as well go with de braves as stay with de scart.

"If de young gen'ration would study dey could make something out deyselves, but dey wont do it. Dey am too wild. Jus' last week, I hears de young cullud preacher at Karnack say, 'Brudders and sisters, style and brightness am what we needs today.' I looks at him and says to myself, 'Thank de Lawd I knows better'n dat.' When I's comin' up it am dark, but I knows better things am ahead for us people and us trusts in de Lawd and was hones' with our white folks and profits by what dey tells us. Dey wasn't no niggers sent to jail when I's comin' up. It dis 'style and brightness' what gits de young niggers in trouble. Dey got de dark way 'head of dem, less dey stops and studies and make somethin' out deyselves."

United States.Work Project Administration

WILLIAM DAVIS

WILLIAM DAVIS was born near Kingston, Tennessee, on the first of April, 1845. His family were the only slaves owned by Jonathan Draper, Baptist minister. In 1869 William joined the army and was stationed at Fort Stockton, Texas. He has lived in Houston since 1870. William is active and takes a long, daily walk.

"Well, suh, jes' sit down in de chair yonder and I'll tell you what I can 'bout times back yonder. Let's see, now. I was born on de first day of April in 1845. De reason I knows was 'cause Miss Lizzie, our missy, told me so when we was sot free. Mammy done told me I was born den, on de Tennessee river, near Kingston. I heared her say de turnpike what run past Massa John's house dere goes over de mountain to Bristol, over in Virginny. Mammy and pappy and all us chillen 'long to de Drapers, Massa Jonathan what us call Massa John, and he wife, Miss Lizzie, and we is de only cullud folks what dey owns.

"Massa John am de Baptist preacher, and while I'm sho' glad to see my folks sot free, I'll tell de truth and say Massa John and Miss Lizzie was mighty good to us. Dey have four chillen; Massa Milton, what am oldes' and kill in de first battle; Massa Bob and Massa George and Massa Canero. Oh, yes, dey have one gal, Missy Ann.

"Course us didn't have no last names like now. Mammy named Sophie and pappy named Billy. Sometimes de owners give de slaves last names 'cordin' to what dey do, like pappy was meat cook and mammy cook pies and cakes and bread, so dey might have Cook for de last name.

"We has a bigger family dan Massa John, 'cause dey eight of us chillen. I ain't seen none of dem since I lef' Virginny in 1869, but I 'member all de names. Dere was Jane and Lucy and Ellen and Bob and Solomon and Albert and John, and I'm de younges' de whole lot.

"I heared Miss Lizzie tell some white folks dat my mammy and pappy give to her by her pappy in Alabama when she get married. Dat de custom with rich folks den, and mammy 'long to de Ames, what was Miss Lizzie's name 'fore she marry. I heared her say when de stars falls, I think she say in 1832, she was 'bout eighteen, and dey think de world am endin'.

"Pappy was a Indian. I knows dat. He came from Congo, over in Africa, and I heared him say a big storm druv de ship somewhere on de Ca'lina coast. I 'member he mighty 'spectful to Massa and Missy, but he proud, too, and walk straighter'n anybody I ever seen. He had scars on de right side he head and cheek what he say am tribe marks, but what dey means I don't know.

"'Bout de first I 'members real good am where we am in Virginny and Massa John runs de Washington College, in Washington County. I 'member all de pupils eats at massa's house and dat de first job I ever had. 'Scuse me for laughin', but I don't reckon I thunk of dat since de Lawd know when. Dat my first job. Dey has a string fasten to de wall on one side de room, with pea fowl tail feathers strung 'long it, and it runs most de length de room, above de dinin' table, and round a pulley-like piece in de ceilin' with one end de string hangin' down. When mealtime come, I am put where de string hang down and I pulls it easy like, and de feathers swishes back and forth sideways, and keeps de flies from lightin' while folks am eatin'. 'Ceptin' dat, all I does is play round with Massa

George and Missy Ann.

"Dey ain't no whuppin' on our place and on Sunday us all go to church, and Massa John do de preachin'. Dey rides in de buggy and us follow in de wagon. De white folks sets in front de church and us in back.

"I can't tell you how long us stay at de college, 'zactly, but us moves to Warm Springs to take de baths and drink de water, in Scott County. Dat two, three years befo' de war, and Massa John run de hotel and preach on Sunday. I think dere am three springs, one sulphur water and one lime water and one a warm spring. I does a little bit of everything round de hotel, helps folks off de stage when it druv up, wait on table and sich. When I hears de horn blow—you know, de stage driver blow it when dey top de hill 'bout two miles 'way, to let you know dey comin'—I sho' hustle round and git ready to meet it, 'cause most times folks what I totes de grips for gives me something. Dat de first money I ever seed. Some de folks gives me de picayune—dat what us call a nickel, now, and some gives me two shillin's, what same as two-bits now. A penny was big den, jes' like a two-bit piece, now.

"But when war begin 'tween de Yankees and de South, it sho' change everything up, 'cause folks quit comin' to de Springs and de soldiers takes over de place. Massa Milton go to jine de South Army and gits kill. Morgan and he men make de Springs headquarters most de war, till de Yankees come marchin' through toward de last part. I know pappy say dem Yankees gwine win, 'cause dey allus marchin' to de South, but none de South soldiers marches to de North. He didn't say dat to de white folks, but he sho' say it to us. When de Yankees come marchin' through, de Morgan soldiers jes' hide out till dey gone. Dey never done no fightin' round Warm Springs. Lots of times dey goes way for couple weeks and den comes back and rests awhile.

"Den one mornin'—I 'members it jes' like it yestiddy, it de fourth of July in 1865—Miss Lizzie say to me, 'Willie, I wants you to git you papa and de rest de family and have dem come to de porch right away.' I scurries round quick like and tells dem and she comes out of de house and says, 'Now, de Yankees done sot you free and you can do what you wants, but you gwineter see more carpet baggers and liars dan you ever has seed, and you'll be worse off den you ever has been, if you has anythin' to do with dem. Den she opens de book and tells us all when us born and how old us am, so us have some record 'bout ourselves. She tells me I'm jes' nineteen and one fourth years old when I'm sot free.

"She tell pappy Massa John want to see him in de house and when he comes out he tells us Massa John done told him to take a couple wagons and de family and go to de farm 'bout ten miles 'way on Possum Creek and work it and stay long as he wants. Massa has us load up one wagon with 'visions. Pappy made de first crop with jes' hoes, 'cause us didn't have no hosses or mules to plow with. Us raise jes' corn and some wheat, but dey am fruit trees, peaches and apples and pears and cherries. Massa John pay pappy $120 de year, 'sides us 'visions, and us stays dere till pappy dies in 1868.

"Den I heared 'bout de railroad what dey buildin' at Knoxville and I leaves de folks and gits me de job totin' water. Dey asks my name and I says William Davis, 'cause I knows Mr. Jefferson Davis am President of de South durin' de war, and I figgers it a good name. In 1869 I goes to Nashville and 'lists in de army. I'm in de 24th Infantry, Company G, and us sent to Fort Stockton to guard de line of Texas, but all us do am build 'dobe houses. Col. Wade was de commander de fort and Cap'n Johnson was captain of G. Co. Out dere I votes for de first time, for Gen. Grant, when Greeley and him run for president. But I gits sick at de Fort and am muster out in 1870 and comes to Houston.

"I gits me de deckhand job on de Dinah, de steamboat what haul freight and passengers 'tween Galveston and Houston. Den I works on de Lizzie, what am a bigger boat. Course, Houston jes' a little bit of place to what it am now—dey wasn't no git buildin's like dey is now, and mud, I tell you de streets was jes' like de swamp when it rain.

"Long 'bout 1875 I gits marry to Mary Jones, but she died in 1883 and I gits marry 'gain in 1885 to Arabelle Wilson and has four girls and one boy from her. She died 'bout ten years back. Course, us cullud folks marry jes' like white folks do now, but I seen cullud folks marry 'fore de war and massa marry dem dis way: dey goes in de parlor and each carry de broom. Dey lays de brooms on de floor and de woman put her broom front de man and he put he broom front de woman. Dey face one 'nother and step 'cross de brooms at de same time to each other and takes hold of hands and dat marry dem. Dat's de way dey done, sho', 'cause I seed my own sister marry dat way.

"I has wished lots of times to go back and see my folks, but I never has been back and never seed dem since I left, and I guess dey am all gone 'long 'fore now. I has jobbed at first one thing and 'nother and like pappy tells me, I has trials and tribulations and I has good chillen what ain't never got in no trouble and what all helps take care dere old pappy so I guess I ain't got no complainin' 'bout things.

"I dreams sometimes 'bout de peach trees and de pear trees and de cherry trees and I'd give lots to see de mountains 'gain, 'cause when de frost come, 'bout now, de leaves on de trees put on pretty colors and de persimmons and nuts is ready for pickin' and a little later on us kill de hawgs and put by de meat for de winter.

"De Lawd forgive me for dis foolishness, 'cause I got a good home, and has all I need, but I gits to thinkin' 'bout Virginny sometimes and my folks what I ain't seed since I left, and it sho' make me want to see it once more 'fore I die.

ELI DAVISON

ELI DAVISON was born in Dunbar, West Virginia, a slave of Will Davison. Eli has a bill of sale that states he was born in 1844. His master moved to Texas in 1858, and settled in Madison County. Eli lives in Madisonville, with one of his sons.

"My first Old Marse was Will Davison. My father's name was Everett Lee and mama was Susan, and he come to see her twict a month, 'cause he was owned by 'nother master.

"Marse Davison had a good home in West Virginia, where I's born, in Dunbar, but most of it 'longed to he wife and she was the boss of him. He had a great many slaves, and one mornin' he got up and 'vided all he had and told his wife she could have half the slaves. Then we loaded two wagons and he turned to his oldest son and the next son and said, 'You's gwine with me. Crawl on.' Then he said to he wife, 'Elsie, you can have everything here, but I'm takin' Eli and Alex and these here two chillen.' The other two gals and two boys he left, and pulled out for Texas. It taken us mos' two years to git here, and Marse Will never sot eyes on the rest of his family no more, long as he lived.

"Marse never married any more. He'd say, 'They ain't 'nother woman under the sun I'd let wear my name.' He never said his wife's name no more, but was allus talkin' of them chillun he done left behind.

"We gits here and starts to build a one room log house for Marse Will and his two boys. My quarters was one them covered wagons, till he trades me off. He cried like a baby, but he said, 'I hate to do this, but its the only way I'll have anything to leave for my two boys.' Looks like everything done go 'gainst him when he come to Texas, and he took sick and died. The boys put him away nice and loaded up and went back to Virginia, but the home was nailed up and farm lying out, and it took them mos' a year to find they folks. The mother and one gal was dead, so they come back and lived and died here in Texas.

"Marse Will was one more good man back in Virginia. He never got mad or whipped a slave. He allus had plenty to eat, with 1,200 acres, but after we come here all we had to eat was what we kilt in the woods and cornbread. He planted seven acres in corn, but all he did was hunt deer and squirrels. They was never a nigger what tried to run off in Texas, 'cause this was a good country, plenty to eat by huntin' and not so cold like in Virginia.

"After I was traded off, my new master wasn't so good to me. He thunk all the time the South would win that war and he treated us mean. His name was Thomas Greer. He kept tellin' us a black nigger never would be free. When it come, he said to us, 'Well, you black ——, you are just as free as I am.' He turnt us loose with nothin' to eat and mos' no clothes. He said if he got up nex' mornin' and found a nigger on his place, he'd horsewhip him.

"I don't know what I'd done, but one my old Marse Will's chillun done settle close by and they let me work for them, and built me a log house and I farmed on halves. They stood good for all the groceries I buyed that year. It took all I made that year to pay my debts and that's the way its been ever since.

"I married Sarah Keys. We had a home weddin' and 'greed to live together as man and wife. I jus' goes by her home one day and captures her like. I puts her on my saddle behind me and tells her she's my wife then. That's all they was to my weddin'. We had six chillun and they's all farmin' round here. Sarah, she dies seventeen years ago and I jus' lives round with my chillen, 'cause I's too old to do any work.

"All I ever done was to farm. That's all this here nigger knew what to do. O, I's seed the time when I never had nothin' to eat and my big bunch of chillun cryin' for bread. I could go to the woods then, but you can't git wild game no more. In them days it was five or ten mile to your nearest neighbor, but now they's so close you can stand in your yard and talk to them.

"I never done no votin', 'cause them Klu Kluxers was allus at the votin' places for a long time after the niggers was freed. The niggers has got on since them old days. They has gone from nothin' to a fair educated folks. We has been kind of slow, 'cause we was turnt loose without nothin', and couldn't read and write.

"I's worked for fifteen and thirty cents a day, but Lawd, blessed to our president, we gits a li'l pension now and that's kep' me from plumb starvin' to death. Times is hard and folks had to do away with everything when they had that Hoover for president, but they will be straightened out by and by if they'll listen to the president now. 'Course, some wants to kill him, 'cause he helps the poor, but it do look like we ought to have a li'l bread and salt bacon without upsettin' 'em, when they has so much.

United States.Work Project Administration

ELIGE DAVISON

ELIGE DAVISON was born in Richmond, Virginia, a slave of George Davison. Elige worked in the field for some time before he was freed, but does not know his age. He lives with one of his grandsons, in Madisonville, Texas.

"My birth was in Richmond. That's over in old Virginny, and George Davison owned me and my pappy and mammy. I 'member one sister, named Felina Tucker.

"Massa and Missus were very good white folks and was good to the black folks. They had a great big rock house with pretty trees all round it, but the plantation was small, not more'n a hunerd acres. Massa growed tobaccy on 'bout 30 of them acres, and he had a big bunch of hawgs. He waked us up 'bout four in the mornin' to milk the cows and feed them hawgs.

"Our quarters was good, builded out of pine logs with a bed in one corner, no floors and windows. Us wore old loyal clothes and our shirt, it open all down the front. In winter massa gave us woolen clothes to wear. Us didn't know what shoes was, though.

"Massa, he look after us slaves when us sick, 'cause us worth too much money to let die jus' like you do a mule. He git doctor or nigger mammy. She make tea out of weeds, better'n quinine. She put string round our neck for chills and fever, with camphor on it. That sho' keep off diseases.

"Us work all day till jus' 'fore dark. Sometimes us got whippin's. We didn't mind so much. Boss, you know how stubborn a mule am, he have to be whipped. That the way slaves is.

"When you gather a bunch of cattle to sell they calves, how the calves and cows will bawl, that the way the slaves was then. They didn't know nothin' 'bout they kinfolks. Mos' chillen didn't know who they pappy was and some they mammy 'cause they taken 'way from the mammy when she wean them, and sell or trade the chillen to someone else, so they wouldn't git 'tached to they mammy or pappy.

"Massa larn us to read and us read the Bible. He larn us to write, too. They a big church on he plantation and us go to church and larn to tell the truth.

"I seed some few run away to the north and massa sometime cotch 'em and put 'em in jail. Us couldn't go to nowhere without a pass. The patterrollers would git us and they do plenty for nigger slave. I's went to my quarters and be so tired I jus' fall in the door, on the ground, and a patterroller come by and hit me several licks with a cat-o-nine-tails, to see if I's tired 'nough to not run 'way. Sometimes them patterrollers hit us jus' to hear us holler.

"When a slave die, he jus' 'nother dead nigger. Massa, he builded a wooden box and put the nigger in and carry him to the hole in the ground. Us march round the grave three times and that all.

"I been marry once 'fore freedom, with home weddin'. Massa, he bring some more women to see me. He wouldn't let me have jus' one woman. I have 'bout fifteen and I don't know how many chillen. Some over a hunerd, I's sho'.

"I 'member plenty 'bout the war, 'cause the Yankees they march on to Richmond. They kill everything what in the way. I heared them big guns and I's scart. Everybody scart. I didn't see no fightin', 'cause I gits out the way and keeps out till it all over.

But when they marches right on the town I's tendin' hosses for massa. He have two hosses kilt right under him. Then the Yankees, they capture that town. Massa, he send me to git the buggy and hoss and carry missus to the mountain, but them Yankees they capture me and say they gwine hang that nigger. But, glory be, massa he saves me 'fore they hangs me. He send he wife and my wife to 'nother place then, 'cause they burn massa's house and tear down all he fences.

"When the war over massa call me and tells me I's free as he was, 'cause them Yankees win the war. He give me $5.00 and say he'll give me that much a month iffen I stays with him, but I starts to Texas. I heared I wouldn't have to work in Texas, 'cause everything growed on trees and the Texans wore animal hides for clothes. I didn't git no land or mule or cow. They warn't no plantations divided what I knowed 'bout. Mos' niggers jus' got turn loose with a cuss, and not 'nough clothes to cover they bodies.

"It 'bout a year 'fore I gits to Texas. I walks nearly all the way. Sometimes I git a li'l ride with farmer. Sometimes I work for folks 'long the way and git fifty cents and start 'gain.

"I got to Texas and try to work for white folks and try to farm. I couldn't make anything at any work. I made $5.00 a month for I don't know how many year after the war. Iffen the woods wasn't full of wild game us niggers all starve to death them days.

"I been marry three time. First wife Eve Shelton. She run off with 'nother man. Then I marries Fay Elly. Us sep'rate in a year. Then I marry Parlee Breyle. No, I done forgot. 'Fore that I marries Sue Wilford, and us have seven gals and six boys.

They all in New York but one. He stays here. Then I marries Parlee and us have two gals. Parlee die three year ago.

"The gov'ment give me a pension and I gits li'l odd jobs round, to get by. But times been hard and I ain't had much to eat the las' few years. Not near so good as what old massa done give me. But I gits by somehow.

"I done the bes' I could, 'sidering I's turned out with nothin' when I's growed and didn't know much, neither. The young folks, they knows more, 'cause they got the chance for schoolin'.

JOHN DAY

JOHN DAY, 81, was born near Dayton, Tennessee, a slave of Major John Day. John lives in McLennan Co., Texas.

"I was born near three mile from Dayton. That's over in Tennessee, and it was the sixteenth of February, in 1856. Master's name was Major John Day and my father's name was Alfred Day, and he was a first-class blacksmith. Blacksmithin' was a real trade them days, and my father made axes and hoes and plow shares and knives and even Jew's harps.

"Master was good to my father and when he done done de day's work he could work and keep the money he made. He'd work till midnight, sometimes, and at de end that war he had fifteen hundred dollars in Confederate money. I never seen such a worker.

"Master John thunk lots of father but he took de notion to sell him one time, 'cause why, he could git a lot of money for him. He sold him, but my mama and even Old Missy, cried and took on so dat Master John went after de men what bought him, to git him back. Dey already done crossed de river, but master calls and dey brung my father back and he give dem de money back. Dat de only time master sold one of us.

"He was a preacher and good to us, never beat none of us. He didn't have no overseer, but saw to all de work heself. He had twenty-five slaves and raised wheat and corn and oats and vegetables and fruit. He had four hundred acres and a house with twelve rooms.

"A man what owned a farm jinin' ourn, de houses half a mile apart. He had two slaves, Taylor and Jennie, and he whip dem every day, even if dey hadn't done nothin'. He allus beatin' on dem, seemed like. One awful cold day in February, Taylor done go to Denton for somethin', and when he come back his master starts beatin' on him, and cursed him somethin' awful. He kep' it up till my mama, her name was Mariah, gits a butcher knife and runs out dere and say, 'Iffen you hits him 'nother lick, I'll use this on you.' Old Missy was watchin' and backed her up. So he quit beatin' on Taylor dat time. But one day dat white man's own son say to him, 'Iffen you don't quit beatin' on dem niggers, I'll knock you in de head.' Den he quit.

"Master was in de Confederate army. He gits to be a major and after he done come out dat war he sho' hated anythin' what was blue color. I got hold a old Yankee cap and coat and is wearin' dem and master yanks dem off and burns dem.

"We heared dem guns in de Lookout Mountain battle. Dey sounded like thunder, rumblin' low. One day de Feds done take Dayton and de soldiers goes by our place to drive dem Feds out. Dere a valley 'bout two miles wide 'twixt our place and Dayton and we could see de Confederate soldiers till dey go up de hill on de other side. Long in evenin' de Confederates come back through dat valley and they was travelin' with dem Yankees right after dem. Dey come by our house and we was gittin' out de way, all right. Old Missy took all us chillen, black and white, and puts us under half a big hogshead, down in de stormhouse.

"De Yankees got to de place and 'gin ransack it. Old Missy done lock dat stormhouse door and sot down on it and she wouldn't git up when dey done tell her to. So dey takes her by de arms and lifts her off it. Dey didn't hurt her any. Den dey brekks de lock and comes down in dere. I didn't see why dey hadn't found us kids, 'cause my heart beatin' like de hammer. Dey turned dat hogshead over and all us kids skinned out dere like de Devil after us. One de Yanks hollers, 'Look what we done hatch out!'

"I tore out past de barn, thinkin' I'd go to mama, in de field, but it look like all de Yanks in de world jumpin' dere hosses over dat fence, so I whirls round and run in dat barn and dives in a stack of hay and buries myself so deep de folks like to never found me. Dey hunted all over de place befo' dey done found me. Us kids scart 'cause we done see dem Yanks' bayonets and thunk dey was dere horns.

"Dem Yanks done take all de flour and meal and wheat and corn and smoked meat. After dat master fixes up a place in de ceilin' to store stuff, and a trap door so when it closed you couldn't tell its dere.

"I lives in and round de old place till 1910, den comes to Texas. I jist works round and farms and gits by, but I ain't never done nothin' worth tellin'.

United States.Work Project Administration

NELSEN DENSON

NELSEN DENSON, 90, was born near Hamburg, Arkansas, a slave of Jim Nelson, who sold Nelsen and his family to Felix Grundy. Nelsen's memory is poor, but he managed to recall a few incidents. He now lives in Waco, Texas.

"I'll be ninety years old this December, (1937). I was born in Arkansas, up in Ashley County, and it was the twenty-second day of December in 1847. My mammy was from Virginny and pappy was from old Kentucky, and I was one of they eight chillen. Our owner, Marse Jim Densen, brung us to Texas and settled near Marlin, but got in debt and sold as all to Marse Felix Grundy, and he kep' us till freedom, and most of us worked for him after that.

"Marse Jim Densen had a easy livin' in Arkansas, but folks everywhere was comin' to Texas and he 'cides to throw in his fortunes. It wasn't so long after that war with Mexico and folks come in a crowd to 'tect theyselves 'gainst Indians and wild animals. The wolves was the worst to smell cookin' and sneak into camp, but Indians come up and makes the peace sign and has a pow wow with the white folks. Marse git beads or cloth and trade for leather breeches and things.

"I want to tell how we crosses the Red River on de Red River Raft. Back in them days the Red River was near closed up by dis timber raft and de big boats couldn't git up de river at all. We gits a li'l boat, and a Caddo Indian to guide us. Dis Red River raft dey say was centuries old. De driftwood floatin' down de river stops in de still waters and makes a bunch of trees and de dirt 'cumulates, and broomstraws and willows and brush grows out dis rich dirt what cover de driftwood. Dis raft growed 'bout a mile a year and de oldes' timber rots and breaks away, but dis not fast 'nough to keep de river clear. We found bee trees on de raft and had honey.

"It was long time after us come to Texas when de gov'ment opens up de channel. Dat am in 1873. 'Fore dat, a survey done been made and dey found de raft am a hundred and twenty-eight miles long. When we was on dat raft it am like a big swamp, with trees and thick brush and de driftwood and logs all wedge up tight 'tween everything.

"'Fore Texas secedes, Marse Jensen done sell us all to Marse Felix Grundy, and he goes to war in General Hardeman's Brigade and is with him for bodyguard. When de battle of Mansfield come I'm sixteen years old. We was camped on the Sabine River, on the Texas side, and the Yanks on the other side a li'l ways. I 'member the night 'fore the battle, how the campfires looked, and a quiet night and the whippoorwills callin' in the weeds. We was 'spectin' a 'tack and sings to keep cheerful. The Yanks sings the 'Battle Cry of Freedom' when they charges us. They come on and on and, Lawd, how they fit! I stays clost to Marse Grundy and the rebels wins and takes 'bout a thousand Yanks.

"Most the slaves was happy, the ones I knowed. They figgers the white men fightin' for some principal, but lots of them didn't care nothin' 'bout bein' free. I s'pose some was with bad white folks, but not round us. We had more to eat and now I'm so old I wouldn't feel bad if I had old marse to look after me 'gain.

VICTOR DUHON

VICTOR DUHON was born 97 years ago in Lafayette Parish, La., a slave of the Duhon family. His blue eyes and almost white skin are evidence of the white strain in his blood. Even after many years of association with English speaking persons, he speaks a French patois, and his story was interpreted by a Beaumont French teacher.

"My papa was Lucien Duhon and my mama Euripe Dupuis. I was born over in Louisiana in Lafayette Parish, between Broussard and Warville. I'm 97 years old now.

"I didn't have brothers or sisters, except half ones. It is like this, my mama was a house servant in the Duhon family. She was the hairdresser. One day she barbered master's son, who was Lucien. He says that he'll shave her head if she won't do what he likes. After that she his woman till he marries a white lady.

"My grandmama was stolen from Africa and she lived to be 125 years old. She died last year in April. I think I'll live long as she did. There were fifteen slaves on the land what Duhon's had but I never ran around with them. I had room at the back of the big house. You know, Madame Duhon was my grandmama. She was good to me. The only thing I did was look to my master's horse and be coachman for Madame. Master had four sons. They were Ragant and Jaques and Lucien and Desire. Desire was shot at the dance.

"Master had about 100 acres in cotton and the corn. He had a slave for to hunt all the time. He didn't do other things. The partridge and the rice birds he killed were cooked for the white folks. The owls and the rabbits and the coons and the possums were cooked for us. They had a big room for us to eat in. Where they cook they had a long oven with a piece down the middle. They cooked the white folks things on one side. They cooked their own things on the other. They had each ones pots and skillets.

"I didn't play much with the black children. My time went waiting on my white folks.

"Sometimes the priest came to say Mass. The slaves went to Mass. The priest married and baptized the slaves. They gave a feast of baptizing. We all had real beef meat that day.

"When my mama had 22 years she married a Polite Landry slave. Then she went to the Landry plantation. There was often marrying between the two plantations. When they married the wife went to her man's plantation. That made no difference. It wouldn't be long before a girl from the other place marry into the man's plantation. That kept things in balance.

"My mama married Fairjuste Williams. They had two sons and a daughter. I didn't know them so much. They were half brothers and sister.

"I had 22 years when war came. You know what war I mean. The war when the slaves were set free. I wasn't bothered about freedom. Didn't leave master till he died. Then I went to work for Mr. Polite Landry.

"I was always in good hands. Some slaves ware treated bad. Mr. Natale Vallean beat up a slave for stealing. He beat him so hard he lay in front of the gate a whole day and the night.

"I worked on farms all my life. Then I came to Beaumont. About 23 years ago, it was. I worked at anything. Now I'm too old. I live with my daughter.